TAUGHT BY LOVE

TAUGHT BY LOVE

Worship Resources for Year A

L AVON B AYLER

The Pilgrim Press
Cleveland

TO ALL MY COLLEAGUES, BOTH CLERGY AND LAITY, WITH
WHOM I HAVE LABORED DURING ALMOST FORTY YEARS
OF ORDAINED MINISTRY

The Pilgrim Press, 700 prospect Avenue, Cleveland, Ohio 44115-1100
pilgrimpress@ucc.org
www.pilgrimpress.com

© 2002 by the Pilgrim Press

Printed in the United States of America on acid-free paper

07 06 05 04 03 02   8 7 6 5 4 3 2

Library of Congress Cataloging-in-Publication Data

Bayler, Lavon, 1933–
    Taught by love : worship resources for year A / Lavon Bayler.
     p. cm.
    Includes indexes.
    ISBN 0-8298-1235-0 (pbk. : alk. paper)
    1. Worship programs.   2. Church year.   I. Title.
BV198.B2935   1998
264—dc21   97-44052
                                            CIP

C o n t e n t s

Preface

Today I have the strange feeling that I am writing the end of a long chapter in my life rather than a preface to a book I've just completed. In the midst of a sabbatical from my responsibilities as minister to the clergy and congregations of the Fox Valley Association of the Illinois Conference, United Church of Christ, I reflect that it was twelve years ago, on a similar sabbatical, that I set out to prepare a volume of worship resources based on Year A of the *New Common Lectionary*. At that time I knew little about lectionaries, never perceived of myself as a hymn writer, and had no consistent format in mind. But that book, *Fresh Winds of the Spirit* (titled by the editor, Marion Meyer), was well received. Suddenly it was no longer a one-shot sabbatical project. The request came for follow-up volumes devoted to Years B and C. As I learned along the way, *Whispers of God* and *Refreshing Rains of the Living Word* came into being. Writing became part of my daily personal devotions as well as filling many leisure hours on vacation and around events that took me away from home.

The set of three books seemed the end of a project, but that was not to be. It had become apparent that the first book lacked many of the resources that had developed into a consistent pattern in the later volumes. It seemed important to offer a sequel, which became *Fresh Winds, Book 2*. Scarcely was it published when I was made aware of the continuing work of the Consultation on Common Texts. They had reviewed the church's experience through several cycles of the lectionary, deciding on revisions in the order and content of some of the scripture listings while attempting to resolve differences among various lectionaries then in use.

With the 1992 publication of the *Revised Common Lectionary* came the challenge to provide a new series of books consistent with the new design. This current book, *Taught by Love,* completes that project. It joins *Led by Love,* Year B, and *Gathered by Love,* Year C. Meanwhile, in response to several requests, my husband, Bob Bayler, joined me and a number of clergy colleagues in authoring three books of longer (pastoral) prayers related to the lectionary, titled *When We Pray,* years A, B, and C.

After twelve years and ten books, the circle is closing. I started with Year A and its focus on Matthew's Gospel. Today I'm wrapping up a third book—well, actually, a fourth—that addresses many of the same texts in a slightly different arrangement. That's enough of this type of writing. All the books will continue to have some usefulness for the next few years. Since writing is now so much a part of my life, I will probably find a new area of concentration, but for now the project that began with a modest single-manuscript sabbatical effort seems complete.

Special thanks go to my patient spouse and sons, who often observed me in my favorite recliner with notebook, pen, and Bible in hand, rather than otherwise engaged with them. Encouraging comments by users of the resources and colleagues at The Pilgrim Press and United Church Press have kept me writing. My chief typist has been Pat Kitner, a licensed minister and good friend who makes up for my lack of computer skills. Editors and publishers and cover designers, some unknown to me, have added their expertise, and Kim Sadler always keeps me on schedule. To all who have been a part of this venture, I offer my deepest gratitude. Thank you!

Introduction

We are indebted to Vatican II for revived interest in lectionaries. Efforts to renew Roman Catholic worship sparked an ecumenical movement to develop a common listing of scripture texts for Sundays and special occasions in the church year, which begins with Advent, four Sundays before Christmas, and ends with the celebration of the reign of Christ, in late November. The *Revised Common Lectionary* now in use across denomination lines combines the preferences of various traditions of the Christian faith. Most of the New Testament and a significant portion of the Hebrew Scriptures are included in a three-year cycle centered in the Synoptic Gospels.

This lectionary has provided an organizational structure for some church school curricula and numerous study resources for both clergy and laity. Weekly wrestling with biblical texts among community gatherings of pastors has become commonplace—and worship has been enriched by this dialogue. Far from stifling creativity and relevance, texts for a specific occasion often speak profoundly to our particular circumstances. I am frequently amazed at how God seems to work through these suggested scripture selections to meet our specific needs.

One of my favorite ways of describing what I do in preparing resources for lectionary-based worship is to note that the words are there in the texts for the day. I simply rearrange them to fit various elements of worship: call to worship, invocation, call to confession, prayer of confession, assurance of forgiveness, collect, offertory invitation, offertory prayer, commission and blessing, and at least one new hymn based on one or more of the scripture selections. Repetition of biblical phrases throughout each service is important for our hearing, remembering, and follow-up action.

Never do I expect worship planners to use all my suggestions as they are written. There are more words here than any service should contain. My hope is to "prime the pump" for the creative efforts of others as they adapt these resources or generate their own (usually shorter) versions. Permission to use these materials in worship services is granted on the copyright page. Your notation may state "adapted from" rather than the words noted there.

Year A is centered in the Gospel of Matthew. Writing perhaps four decades after the events he described, Matthew was clearly indebted to Mark, and to another source he shared with Luke, for the material he organized into teaching units. The oral traditions of Jesus' words and deeds were retold by Matthew to portray Jesus as the fulfillment of God's purposes revealed in the Hebrew Scriptures. His remembrances of Jesus were influenced by the developing theologies of the first-century Christian church as it gradually found its identity apart from the synagogue and temple. Matthew grouped the teachings of Jesus into five major discourses, the first of which is the collection Christians have come to call the Sermon on the Mount, chapters 5–7. While Matthew's version of the "good news" is primary this year, John's Gospel also appears from time to time, especially for the great festival seasons.

For the first half of the church year, the "first readings" (usually from the Hebrew Scriptures) are selected for their relationship to the Gospel lesson. After Trinity Sunday, two tracks of Old Testament readings are offered. The one used in my writing follows a semicontinuous pattern of readings from Genesis into Exodus and beyond, recalling the Hebrew patriarchs and the ventures of Moses to the time of Joshua. (The other track continues to relate everything to the Gospel. If chosen by worship planners, it should be followed consistently rather than alternating between the two.) The psalm of the day is always intended as a response to the first reading. The "second reading" of the day is usually from the New Testament epistles (letters), featuring this year some semicontinuous readings from 1 Corinthians during the Epiphany season and from Romans during "ordinary time" after Pentecost.

All three of my books related to the *Revised Common Lectionary* bear titles that reveal my most profound conviction about the Spirit who is creating and embracing all time and space: John's assertion that "God is love." It is our understanding that in God "we live and move and have our being." When we are open to the Love that surrounds us in all times and places, we have the potential of living our best. As Matthew teaches us this year, we will also be *Taught by Love*. I pray that it may be so. Shalom.

—Lavon Bayler

Worship Resources

THE ADVENT SEASON

Isaiah 2:1–5   Romans 13:11–14
Psalm 122   Matthew 24:36–44

CALL TO WORSHIP

Awaken to a season of anticipation.
God is offering peace within and among us.
> *How good it is to gather in God's house!*
> *God draws us together for this time of worship.*

God calls us to celebrate our diversity.
Differences shall no longer divide us.
> *We want to see one another through God's eyes.*
> *We will look for the good in our neighbors.*

Seek the highest and best for each other.
Come to the mountain of God's love.
> *We will follow in the paths where God leads.*
> *Our ears are open to hear God's instructions.*

INVOCATION

You have wakened us from sleep and led us to this place, wondrous God. Now let us feel your presence with us as we encounter your Word. Surely you have blessed us. You have drawn us together and bound us firmly to one another. We give you thanks for giving us an identity as relatives and friends through Jesus Christ. In this season we remember your unexpected appearance among us in the birth of a child. You make yourself known to us again and again. May we know you now! Amen.

CALL TO CONFESSION

In awe before God, who judges our motives and our actions, we come to this time of confession. Often we are reluctant to examine our intentions or our deeds. We postpone changes that would make us ready to receive Christ into our lives. Let us delay no longer.

PRAYER OF CONFESSION

Eternal God, you have brought us to this moment of confrontation. We cannot escape your judgment of our hidden deceits. You know when we are jealous of others. You observe our quarrels with one another. You see how we seek self-gratification rather than the ways you intend for us. Our physical desires are more important to us than the spiritual hungers we suppress. Come among us now to turn us toward the paths where you want to lead us. Amen.

Assurance of Forgiveness

The word of God comes to us for our instruction. The forgiveness of God prompts our thanksgiving. The peace of God turns us from our weapons of destruction to fashion instruments of sharing. God's will for us is security and peace in a community of mutual caring. We are offered this pathway to true prosperity, seeking one another's good. Let us put on Jesus Christ that others may discern Christ's coming through us.

Collect

God of peace, whose ways are not our own and whose coming among us cannot be predicted, we dare to welcome your surprises, seeking to be awake and alert to fully embrace the unexpected, that we might be changed by your appearing and transformed into a peaceful, loving community, for the sake of your house. Amen.

Offertory Invitation

We are stewards of God's household, managers of the earth's treasures for a little while. This time of offering gives us opportunities to invest in causes consistent with God's will for us, to offer the light of God's love to sisters and brothers living in despair. Let us not rob God by withholding what is already God's own.

Offertory Prayer

Thank you, God, for the privilege of sharing your bounty with those in need. Thank you for prospering our work and witness. We seek to walk in your light and follow the pathways where you lead. We want to share the good news of salvation through these gifts and by the way we live. May all your people be made ready for Christ's coming. Amen.

Commission and Blessing

Let us live honorably as in the day.
May we have nothing to hide from God or others.
> **We seek to live in the light of God's love.**
> **We want to be ready when Christ comes.**
We have been privileged to ascend God's mountains.
We are honored by God's call to us.
> **It has been good to meet together in God's house.**
> **It is good to serve together in God's world.**
May we carry the peace of God wherever we go.
Let us share that peace with all whom we meet.
> **For the sake of all, we say, "Peace be with you."**
> **To all the world, we promise, "We will seek your good."**
Amen. **Amen.**

(See hymn 1. Additional worship resources for each Sunday in Advent, based on the same scriptures, may be found in *Fresh Winds of the Spirit*, books 1 and 2.)

Isaiah 11:1–10   Romans 15:4–13
Psalm 72:1–7, 18–19   Matthew 3:1–12

CALL TO WORSHIP
Rejoice together, people of God.
Let all the earth praise our Creator.
> *We have gathered to honor our God.*
> *In awe and reverence, we seek God's Word.*
Welcome one another as Christ welcomes you.
Let each other know of Christ's presence.
> *Surely Christ has come to change us.*
> *Christ is coming still to redirect us.*
This is a time to take delight in the Spirit.
This is the hour to seek knowledge and counsel.
> *We are ready to learn what the Spirit teaches.*
> *We are awakening to the Spirit's gifts.*

INVOCATION
Come, Spirit of God, to rest on our community, embracing the poor, bringing equity to the meek, turning away all expressions of evil. Come into this congregation to enliven our worship, to immerse us in righteousness, to prompt our faithfulness. Rain on us your hope and joy and peace, filling the whole earth with your glory. Amen.

CALL TO CONFESSION
We, who have neglected the instruction of the Scriptures, are called to repent, for God's realm is at hand. How can we help to prepare the way if we are caught up in sin or fascinated by wickedness? Let us confess all that isolates us from the source of life.

PRAYER OF CONFESSION
Awesome God, we have disregarded your Word, failing to inquire after your will for us. We have ignored the needy, defended our advantages, and neglected our prayers. We have not appreciated or witnessed to your sustaining love. Instead we destroy the resources of the earth with little regard for those who follow us. We value our prosperity more than the harmony you envision for your people. O God, we do not like ourselves this way. Deliver us, we pray. Amen.

ASSURANCE OF FORGIVENESS

Remember your baptism! Feel again the refreshing waters that cleanse and make whole. Anticipate the baptism of the Spirit, the unquenchable fire that burns away the chaff. Receive these gifts and bear fruit worthy of repentance.

COLLECT

Just and righteous God, whose wondrous deeds cause love to abound, and whose steadfast love and encouragement grant us to live in harmony with one another through our Savior Jesus Christ, open our spirits to receive your gracious gifts so peace may flourish within and among us until your glory fills all the earth. Amen.

OFFERTORY INVITATION

As we join our voices in prayer and praise, so, too, we bring together the symbols of our life investment: money we have earned, the hours we have before us, the abilities that are ours alone. Let us give ourselves with joy.

OFFERTORY PRAYER

What a joy to give! What a delight to join our efforts to your purposes, amazing God! You inspire us to oppose wickedness, to stand up for the oppressed, to work for harmony among all your children. Lead us, together, to your holy mountain, where all are valued and no one is excluded. May our offerings spread the knowledge of your ways across this earth, widening the circle of inclusion to embrace all your children, in Jesus' name. Amen.

COMMISSION AND BLESSING

The God of steadfastness sends you into the world.
The God of encouragement bids you to live in harmony.
>   *In our daily living, we will rejoice in God's presence.*
>   *We are thankful that God helps us to understand.*
Live each day with hope, welcoming one another.
Rejoice that Christ welcomes you and claims you.
>   *Praise God, whose Holy Spirit empowers us.*
>   *Praise God, who offers us joy and peace.*
Join with God in seeking justice for all.
Lend your resources to help the poor and needy.
>   *May righteousness flourish and peace abound.*
>   *May God's glory fill the earth, through us.*
Amen. **Amen.**

(See hymns 2, 3.)

Isaiah 35:1–10   James 5:7–10
Psalm 146:5–10 or Luke 1:47–55   Matthew 11:2–11

CALL TO WORSHIP

Come away from haste and frantic busyness.
This is the season for quiet waiting.
> *It is hard to still our souls when we are so busy.*
> *It is hard to be patient with ourselves or others.*

Receive God's mercy and strengthen your hearts.
A Savior is coming; God's love is near.
> *We want to hear and believe God's promises.*
> *We want to become patient, loving seekers.*

God presents us with a high and holy way.
Come before God now with praise and singing.
> *We sense the joy God offers to us.*
> *Our spirits rejoice in God our Savior.*

INVOCATION

Mighty One, we rejoice that you strengthen our weak hands and make firm our feeble knees. You open our eyes and unstop our ears. You meet our hungers with good things. You disturb our false pride while helping us discover our true strength. You topple us from our pretensions while lifting up the lowly to claim the inner power you alone can provide. We have assembled to worship you. Awaken the gladness that comes when we recognize your presence. We long to know you in this hour. Amen.

CALL TO CONFESSION

To all whose lives seem like a desert wasteland, God invites: Come to the living waters. To all who feel they are wrestling with lions, God offers a refuge. The Judge who is standing before us awaits our confession with compassion and the promise of healing.

PRAYER OF CONFESSION

Come into our emptiness, gracious God. We feel empty because we have shut you out of our lives. Break through our pretensions, Holy One. We pretend to be powerful because we have not claimed the peace that is available deep within when you dwell with us. Quiet our grumbling and complaining. We are impatient because we have focused on things, not on you. Enter our lives with the forgiveness you have promised to all who are truly sorry for their unfaithfulness. Release us from our self-created prisons. Amen.

ASSURANCE OF FORGIVENESS

God speaks to our fearful hearts: Be strong. Do not fear. I will come to save you. Sorrow and sighing flee away. Joy and gladness are yours. "The blind receive their sight, the lame walk, the lepers are cleansed, the deaf hear, the dead are raised, and the poor have good news brought to them." Praise God!

COLLECT

O Healing Presence, whose claim on us is strong enough to change our direction, look with favor on this gathered congregation, that none may go astray but all may respond with joy to your promises and go out to share your good news with the hungry and needy and oppressed. Amen.

OFFERTORY INVITATION

God continues to lift up the lowly and to topple the powerful from their thrones. God judges us, not by worldly standards of greatness but according to the genuineness of our compassion and the extent of our faithfulness. Our offerings are one measure of our priorities.

OFFERTORY PRAYER

Majestic God, thank you for inviting us to share the blessings you pour out on us. We want to extend the healing ministry of Jesus who gave sight to those who were blind and new insight to some who only pretended to see. Use our resources to heal attitudes as well as bodies, to bring wholeness, not just cures. Help us to address the inequities of the earth that leave so many without food or shelter or hope. Lead us into your realm in the midst of our daily living. Amen.

COMMISSION AND BLESSING

God has been present with us here today.
God also sends us out into the world.
> **The world we are about to enter is God's world.**
> **We can count on God to be with us every day.**
God's judgment is sure, but so is God's love.
God lifts up the lowly and offers them strength.
> **Our eyes and ears have been opened to God's truth.**
> **We have good news for all who need to hear it.**
Be patient with others and do not grumble.
Be patient with yourselves as you seek the Holy Way.
> **Like the prophets, we seek to speak in God's name.**
> **Like lowly servants, we are eager to help others.**
Amen. **Amen.**

(See hymn 4.)

Third Sunday of Advent

Isaiah 7:10–16

Psalm 80:1–7, 17–19

Romans 1:1–7

Matthew 1:18–25

CALL TO WORSHIP

Come away from times of weariness.
Dare to accept the energy God offers you.
> *Restore our energy, O Source of all power.*
> *Let your goodness flow through us.*

Come away from all your insignificant distractions.
Dare to let God show you a larger picture.
> *Help us to examine the flow of our lives.*
> *Reveal to us what is really important.*

Come away from the scorn of enemies.
Dare to laugh with those who have laughed at you.
> *Lead us to think of others in new ways.*
> *Let us find grace and peace in Emmanuel.*

INVOCATION

Shepherding God, whose signs are everywhere, restore in us your light that we may discern what you are about. Shine upon this assembly to give life to our tired routines. Fill our longing hearts with quiet confidence. Awaken the child in us to experience your revelation. By your presence with us, deepen the prayers we utter, and turn our fears to eager anticipation. Touch us to lend strength and confidence as we reach out to one another for help and healing. Amen.

CALL TO CONFESSION

How often we have chosen evil and refused what is good! The result of our choices is not what we intend. Listen, God is waiting to share pardon with all who have erected barriers to shut out God's love.

PRAYER OF CONFESSION

O God, you have called us to be apostles of your grace, but we have been judgmental instead of gracious. We condemn in others what is also, all too often, in us. We refuse to listen to others' pain or to understand the source of their tears. We avoid those who are angry or scornful or embittered. It is easier to dismiss the feelings of others than to offer true empathy. We would rather reject than encounter them. Yet you come to us, Emmanuel, and we want to repent. You reach out to us, and our hearts melt. We want to embrace this new life. Amen.

ASSURANCE OF FORGIVENESS

God's promises are fulfilled. We awaken from the nightmare of our neglect to a vision of what may yet be. We arise from our preoccupation with immediate problems to catch the larger vision and purpose God sets before us. Jesus is coming to save us from our sins. Emmanuel is God with us.

COLLECT

Righteous God, whose gifts of grace and peace are delivered in strange and unexpected places, let your promise of Emmanuel be a sign to us of salvation near at hand. Restore us to that quality of life and relationships which has been your intention for humanity since the beginning of time, that we may be saints who serve, for the sake of all your hurting children. Amen.

OFFERTORY INVITATION

In thanks for all God's gifts, and in response to the tears of so many of God's children, we now gather all that we have brought to share, praying that these resources will accomplish much good among us and far beyond our individual reach.

OFFERTORY PRAYER

Loving God, we would not weary you with empty words or with routine tips of obligation. You have granted us life with such abundant possibilities that we can never do enough to express our gratitude. You have honored us by calling us saints and apostles. Therefore we offer ourselves and our abundance in the confidence that you will continue to provide for us in whatever circumstances we face. Use us as ministers of your grace. Amen.

COMMISSION AND BLESSING

The word of the prophet is finding fulfillment.
Emmanuel is arriving; God is with us.
> *Outcasts have become a holy family.*
> *Rejected ones carry the promise of salvation.*
God widens the circle of acceptance to include us.
God welcomes us to the obedience of faith.
> *Some laugh at our beliefs and taunt us.*
> *Sometimes we are scorned for trusting.*
Surely God's face shines on us to strengthen us.
Gifts of grace and peace are ours to receive.
> *God helps us turn away from doing evil.*
> *God equips us to choose what is good.*
Amen. **Amen.**

(See hymns 5, 6.)

Fourth Sunday of Advent　　11

THE CHRISTMAS SEASON

CHRISTMAS
(PROPER 1)—A, B, C

Isaiah 9:2–7   Titus 2:11–14
Psalm 96   Luke 2:1–14 (15–20)

CALL TO WORSHIP
The grace of God has appeared among us.
A child has been born, bringing God's salvation.
> *We have seen anew the light of God's love.*
> *How splendid is God's gift to us!*

Sing to our God a joyous new song.
Sing to God, all nations of the earth.
> *Great is our God and greatly to be praised.*
> *Ascribe to God the glory that is due.*

Let the heavens be glad as the earth rejoices.
Glory to God in the highest heaven.
> *The child of Bethlehem will help us know God.*
> *We gather to contemplate what God has done.*

INVOCATION
We tremble before you, holy God, for your ways are far beyond our knowing. You surprise us in unexpected places. You come to us in people we may overlook. Your light exposes our shallow commitments and misplaced loyalties. Yet we dare to come before you, to bow down at the manger in awe and wonder. This humble scene moves us more than we could have guessed. It shakes all our pretensions. We are filled with hope that a new day is dawning. Establish among us your way of righteousness. Amen.

CALL TO CONFESSION
Will the light make a difference in our lives? Will the new life appearing in Bethlehem awaken new life within us? We are invited to make a life-changing confession before the God of justice who calls us to renounce impiety and worldly possessions.

PRAYER OF CONFESSION
God of light, we are frightened by what you might expect of us if we get too close to the manger. Many enticements draw our attention away from this holy place. Our worldly passions have led us into comfortable ruts. We admit that some are mere time-killers but others seem to have real value to us. What more can a baby offer us? Of what use is a Messiah who ends up on a cross?

O God, teach us what salvation is all about. Heal the emptiness that gives rise to our misplaced loyalties and distorted dreams. We want to be whole people, experiencing wholesome relationships, giving ourselves to worthy causes. Amen.

Assurance of Forgiveness

The child of Bethlehem becomes for us the Wonderful Counselor whose life points us to new priorities. Away from our frantic busyness, we find true peace on our knees. The truth is dawning in us and among us. Good news of great joy fills us with hope. Glory to God in the highest heaven!

Collect

God of peace, whose judgment is righteous and whose way is truth, draw us toward the new life you send to bless us, that light may shine on our daily paths, awakening our sense of wonder, helping us to appreciate each moment, and equipping us with strength to face life's challenges with zeal for good deeds. Amen.

Offertory Invitation

Ascribe to the Sovereign the glory that is due; bring an offering in response to God's mighty acts. Come with thanksgiving to the place where new birth occurs and the boots of trampling warriors are stilled. Worship God with your gifts.

Offertory Prayer

Amazing God, we want to invest in your promise of endless peace when the authority of your holy child is established. Let your peace come here and now as we dedicate ourselves and our offerings for the purpose of upholding justice and extending the gift of salvation to all people. May our offerings and our lives be a blessing to others, proclaiming good news of great joy in ways that all of us can understand. Amen.

Commission and Blessing

Let us look up, lest we miss the light.
Let us go where God leads, lest we miss the good news.
> *Let us leave behind the burdens God has lifted.*
> *We want to embrace the hope of God's justice.*
Sing a new song to the God of our salvation.
Declare God's glory by the way we live.
> *We want our lives to be songs of praise.*
> *We want to communicate the joy we have found.*
God's truth and righteousness will prevail.
The child of Bethlehem will lead us.
> *Then we will follow where Christ leads.*
> *Glory to God and peace on earth!*
Amen. **Amen.**

(See hymns 7, 8.)

Isaiah 62:6–12   Titus 3:4–7
Psalm 97   Luke 2:(1–7) 8–20

CALL TO WORSHIP

A Savior has appeared in a Bethlehem manger.
Hurry to receive God's loving-kindness.
> **Our God has called us a holy people.**
> **God has gathered us to redeem us.**

This is a time for renewal and rebirth.
Dare to embrace the hope of eternal life.
> **Light is dawning; glory is revealed.**
> **Rejoice and give thanks to our God.**

Let God's healing grace transform you.
Receive the salvation God has promised.
> **We have come to receive God's gifts.**
> **We have come to worship and praise our God.**

INVOCATION

Holy God, as you came to live among people long ago, become real to us as we unite in this special remembrance of Jesus' birth. Establish your realm within and beyond the church, that your name may be renowned through all the earth. Penetrate our sophistication that we, who are so seldom amazed by anything new, may tremble before the power of love. Bring us to our knees before the manger, that we may then stand with confidence before the dangers that are all around us. Amen.

CALL TO CONFESSION

Come away from the idols we have created. Turn away from preoccupation with the things that have become so important to us. Take a break from the routines that keep us from seeking communion with our Creator.

PRAYER OF CONFESSION

O God, we have been too busy to pray and too proud to kneel. We are skeptics in a skeptical age. Yet, we are drawn to the birth of a child. We are inspired by the song of angels. We are challenged by the responsive faithfulness of shepherds. Have mercy on us and help us to put all our concerns in the new perspective of your constant presence and unfailing care. Amen.

ASSURANCE OF FORGIVENESS

The birth in Bethlehem holds for us the promise of rebirth. The faithful response of the shepherds renews among us the courage to trust and to act on our convictions. Our salvation has come. Our healing is assured. The discordant pieces of our lives are reconciled in a wholeness we are free to accept and enjoy. We are God's holy people, redeemed and not forsaken. Praise God!

COLLECT

Good and loving God, whose offering of rebirth and renewal has been richly poured out for us in Jesus Christ, take us again to the manger where we may receive your gifts in awe and humility, that our lives may reflect the joy you intend, winning others to the wholesomeness you offer and giving glory to your holy name. Amen.

OFFERTORY INVITATION

All the good things in life that we enjoy, all the relationships that enrich our lives, all the experiences we have been privileged to encounter are tokens of God's greatest gift to us. God has entered human flesh. God comes to us, offering life in all its fullness. Our offerings are one way to accept these gifts with great thanksgiving.

OFFERTORY PRAYER

Gracious God, your claims on us fill us with awe. You have not abandoned us when we forgot you or turned away as we denied you. Instead, you call us once more to be a holy people, heirs of hope, conveyors of good news. As we return to you some of the riches you have entrusted to us, let our offerings be a down payment on our recommitment of life itself to carrying out the mission to which you call us. Amen.

COMMISSION AND BLESSING

Carry with you the quiet joy ignited in your hearts.
You are a part of God's gift to the world.
>   *Our hearts have been cleansed at the manger.*
>   *We want to respond with faithfulness.*
Return again and again to Bethlehem.
Take time to remember and rejoice in our salvation.
>   *We cannot be silent, for we have received God's gift.*
>   *We cannot rest until everyone hears the good news.*
The goodness and loving-kindness of God go with us.
God's mercy renews us day by day.
>   *Glory to God in the highest heaven.*
>   *Peace on earth for all whom God favors.*
Amen. **Amen.**

(See hymns 8, 9.)

Isaiah 52:7–10   Hebrews 1:1–4 (5–12)
Psalm 98   John 1:1–14

CALL TO WORSHIP

Before all time and all worlds, there was the Word.
That Word came to our time and place as a human being.
The Word was the truth of God.
That Word has come to us in Jesus Christ.
God has spoken through creation, and through prophets.
Yet the person of Jesus speaks to us most clearly.
In Christ, we see the glory and kindness of God.
Through Christ, we know we are God's children.
Come, then, to sing new songs of praise.
Rejoice that God sends messengers of good news.
We bring the melodies of our hearts and voices.
Praise God with harp and trumpet and horns!

INVOCATION

Amid the joyful songs of Christmas, we pause, O God, to let the joy seep into the pores of our being. We take these moments to ponder your faithfulness, even when we have ignored you. We reach for your peace that turns us from our frantic preoccupation with so much that denies life. May the brightness of your glory be reflected on us in a time of genuine worship. May it shine through us, changing what we see and hear as we pass through your world. Amen.

CALL TO CONFESSION

What a rare gift this season brings. Families come together. Little children are heard. We claim our church family as our own link to God's love. God works miracles among us. Let us confess our need.

PRAYER OF CONFESSION

O God, we almost missed your light. We confess our neglect of worship, our forgetfulness of your gifts. We have failed to see evidences of your love. We have not heard your cries for justice. We have viewed salvation as strange rhetoric rather than healing transformation. We have mouthed tired platitudes while you call for a new song of true joy and peace. Is there forgiveness for us in this season? Is there hope for new life? Amen.

Assurance of Forgiveness

There is good news. The light still shines, and it is for you, for me, for all of us together. God still works miracles within us and among us. The hills are singing, the oceans roar, and the rivers clap. Let all the people shout for joy. Celebrate God's saving power, God's compassion, God's acceptance of us. God's forgiveness helps us confront and overcome the evil in our lives. God offers us peace that has no other source than God's faithfulness.

Collect

Creator God, who laid the foundations of the earth and breathed into its many forms the great mystery of life, work your miracles of transformation among us now, that we may not leave this place without a passionate commitment to your truth and the pursuit of justice for all people, in the name of Christ, the word made flesh in Jesus long ago, and in us today. Amen.

Offertory Invitation

All creation proclaims God's saving power and faithfulness. Our offerings can also make a powerful witness. They are expressions of gratitude but also proclamations of commitment. They celebrate God's covenant with us, demonstrated in the gift of Jesus. Let us give as we have been blessed.

Offertory Prayer

Loving God, we have heard good news. We want to pass it on. We have seen your beauty. We want to make it a part of who we are so others may praise you. We have felt your presence. We want others to know the peace that you alone can bring. So we dedicate our offerings and ourselves to your movement of justice and the building of true community. Amen.

Commission and Blessing

We are being sent out unto the world.
We are commissioned as messengers of good news.
> *God grant us good hearing and wise speaking.*
> *God grant us discerning sight and deep insight.*
We are sent out to reflect the glory of God.
We are called to announce salvation and peace.
> *God grant us honest speech and warm compassion.*
> *God grant us continuing commitment to justice.*
We have been blessed in the gift of a child.
We are upheld by the gift of the Word made flesh.
> *We go out to serve with joy and confidence.*
> *Let all the world join our happy songs.*
Amen. **Amen.**

(See hymn 10.)

Isaiah 63:7–9   Hebrews 2:10–18

Psalm 148   Matthew 2:13–23

CALL TO WORSHIP

Praise God, all who dwell on this earth.
Praise God in the heights and depths of life.
> **We will recount the deeds of God.**
> **Surely God has shown us goodness and mercy.**
Praise God, sun and moon and stars.
Praise God, fire and hail, snow and frost.
> **Men and women, young and old, together:**
> **Let us praise and honor our Creator.**
Let God's name be praised and exalted.
God's glory is above heaven and earth.
> **By God's steadfast love, we are drawn to worship.**
> **Our gracious Savior leads us in new ways.**

INVOCATION

Redeemer of all who put their trust in you, we seek your presence here. Only our own attitudes can separate us from you. Re-create us in your own image so we may be true to your intentions for us and in tune with your purposes for our life together. In our times of distress, pour out your pity and your love that we may know we are not alone. Lift us up and carry us when our strength fails. Now, in the midst of this congregation, we would praise you and honor your name. Amen.

CALL TO CONFESSION

Surely God longs to draw us close, to enter our thoughts and clarify our vision. It is God's will and purpose to free us from our fears and our frantic, self-protective ways. We cannot be whole people apart from God, so we come to confess how lost we are.

PRAYER OF CONFESSION

O God, we have been so busy with things that do not satisfy! We have tried to fill our emptiness with activities and possessions that drain our energies rather than give life meaning. We do not know how to live, and we are afraid to die. We excuse our own sin at the same time that we deplore the abuse and violence we see in others. We deny the witness of the One who shared our common lot, for we are not willing to take the risks of genuine love. O God, save us from ourselves. Amen.

Assurance of Forgiveness

Christ identified with us to show us whose we are. Christ suffered for us to help us in our times of testing. Christ died to lead us to life in all its fullness. Now our merciful and faithful High Priest welcomes us to be at one with God and our own best selves. We are forgiven, we are redeemed, we are lifted up to a life of true freedom.

Collect

God of the prophets, God of our dreams and our waking moments, God of our times of weeping and our days of gladness, lead us, we pray, from all that would destroy the best you have placed within us. Lead us toward those times and places where we can grow in the likeness of Jesus. Help us to discern the warnings and the invitations that come from you so our lives may be a beacon to lead others to fulfillment and joy. Amen.

Offertory Invitation

We are invited to praise God with the offerings of our best. In the generous spirit of this season, we give thanks for God's providence with an answering generosity. The needs of our brothers and sisters, both spiritual and material, cry out for the help we can give. What a privilege to act for God through our giving!

Offertory Prayer

Awesome God, when we recount your gracious deeds and praiseworthy acts, we want to imitate them. Because of your mercy and favor and the abundance of your steadfast love, we are moved to respond. Thank you for the gift of life, for all you have entrusted to us, for your watchful care over us, for surrounding us with love when loss and suffering overwhelm us. It is when we give with generous hearts that we begin to understand how much we have been given. Thank you, God. Amen.

Commission and Blessing

Engage your world as brothers and sisters of Jesus.
Treat all God's children as next of kin.
> *God has called us into community.*
> *Jesus leads us into a life of service.*
Praise God for all creation, including yourself.
Praise God for the variety of people who surround us.
> *We share one flesh and blood with all humanity.*
> *We share one flesh and blood with Jesus Christ.*
Surely we are loved, welcomed, and blessed.
God's presence goes with us in all we do.
> *Wherever we go, we can count on God's care.*
> *Whatever we face, Christ will meet us there.*
Amen. **Amen.**

(See hymn 11.)

Numbers 6:22–27   Galatians 4:4–7 or Philippians 2:5–11
Psalm 8   Luke 2:15–21

CALL TO WORSHIP

Heirs of God, come to claim your identity.
Inheritors of glory, gather to worship our Creator.
> *How majestic is God's name in all the earth!*
> *How generously you have blessed us, O God!*
The beauty of heaven and earth is God's gift.
The awesome mystery of new life is entrusted to us.
> *We are given dominion over God's creation.*
> *The care of this planet is referred to us.*
Plants and animals depend on our faithfulness.
Air and soil and water require our stewardship.
> *How awesome are the wonders around us!*
> *How amazing is the trust God places in us!*

INVOCATION

Bless us and keep us this day, O God, for we need your regular visitation to order our priorities. We forget that we are called to act in your name, for the interest of all people. We need to be reminded that the glory and honor given to us are meant for all to share. In the name of Jesus, who humbly accepted your authority, we seek the guidance of your Spirit in this time of worship, and in every day of service. Amen.

CALL TO CONFESSION

Let the same mind be in you that was in Christ Jesus, who did not exploit his relationship with God but took on the humble role of servant. Put aside false pride and self-seeking, that the fullness of God may dwell in you.

PRAYER OF CONFESSION

O God, we confess that we have resisted your rule in our lives. We act in our own name for our own advantage. We want glory and honor without sacrifice. We want to be your children and heirs without accepting your sovereignty. We want to claim your name without taking on the responsibilities given to members of your household. O God, we have violated your trust in us. How can you forgive us again? Amen.

Assurance of Forgiveness

Children of God, you are forgiven in the name of Jesus. The Spirit of Christ is a gift available to each one of us today. Through Christ, we recognize God as a loving parent who wills the very best for us in all circumstances. Bow in amazement before the One who became flesh to dwell among us. Praise and glorify God in this time of worship. Prepare to testify to this good news wherever you go this week. God is mindful of us and restores us to full communion with the Eternal One.

Collect

Sovereign God, whose majesty can be seen whenever we open our eyes, and whose revelation is most clearly discerned in the life of Jesus, show us again the good news we so often ignore. Take us to the humble manger that we may live with amazement and praise, welcoming others in the name of Jesus. Amen.

Offertory Invitation

When shepherds heard the message of angels, they made immediate response. Once again, we have heard the story. What is our response? In these moments, we have the opportunity to glorify and praise God through our giving—in the name of Jesus.

Offertory Prayer

In the name of Jesus, who emptied himself for us, we pour out our gratitude in these symbols of commitment. In joyful obedience, we give as we have been blessed. We want to participate with our Creator in reaching out to sisters and brothers who have not experienced God's care. We commit ourselves to be champions of children, whose eager openness can teach us so much. We offer our lives in humble obedience to you, amazing, majestic God. Amen.

Commission and Blessing

God bless you and keep you.
God's face will shine on you and be gracious to you.
> *We receive God's blessing with joy.*
> *We embrace the peace God offers.*

Let the enemies of truth be silenced.
Let the children of God bear witness to the world.
> *We would glorify and praise God together.*
> *We will carry the message into our world.*

We are heirs of God's mercy and favor.
We have been crowned with glory and honor.
> *O God, our God, how majestic is your name.*
> *All earth and heaven reflect your glory!*

Amen. **Amen.**

(See hymn 12.)

NEW YEAR'S DAY
(JANUARY 1)—A, B, C

Ecclesiastes 3:1–13   Revelation 21:1–6a
Psalm 8   Matthew 25:31–46

CALL TO WORSHIP

Welcome this new year as the time of God's presence.
Our Creator offers us a new heaven and a new earth.
> *This is the season for rebirth of our best.*
> *God has gifted us with new opportunities.*

God is making all things new.
Mourning, crying, and pain cannot prevail.
> *We are invited to find enjoyment in living.*
> *We are meant to discover pleasure in our toil.*

God is mindful of our needs and our strengths.
We receive resources for the tasks God gives us.
> *We have come to thank and praise God.*
> *How majestic is God's name in all the earth!*

INVOCATION

In-dwelling God, we greet you in this new year. As centuries come and go, your presence is ever new when we open our senses to receive you. We ask now that you sharpen our awareness of your creative energy at work within and around us. Let us welcome you in the stranger who is not yet a friend, in the hungry who need the food and care we might provide, in the nurse who fulfills our thirst for water and kindness. Show us your expectations for us in this season. Amen.

CALL TO CONFESSION

In awe before God's creation—a sky full of distant suns, and a tiny planet nurtured by one small star among them—we see our own relative insignificance. Yet God tells us that each one of us is known and valued. Before such a God, we bow in humble repentance.

PRAYER OF CONFESSION

God of all creation, how can you accept our empty praying? The world of our prayers is so small, and the needs of your people are so great. Yet, we must be personal in our confession, for we are a people of misplaced values, and our wrongful priorities have brought us much distress. We have missed your realm among us when we ignored those around us who were thirsty and hungry, when we turned away from prisoners and people suffering from AIDS. Restore us to membership in your family. We want to be forgiven, we want to change. Amen.

ASSURANCE OF FORGIVENESS

The promise of eternal life is meant for each one of us, and all of us together. Our lives begin to experience eternity when they focus beyond ourselves. Experience anew the wonders of God's creation. Take time to discover God's presence in another human being today. The new heaven and earth will be yours.

COLLECT

Sovereign God, before whom our thoughts and deeds are judged, we have gathered before you, sheep and goats together, praying that all of us might be compassionately responsive to sisters and brothers who are hungry, thirsty, ill-clothed, sick, or imprisoned, not that we might be rewarded, but that they might be helped and your realm brought near. Amen.

OFFERTORY INVITATION

For everything there is a season. Always there is occasion for gratitude. One expression of our thanks to God is this time of tangible sharing. We give that God's will may be more fully realized as we dedicate ourselves and our gifts toward meeting others in their time of need.

OFFERTORY PRAYER

May our hands extend a blessing to friends and strangers who hunger, or thirst, or shiver in the cold. May our presence comfort and inspire persons who are sick or in prison. May our witness to your gift of newness help to make it real to those who can only look backward. Help us all to face the future, trusting you, as we join you in wiping away tears and caring for the least and the lost. Amen.

COMMISSION AND BLESSING

Go from this time of seeking to seasons of sharing.
God gives us many opportunities to love and to care.
> **We know lonely ones whom we can visit.**
> **There are hungry people we can help to feed.**
God sets before us a new heaven and a new earth.
God makes all things new—even us.
> **We have been made a little lower than God.**
> **We are crowned with glory and honor.**
God gives us dominion and stewardship.
We have awesome responsibility over God's creation.
> **God gives us tasks to be busy with.**
> **We want to do what God intends in this new year.**
Amen. **Amen.**

(See hymn 13.)

SECOND SUNDAY AFTER CHRISTMAS— A, B, C

Jeremiah 31:7–14   Ephesians 1:3–14
Psalm 147:12–20   John 1:(1–9), 10–18

CALL TO WORSHIP

God has been good to us.
Let us sing our songs of praise.
> **God brings us together from many places.**
> **Let us celebrate our diversity.**

Come to hear God's word for our day.
Listen that you might understand and share it.
> **God's commands run swiftly over the earth.**
> **God's word comes to us as a mighty wind.**

Give thanks for the bounty God supplies.
Gain strength from the peace God offers.
> **God's word fills us with radiance.**
> **We are ready to dance with joy.**

INVOCATION

All blessing and honor be to you, Holy God, for the wisdom and insight you have
offered us in Jesus Christ. Through him, the mystery of your will is becoming
clearer to us. You introduce us to life in all its fullness, lived in the light of your
grace and truth. Thank you for this holy season. Continue, we pray, to reveal yourself to us in this hour. Amen.

CALL TO CONFESSION

As the celebration of Christmas draws to a close, we are tempted to let the light
of God's revelation among us fade into the shadows of our busyness. We stumble
as skeptics, doubting God's visitation and squandering our inheritance as children
of light. God longs for our return.

PRAYER OF CONFESSION

Save your people, God of goodness and light. You have blessed us with the peace
of Christmas, but we reject your gift in our frantic striving. You destine us for adop-
tion, but we go our own way. You send the Holy Spirit to lead us, but we block
out awareness of your will for us in favor of our own selfish ambition. Restore to
us the ability to discern and respond to the light you offer, we pray in Jesus' name.
Amen.

ASSURANCE OF FORGIVENESS

God promises us rescue and comfort and joy. In Christ we receive forgiveness of our trespasses, according to the riches of God's grace. The gospel of salvation is for all who repent and believe. In Christ, the Word became flesh to dwell among us and assure us of God's love. Let us give thanks for the truth available for our living. Amen.

COLLECT

Gracious God, in whose love we are chosen and blessed, let your Word become flesh once more as we embrace the light of Jesus Christ in our walk and in our talk. Strengthen our belief and our testimony, that enlightenment may be available to all your children and fulfillment of your will for us may be realized among all the earth's people. Amen.

OFFERTORY INVITATION

How will we express our thanks for all God's bounty? We can extend God's invitation to those who are blind and those who are lame, to the scattered and lost, to people of all ages and conditions in need of a shepherd. We can use well the resources God entrusts to us. Let us dedicate our gifts.

OFFERTORY PRAYER

How good you have been to us, wondrous God! Our lives are like a watered garden when we are responsive to your will for us. You turn mourning into joy and give gladness for sorrow. We are radiant with thankfulness when we remember the glory of your Word made flesh. In response to your grace, we dedicate this offering to extend your reign among us. May we be part of your plan for the fullness of time. Amen.

COMMISSION AND BLESSING

We are made next of kin to Jesus Christ.
Let us live in the light God sent.
> *Like John, we wish to testify to that light.*
> *May all come to faith through Christ.*
Believe that we are all children of God.
We are here according to the will of God.
> *Through Christ we have received grace upon grace.*
> *The truth of the gospel is revealed to us.*
Let your praise be heard throughout this week.
Give thanks for all the spiritual blessings you receive.
> *We are redeemed as God's own people.*
> *God declares us holy and blameless. Praise God!*
Amen. **Amen.**

(See hymn 14.)

EPIPHANY AND THE SEASON FOLLOWING

EPIPHANY—A, B, C

Isaiah 60:1–6   Ephesians 3:1–12
Psalm 72:1–7, 10–14   Matthew 2:1–12

CALL TO WORSHIP

Have you seen the star? Have you heard the good news?
God, who created all things, has come to earth.
> **We have heard of a baby born in Bethlehem.**
> **We have seen evidence that God is with us.**
Have you allowed God to reign in your life?
Have you laid your gifts before the Holy Child?
> **We have noticed the generous travelers from the east.**
> **They inspire in us a willingness to share.**
God's call to us is for justice, beyond generosity.
Are you ready for God's eternal purpose in Christ?
> **We have been afraid to trust God completely.**
> **Yet we want to respond to God's dreams for us.**

INVOCATION

Arise upon us, holy God, and let your glory appear over us today. Come in the
brightness of your dawn to bring light to all the nations of earth. Gather us together in such harmony that we may discern your will for us and be led in your
ways. Fill us with that radiant joy that allows us to reflect your goodness. Let all
people praise you, O God. Let our praise resound through all the world. Amen.

CALL TO CONFESSION

Amid the oppression and violence all too evident in the world around us, we are
called to rid ourselves of resentment and hatred and misuse of power. Aware of
vast inequalities of opportunity and resources, we are summoned to examine our
roles in creating or eliminating injustice. Let us confess our sin.

PRAYER OF CONFESSION

Just and righteous God, we tremble before your all-knowing awareness of us. You
have blessed us with abundance we have not counted and riches we have not fully
appreciated. Our gratitude is found wanting before your judgment. Our attention
to the needs of the poor and oppressed is less than you desire. Forgive us, God, for
misplaced anger and callous disregard of ways we trample others. We seek redemption from oppression and violence to embrace new life in Christ. Amen.

Assurance of Forgiveness

God in Christ delivers the needy when they call, the poor and those who have no helper. God forgives us when we are truly penitent and know we have nowhere to turn but to the grace that Love provides. We are the church to which God entrusts a rich variety of wisdom. Let us together accept the gifts of God and make them known.

Collect

God of mystery and grace, whose revelation comes to those willing to hear and see and feel, send your word, your star, your dreams, to confront us with the gospel of salvation, that we might respond with a radiance that is contagious to those around us and faithful in proclaiming your praise. Amen.

Offertory Invitation

The riches of our land far surpass the resources of the visitors from the east who came to worship the infant Jesus. As they opened their treasure chests, may we open our wallets and our lives in expressions of thanksgiving and commitment. This offering is an expression of our priorities.

Offertory Prayer

We bring our wealth to praise you, God. All the riches of our abundance you have provided. The land has yielded prosperity for us so that even the poorest among us have something to give. Above all, we are thankful for your revelation in Jesus Christ that gives us good news to share. May this offering accomplish among us, and far beyond us, the mission you give to each one of your people. Amen.

Commission and Blessing

To the least of God's saints, grace is given.
Thus we have received grace upon grace.
> **The boundless riches of Christ are ours to share.**
> **Our faith in Christ gives us access to God.**
Go forth in boldness and confidence.
God in Christ will meet our needs and give us voice.
> **How exciting it is to proclaim God's praise.**
> **Our hearts thrill and rejoice, and we are radiant.**
God's work of justice is our work.
God's peacemaking is our mandate.
> **We are servants of God's purposes.**
> **We will follow the road of justice and peace.**
Amen. **Amen.**

(See hymn 15.)

Isaiah 42:1–9   Acts 10:34–43
Psalm 29   Matthew 3:13–17

CALL TO WORSHIP

A voice of power and majesty calls out to us:
I am your God; I have called you in righteousness.
> **We are amazed that God knows us and calls us.**
> **By God's breath and spirit, we receive life.**
God takes us by the hand and leads us.
In covenant with God, we extend light to the world.
> **Eyes are opened and prisoners are freed.**
> **Justice and peace prevail, by God's strength.**
Worship with joy and give glory to God's name.
Listen for the new thing God declares.
> **We remember that we have been baptized.**
> **May we live as those with whom God is pleased.**

INVOCATION

Come, Holy Spirit, to dwell in us and among us. Make us more than dimly burning wicks, that we might share enough light to make a difference in your world. Where there is injustice, help us as we work to change the minds and hearts of those who benefit from it. Show us again the new possibilities you have in mind for us. May we reflect your peace amid the frantic busy pace of the marketplace. Amen.

CALL TO CONFESSION

As we remember today the baptism of Jesus, we rejoice that we, too, have been baptized into the family of faith. Our lives have been committed to the way of Jesus. Yet, we have wandered from that way of life. Confession allows us to turn around and rediscover the paths God intends for us.

PRAYER OF CONFESSION

God of glory, we confess that our lives have not glorified you. God of justice, we admit our complicity with systems of injustice. God of light, we are aware of the shadows we create that keep others from seeing you. All-inclusive God, we repent of our narrow vision and our tendency to exclude. Purge us of the idols that keep us from full commitment to the way of Jesus, in whose name we pray. Amen.

ASSURANCE OF FORGIVENESS

The prophets testify that all who believe in God's messenger receive forgiveness of sin through his name. We believe that Jesus is that beloved messenger, with whom God is well pleased. Through this One on whom God's spirit was poured out, like a descending dove, we know ourselves to be beloved by God, forgiven and freed from the bonds of sin.

COLLECT

Creator of all worlds, who appoints us to serve as ministers of justice, examples of righteousness, and teachers of truth, help us to see the fulfillment of your word and the new things you now declare, so we may receive the strength you promise and thereby give a believable testimony to your world. Amen.

OFFERTORY INVITATION

How can we share the message that God is impartial, that justice and peace are God's intention for all humankind? We combine our individual efforts through the church, joining in programs, projects, and outreach that reflect God's light into the world. Our gifts of gratitude are one way of sharing.

OFFERTORY PRAYER

We pray, O God, that our offerings delight you. We bring them to encourage all who work for justice and peace on our behalf, that they may not grow faint or be crushed by opposition. May the oppressed find healing, the discouraged receive hope, and those who are bound discover freedom, through and beyond our efforts. Amen.

COMMISSION AND BLESSING

The voice of power and majesty has spoken to us.
God gives strength and blesses us with peace.
Though we are bruised reeds, we will not break.
Our dimly burning wicks will not be quenched.
We face another week with renewed strength.
The light we received will continue to shine.
God has healed and forgiven us.
We believe God loves us and is pleased with us.
Let your lives testify to the goodness of God.
Ascribe to God glory and majesty and power.
We are witnesses from the baptized community.
God sends us out to embrace others in Christ's name.
Amen. **Amen.**

(See hymns 16, 17.)

First Sunday after Epiphany   33

Isaiah 49:1–7   1 Corinthians 1:1–9
Psalm 40:1–11   John 1:29–42

CALL TO WORSHIP

Have you understood God's thoughts toward us?
Have you listened to glad news of deliverance?
> *We are here to receive God's message.*
> *Our hearts are open to the Word we will hear.*

Listen, all who are near and all who are far away;
God is calling us as servants and as saints.
> *Usually we do not think of ourselves in that way.*
> *We resist lowly roles, but we do not aspire to sainthood.*

Do not be afraid to serve God with your whole being.
Neither fear the call to join the saints of Jesus Christ.
> *We trust that God will strengthen us for our tasks.*
> *We are ready to be led into new responsibilities.*

INVOCATION

God, we wait for you to hear our cries. We come from desperate situations and many moments of despair. Then, when you call us together, we are challenged to be and to do more than we have already faced. We have spent our strength. How can we do more? Will you renew us here? We feel that we have labored in vain. Will you help us make sense out of our failures? Come with your saving help. Amen.

CALL TO CONFESSION

The church of which we are a part has a long record of faithful worship and service. Yet, it is easy to settle into routines and rituals that lose the urgency of the gospel. We become complacent, and our focus narrows to our own immediate concerns. Let us return to God for cleansing from our sin.

PRAYER OF CONFESSION

We come back to you, O Holy One, to renew our commitment. We confess that pride has led us to embrace false gods. We spend more time with our hobbies than with your cause. We pay more attention to our toys than to your truth. Your law is no longer in our hearts. We have neglected the spiritual gifts entrusted to us. We have forgotten that we have been named and baptized and commissioned for service. O God, bring us back to yourself. Amen.

Assurance of Forgiveness

Hear the glad news of deliverance. God's saving help is available to us. God's mercy is sure. We can leave our idols and reorder our priorities. We are empowered by God's steadfast love and faithfulness to become all we are meant to be. Sing a new song of praise to our God!

Collect

God of peace, whose love has graced this planet in Jesus Christ and baptized us with the Holy Spirit, reawaken our eagerness to follow where Jesus leads so we may fulfill the discipleship to which we are called, lead others to experience your steadfast love and faithfulness, and inspire them to delight in doing your will. Amen.

Offertory Invitation

Remembering all we have spent for nothing and vanity, we now consider how to bring offerings worthy of God's saving grace. Nothing can compare to God's wondrous deeds and thoughts toward us. We can only respond with trust and joy and generosity.

Offertory Prayer

God of the saints in every age and time, we are grateful for the privilege of being numbered among them as we invest our gifts from you. Because of your generosity, we have not lacked for anything we really need. Grant now that our words and deeds may follow our offering into loving service in your realm. Amen.

Commission and Blessing

We have found the Messiah, God's anointed one.
Let us follow where Jesus leads.
> *We want to learn from Jesus how to live.*
> *We are eager to be faithful disciples.*
Know that we can call on Jesus any time.
In every place we go, Christ is available to us.
> *We give thanks for the grace of God in Christ.*
> *By it, our knowledge and speech have been enriched.*
God remains steadfast and faithful.
We will be strengthened for all of life's journey.
> *We put our trust in God for all time and eternity.*
> *We will delight to do God's will.*
Amen. **Amen.**

(See hymn 18.)

Isaiah 9:1–4   I Corinthians 1:10–18
Psalm 27:1, 4–9   Matthew 4:12–23

CALL TO WORSHIP

Come, all who have known gloom and anguish.
Come, all who have walked amid terrors of the night.
> *Sometimes we have felt oppressed and forsaken.*
> *Our losses seem greater than we can bear.*
God is our light and our salvation.
God is our stronghold; we need not fear.
> *Enemies lose their power when we look up to God.*
> *We come now, seeking God's face.*
Come, behold the beauty of our God.
Come to find shelter in a day of trouble.
> *We will sing and make melody to God.*
> *We will dare to lift up shouts of joy.*

INVOCATION

Shine on us today, gracious God, for we need the light and salvation you offer.
Come to each one gathered here, and to all who are a part of this community of
faith. Come to our city, our nation, our world, to still the quarrels and dissolve the
enmity among us. Come with good news of health and wholeness for everyone.
Do not cast us off, do not forsake us, O God of our salvation. Amen.

CALL TO CONFESSION

Jesus came to Galilee with the message of John the Baptist: Repent, for God's realm
has come near. His invitation went out to common everyday folks: Follow me. We,
too, are called to repent and to follow.

PRAYER OF CONFESSION

Turn our lives around, God. Help us to identify in ourselves those parts of us that
need to change if we are to experience your joy. Too long we have been hiding in
the shadows, reluctant to express our faith. Too long we have shunned the light,
afraid of what might be exposed. Too long we have avoided people with whom
we have a quarrel, refusing to build bridges across our differences. Save us from
ourselves that we may enjoy your realm. Amen.

Assurance of Forgiveness

Light has come. Salvation is poured out on those who accept it. God is gracious and reaches out to welcome us. We are free to accept the invitation to follow Jesus. There is good news of forgiveness and healing to be shared. Let's do it.

Collect

God of the people, who sent Jesus to dispel the gloom in which we choose to live and bring us closer to your realm, teach us again today, uniting our hearts and minds around the purpose of serving you, for the sake of all humankind. Amen.

Offertory Invitation

What can we do to send the message of the cross to those who think it is foolishness? How will the gospel be proclaimed to people who are perishing, both within and far beyond this church? One way is through the sharing of resources God has given us—our time, talent, and treasure. Let us give with joy.

Offertory Prayer

Let these gifts follow Christ's lead into the lives of people who live in poverty or despair. O God, use them to heal divisions among your children. Show us how to be instruments of peace. Ready us to follow Jesus, to make an offering of ourselves, not just our money. Teach us so we may teach others. Heal us so we can become instruments of healing. To these purposes we dedicate this offering and our lives. Amen.

Commission and Blessing

People of light, turn to face a new week.
People of joy, enter your daily routines empowered.
> *God is our light and our salvation.*
> *We will not be afraid to live our joy.*
People of unity, seek to overcome divisions.
People of commitment, dare to follow Jesus.
> *Christ is our example and our leader.*
> *We will care enough to fish for people.*
God is gracious to us and blesses us.
We are being saved by the power of God.
> *God offers us life in the heavenly realm.*
> *We can begin to experience it here and now.*
Amen. **Amen.**

(See hymns 19, 20.)

Third Sunday after Epiphany   37

Micah 6:1–8   I Corinthians 1:18–31
Psalm 15   Matthew 5:1–12

CALL TO WORSHIP

Jesus taught: Blessed are the poor in spirit.
He said that the realm of God is theirs.
> *We read that those who mourn are blessed.*
> *Jesus said they will be comforted.*

The meek will inherit the earth.
The merciful will obtain mercy.
> *All who hunger and thirst for rich treasures are blessed;*
> *Jesus said they will be filled.*

Blessed are the pure in heart and the peacemakers;
They are God's children and will see God.
> *Those persecuted and falsely accused are blessed.*
> *Even in the face of evil, we will rejoice.*

INVOCATION

Let the mountains hear our voices raised in prayer and praise, wise and holy God. We gather in this sacred place to honor and adore you. We come humbly, claiming the cross of Jesus Christ as our sign. We give thanks that you lift up the weak and lowly, defy the world's foolishness, and invite us to share in life at its fullest and best as disciples of Jesus. We want to accept your invitation. Amen.

CALL TO CONFESSION

God knows the intent of our hearts as we come to this time of repentance. Are we intent on doing justice? Do we love mercy? Are we ready to walk humbly with our Creator? If so, God is ready to hear our prayers.

PRAYER OF CONFESSION

O God, we confess that we have accepted the world's wisdom as our guide. We have been impressed by the power of weapons and the importance of high positions. We measure worth by the number of possessions we command. We have been unkind in our speech and uncaring in our deeds. We have doubted the power of the cross to save. Turn us around, holy God, that we might be blessed. Amen.

Assurance of Forgiveness

God destroys the wisdom of those who think themselves wise. God chooses the weak and foolish to shame those who think themselves strong and all-knowing. The God who forgives calls us to a life of kindness in word and deed, mercy toward both friend and foe, and justice in all our dealings. Thank God for setting before us standards that surpass our highest aspirations, along with the possibility for joyous fulfillment.

Collect

All-wise God, whose saving power has come to us in Jesus Christ, grant that we may hear and speak the truth and do what is right so our lives may be a blessing to the world and lead others to do justice, love kindness, and walk humbly with you. Amen.

Offertory Invitation

God is neither pleased with burnt offerings nor impressed by the size of our gifts. God wants our full commitment and devotion, of which our giving in these moments is only a symbol. God calls us to lives of mercy and peacemaking, for which our offering can make a beginning.

Offertory Prayer

We devote ourselves and these tokens of our thankfulness toward the realization of your reign among us, holy God. We pray for purity of heart as we hunger and thirst for righteousness and as we seek to be peacemakers. We rejoice in this opportunity to share in the extension of your realm. Bless us and our offering, we pray, in Jesus' name. Amen.

Commission and Blessing

Walk blamelessly before God and do what is right.
Speak the truth to all, from your heart.
> *We will honor and fear God each day.*
> *May our words and deeds resist all evil.*

Consider your call and live righteously.
Know that God chooses you for a blessing.
> *We delight in seeking to do God's will.*
> *We are awed that God appoints and blesses us.*

Rejoice and be glad, for God offers rich rewards.
From God you receive wisdom and true power.
> *We are amazed at the responsibility God gives us.*
> *We rejoice in the blessings God promises.*

Amen. **Amen.**

(See hymn 21.)

Isaiah 58:1–9a (9b–12)   I Corinthians 2:1–12 (13–16)
Psalm 112:1–9 (10)   Matthew 5:13–20

CALL TO WORSHIP

> We delight to draw near to you, gracious God.
> We rejoice in the many gifts you have given us.
>> *We lift up our hearts and voices in praise.*
>> *We humble ourselves before the God of all worlds.*
> We gather to remember God's commandments.
> We seek for ourselves the wisdom God imparts.
>> *The wisdom of God is not like any other.*
>> *It draws us away from the world's agenda.*
> God sends us into the world with new priorities.
> We are grounded in the Spirit that we might be discerning.
>> *We are filled with the mind of Christ.*
>> *We are already citizens of God's realm.*

INVOCATION

May our voices rise like trumpets to greet you, holy God. May our ears be attuned to know your ways. May our hearts be steady, focused on you. Praise be to you, O God, whom we worship with awe and delight. Guide us, we pray, in this time of worship. Touch us at the points of our deepest need. Stir us amidst our entrenched complacency. Make us strong to loose the bonds of injustice, to undo the things of the yoke, to let the oppressed go free. Then your light will break forth like the dawn and we will experience your healing care. Amen.

CALL TO CONFESSION

We have come together, not to be confirmed in our prejudices, but to be changed, not to be affirmed for our righteousness, but to uncover the immaturity of our faith that we might grow. Thus, we confess to God our failure to live by the best we know, and our limited response to the vision God sets before us.

PRAYER OF CONFESSION

O God, you call out to us, saying, "Here I am," but we do not listen. You pour out on us spiritual gifts, but we do not discern them. You call us to build a more just society but we cling to our advantages. Forgive us, we pray, and help us to change. Help us so to know and understand Jesus Christ that we might reflect the God of glory in our daily living. Create in us a generosity that reflects your own. Pour out your spirit on this congregation that we might understand and use it to build and repair and restore. Amen.

ASSURANCE OF FORGIVENESS

What no eye has seen, nor ear heard, nor the human heart conceived, God has prepared for all who love God and are open to the Spirit's revelations. Let the yoke be removed from among us, the pointing finger and evil speech, that we may be about the work to which God calls us: feeding the hungry, satisfying the needs of the afflicted, and building foundations of faith for future generations.

COLLECT

God of mystery and of judgment, who has made us to be salt and light in a tasteless, shadowed world, grant to us such understanding of conditions around us and spiritual discernment that others may see your good works through us, give you the glory, and be moved to serve you. Amen.

OFFERTORY INVITATION

How generous are the gifts of God, poured out on us that we might know the joy of giving! The psalmist reminds us that it is well with those who deal generously and lend, who conduct their affairs with justice and give to the poor. Our offerings proclaim God's will in word and deed.

OFFERTORY PRAYER

Righteous God, accept our gifts of gratitude for the dawning awareness among us of your healing presence. You have satisfied our need in parched places and made our bones strong. Now we wish to offer to the world the amazing wonders we have experienced. Let our righteousness and generosity exceed that of the scribes and Pharisees. Fill us with yearning for the Spirit of Christ that we might become salt and light and be empowered for good works, to your honor and glory. Amen.

COMMISSION AND BLESSING

The wisdom of God empowers us to live wisely.
God's generosity prompts us to be generous.
We go forth to share what we have learned.
We reach out to give as we have received.
The Spirit has touched our spirits and changed us.
Our spiritual awareness has been deepened.
How amazing are the gifts of God to us!
We cannot hide the light God entrusts to us.
God will guide us continually.
God will satisfy our thirst with living water.
We cannot hold back our shouts of joy!
We have received the Spirit that is from God.
Amen. **Amen.**

(See hymn 22.)

Fifth Sunday after Epiphany   41

Deuteronomy 30:15–20   I Corinthians 3:1–9
Psalm 119:1–8   Matthew 5:21–37

CALL TO WORSHIP

Happy are those who seek God with their whole heart.
Their eyes are fixed on all that God commands.
> *We have come to reflect together on God's law.*
> *It is hard to hear, in other places, what God expects.*

Ready yourselves to receive all that God supplies.
Attune your hearts to God's promises and warnings.
> *We expect to be challenged as well as encouraged.*
> *We know that our ways are not God's ways.*

God gives us choices that result in life or death.
We can obey or reject the way of life God intends for us.
> *We seek to know and follow the way of life.*
> *We want to live according to promises we have made.*

INVOCATION

We come to you, gracious God, as people of the flesh whose spirits are under-developed and undisciplined. We make decisions without giving consideration to your will for us. We pursue desires that divert our attention away from your call to us. We make gods of our possessions, our work, our hobbies, even our families. We need to experience your presence and power to bring us to obedience. Make yourself known to us, we pray. Amen.

CALL TO CONFESSION

The apostle Paul confronted the church at Corinth with their jealousy and quarreling. Jesus preached about anger, dishonesty, and estrangement in ways that called for radical reconciliation. Everything that strains our relationship with others also distances us from God. That is why we come to this time of confession.

PRAYER OF CONFESSION

O God, you know the pain of all our broken relationships. Some we have tried to mend, and others we have tried to ignore. We feel your judgment on our estrangements. Hear us as, in silence, we remember them before you . . . O God, we ask for courage to admit our mistakes and overcome them. Show us what we can do to right the wrongs for which we are responsible, and forgive, we pray, what cannot be changed. Empower us as reconcilers and servants of your way. Amen.

Assurance of Forgiveness

God wants to forgive us, but there is no cheap grace for those of us unwilling to change. To all who seek to give up jealousy, insults, anger, quarreling, adultery, self-centered pride . . . God offers a new life. There is solid food to nurture us in new ways. God draws us into the community of forgiven and forgiving sinners, in which we support and help one another.

Collect

God of our ancestors, whose power to bless or to destroy has not diminished through the vastness of time, help us to hear your high expectations of us without defensiveness or denial, that we may be open to the changes you require, respond in ways that bring life, and, working together, become your community of spiritual people who have something special to offer your world. Amen.

Offertory Invitation

Our spending priorities measure our loyalties. They reveal who or what is really our God. In the church, we return to God a portion of all that God entrusts to our stewardship. Our giving is not to support a budget but to give thanks to God. How thankful are we?

Offertory Prayer

Faithful God, we give in gratitude for your abundant gifts to us. You have not forsaken us when we were unfaithful. You have not abandoned us in the hells of our own making. You keep calling to us when we pursue other gods. As we offer our tokens of thanks today, we hear you sending us out to mend broken relationships. Our offering is not a substitute for our own engagement in your reconciling work. Go with us to help us as we accept the assignments you give us. Amen.

Commission and Blessing

Go out as people confronted by the living God.
Dare to be reconcilers, recognizing your own need.
God sends us out to mend broken relations.
May we do no wrong, and walk in God's ways.
Choose life, by loving and obeying God.
Seek daily to partake of spiritual food.
We will study to know what God expects of us.
May we learn and keep God's righteous ordinances.
God will bless those who walk in Christ's way.
Beloved, you will be strengthened to keep your vows.
We will praise God with upright hearts.
May our ways become steadfast in doing good.
Amen. **Amen.**

(See hymn 23.)

Leviticus 19:1–2, 9–18   I Corinthians 3:10–11, 16–23
Psalm 119:33–40   Matthew 5:38–48

CALL TO WORSHIP

Come, foolish people; God is calling us.
The God of all time and space wants our attention.
> *Why are we called foolish in the church?*
> *Does God think we are foolish people?*
Have we embraced the world's talk and actions?
Have we turned away from God's expectations?
> *People call us foolish when we take faith seriously.*
> *The world thinks us strange if we are different.*
God says to us: You shall be holy because I am.
You shall be true and just, generous and loving.
> *How can God expect us to be perfect?*
> *How can we help others if we don't fit in?*

INVOCATION

God, we have come to worship you. We thought we could come on *our* terms, but your word proclaims *your* rule over this gathering and in all your creation. Help us to hear your will for us, not as limiting and oppressive but as the freeing, fulfilling pathway to life. We want to be your faithful children. We want to experience life at its best. Amen.

CALL TO CONFESSION

The wisdom of the world is foolishness with God. We have become enmeshed in the world's foolishness. We speak of rights, and plot ways to get ahead. We live among revenge-seekers who label Christ's way impossible. Let us confess our distance from God's design.

PRAYER OF CONFESSION

Gracious God, we do not understand your ways. We have forgotten that you call us to standards far different from the accepted norms of our society. We confess that we have dealt falsely with others. We have benefited from systems that defraud many of a living wage for their labors. We have slandered people you invite us to love and hated some for whom you have asked us to pray. O God, we admit that we are people of vengeance and grudges. We cry to you for help. Amen.

Assurance of Forgiveness

The grace of God is available to all who repent and put their trust in God. We are, each of us, God's temple. God's Spirit dwells in us, creating in us a holy place. We belong to Christ, who lifts our guilt from us that we might begin again to love ourselves and our neighbors.

Collect

God of the second mile, whose expectations of us honor us as temples of the Holy Spirit, create in us today such a longing to be and to do what you intend that there will be no place within or among us for boasting or defensiveness or retaliation, to the end that our witness serves as a channel for delivering your truth to the world, that more people might experience holiness. Amen.

Offertory Invitation

God expects more of believers than of nonbelievers. God delights in our joyous responses to divine generosity. Our offering proclaims our love of God and neighbor, in many different ways. Let us build on the foundations Christ has laid.

Offertory Prayer

With these gifts, we express our desire to observe your law with wholeness of heart, to delight in your commandments with all that we have and are, to worship you not only when we are together but in many difficult places when we are apart. May our church reach out to care for enemies as well as friends. May we remember that *we* are your church, your temple, your holy ones. Amen.

Commission and Blessing

Go forth as a holy people, filled with the Spirit.
Delight in following God's commandments.
We seek to be honest and caring.
We labor to serve, not for selfish gain.
Show love to neighbors and even to enemies.
Share God's bounty as you work for justice.
We seek to be generous and impartial.
We reach out to help, not to reap rewards.
All things belong to you in Christ.
You are gifted by God to share God's love.
We marvel at how much God trusts us!
We seek to be worthy of that trust.
Amen. **Amen.**

(See hymn 24.)

Isaiah 49:8–16a   I Corinthians 4:1–5
Psalm 131   Matthew 6:24–34

CALL TO WORSHIP

Receive with joy the calm and quiet of worship.
Come with hope to this celebration of salvation.
> *Surely our God will speak to us here.*
> *We come, thirsty for springs of living water.*

Come, as stewards of God's mysteries.
Gather as servants of Jesus Christ.
> *Surely Christ will feed us with living bread.*
> *We will be clothed with garments of righteousness.*

Be ready to receive more than you can ask.
Be ready to give more than you thought you had.
> *God will equip us with everything we need.*
> *We will learn how to live in God's realm.*

INVOCATION

You know everything we need, O Heavenly Parent. Come among us to calm our worries, and help us to put first things first. Remind us of our covenant with you, and show us how to live by it. We want to seek first your realm of righteousness. We intend to lay aside all that blocks our trust in you, for you are more than we can imagine. Feed us here, and clothe us with your truth so we, in turn, may be a blessing to others. Amen.

CALL TO CONFESSION

The Scriptures invite us to come out of the shadows where we have tried to hide all that is not right in our lives. When we show ourselves fully to God, we are reminded that God never forgets us, just as a mother does not forget her weaned child.

PRAYER OF CONFESSION

O God, we confess that we have not fulfilled the trust you have given us as servants of Christ and stewards of your mysteries. Our possessions have become more important to us than your approval. We worry a lot rather than trusting you and seeking to be good citizens of your realm. We ask you to forgive us and draw us back to yourself. We beg you to free us from false gods that enslave and from limited visions that diminish the high potential for good that we have received from your hand. Amen.

Assurance of Forgiveness

Every day with God is a day of salvation. God leads us by springs of water to quench our thirst, and meets our hunger with the food we need. God offers comfort and compassion along with the judgment that offers opportunity for spiritual growth. Give thanks for God's healing presence.

Collect

Amazing God, attentive to all of creation, so that birds are fed and lilies of the field are clothed in splendor, attend, we pray, to the needs of your people gathered here, that we may be freed of burdens we should not be trying to carry but also enlisted in causes you want us to champion, so the mysteries of your love might be shared with the world. Amen.

Offertory Invitation

We have been entrusted with more than our share of the world's resources. Above all, we have received good news of God's loving care for all of creation and for every person. Through our offerings, we respond to the mandate to share God's realm and righteousness with the world.

Offertory Prayer

Thank you, God, for calming our striving and empowering our sharing. It feels good to invest ourselves and our resources in disciple-making, responding to the hunger and thirst of your children. We seek to join you in compassion for those who suffer and think themselves forgotten. Use us and all our gifts to this end, we pray. Amen.

Commission and Blessing

By God's generous provision, we have been fed.
Water is provided to quench our thirst.
> **We need not worry about food or drink.**
> **Great abundance surrounds us.**
God frees people from their prisons.
God frees us from all that enslaves us.
> **We are in covenant with God to help others.**
> **We are called to reach out to those in need.**
Think of yourselves as servants of Christ.
Go out as stewards of God's mysteries.
> **We seek to be worthy of this trust.**
> **We long to receive God's commendation.**
Amen. **Amen.**

(See hymn 25.)

Deuteronomy 11:18–21, 26–28　　　　　　Romans 1:16–17; 3:22b–28 (29–31)
Psalm 31:1–5, 19–24　　　　　　　　　　　　　　　　　Matthew 7:21–29

CALL TO WORSHIP

Come together to hear the word of our God.
Listen carefully to the commandments we are given.
> *We are not ashamed of the gospel.*
> *It is the power of God for our salvation.*

Receive God's word in your minds and your souls.
Discuss that word with one another at home.
> *We seek to live by faith and trust.*
> *We want our children to know God's truth.*

God offers a blessing to all who obey.
Those who follow other gods find themselves cursed.
> *We need one another to live faithfully.*
> *We are here to support one another in this quest.*

INVOCATION

Faithful God, incline your ear to us and deliver us from haughty disregard of your law. Be for us a rock and refuge, a strong fortress to save us. Lead us and guide us for your name's sake. We want to hear your word in ways that will empower faith and good works among us, in Jesus' name. Amen.

CALL TO CONFESSION

Who are we to come before God? Can we claim that God's word is our foremost concern? Do we teach and discuss and write and pray, morning and night and all through the long day, in conscious response to our God? Come now to speak honestly to our Creator.

PRAYER OF CONFESSION

Glorious God, we admit that we find it difficult to give you serious consideration except, perhaps, on Sunday morning. Our lives are filled with so many competing interests. It's hard for us to remember you amid the demands of our work, the frustrations of commuting, the distractions of the news and sports and sitcoms. Our families do not fit the ideal of our dreams. Our church often falls short of our expectations. Are you here for us, God? Do you care? Can you help us change for the better? Amen.

ASSURANCE OF FORGIVENESS

All have sinned and fall short of the glory of God. We have recognized how far we wander away from God's intention for us. In Christ, we received undeserved forgiveness and grace to change the course of our lives, to become more caring, responsive, and committed disciples, living by faith. Be strong, take courage, and dare to build a new life on the foundation freely offered to us: Jesus Christ.

COLLECT

God of all worlds, whose realm is present wherever your will is done, lead us in this time together to a fresh understanding of your purposes and a deepened resolve to live the faith we profess, that all around us may discern your abundant goodness and embrace new life, in the name of Jesus Christ, who taught your ways with authority. Amen.

OFFERTORY INVITATION

We give to express thanks for the abundant goodness of our God. We devote our offerings to passing on the astonishing teachings of Jesus Christ. We here dedicate ourselves anew to living, and passing on, the word of God in all its power.

OFFERTORY PRAYER

Into your hands, faithful God, we commit our spirits, our substance, our plans. We offer the best we have to give in thanks for your abiding love. Claim our time, not just the wealth we are willing to share. Receive our energies and creativity, not just the leftovers from our busy days. Let your church become more fully a beacon of hope in our needy world. We celebrate the opportunity to be a part of your plan as it unfolds, for the healing of this planet. Amen.

COMMISSION AND BLESSING

God is our rock and fortress, our refuge.
We are surrounded by God's steadfast love.
> *We will call on God night and day.*
> *We will remember always that God is with us.*
Love God, all you who are called to be saints.
Receive the strength and courage God offers.
> *With heart and soul, we will praise God.*
> *We will teach God's ways to our children.*
Serve God with fear and trembling.
Those who act haughtily cannot know God.
> *We will seek to live faithfully all God teaches.*
> *We will put away boasting and false pride.*
Amen. **Amen.**

(See hymns 26, 27.)

Ninth Sunday after Epiphany

LAST SUNDAY AFTER EPIPHANY (TRANSFIGURATION)

Exodus 24:12–18   2 Peter 1:16–21
Psalm 2 or Psalm 99   Matthew 17:1–9

CALL TO WORSHIP

The coming of a new day calls us to anticipate God's dawn.
The day of God's dawning is like a morning star rising.
> *The light of God is like a devouring fire.*
> *God's brightness is too intense for our gaze.*

Come up to the mountain of God's presence.
Wait for God to reveal divine intentions for us.
> *We are eyewitnesses to God's majesty.*
> *We have sensed God's presence in stories of Jesus.*

Look up, and do not be afraid.
Jesus, whom you seek, is transfigured before you.
> *We will serve our God with fear and trembling.*
> *Happy are those whose refuge is in God.*

INVOCATION

Amazing God, as leaders of old sought high places of encounter with you, lift us up above the fogs of our technology and theology that we might meet you in this hour. If you have instructions for us, we want to hear them. If our lives need a change of direction, turn us around. If there is a prophecy we have ignored, reveal to us its meaning for us. If the Scriptures hold truth we have overlooked, awaken our attention and grant us courage to respond in new and positive ways. Amen.

CALL TO CONFESSION

Day after day we are surrounded by the majesty of God, yet our eyes do not see nor our thoughts comprehend the wonders of creation or the gift of transcendence. God calls us to be eyewitnesses of good news, to believe what we have eyes to see and to trust in the One beyond our knowing. Let us come to God, confessing our need.

PRAYER OF CONFESSION

God of dazzling splendor, we confess that we have lived in a cloud, hiding from your glory and pretending not to notice the wonders of your majesty. The mystery of life eludes us because we take for granted what seems commonplace and refuse to deal with matters beyond our understanding. We have tried to put our religion in a compartment separate from the rest of life. We have not thought to serve you in everyday encounters. Shake our complacency, we pray, and awaken us to new life in all its fullness. Amen.

ASSURANCE OF FORGIVENESS

Happy are all who take refuge in God. We are accepted as God's own children. To us, the Holy Spirit comes as a gift, interpreting to us the truth of the Scriptures. Do not be afraid of the vision God sets before us. A new day is dawning among us as we become aware that God is with us.

COLLECT

God of mountaintops and valleys, whose rule extends beyond the ends of the earth to embrace the unfathomed reaches of time and space, grant to us a vision of your intention for our lives and equip us to fulfill the destiny you entrust to us as followers of Jesus Christ. Banish our fear of one another that we may experience together the awesome wonder of community, serving you in awe and wonder. Amen.

OFFERTORY INVITATION

As we encounter the mystery of God's revelation, we approach the season of Lent with its opportunities for reflection and waiting on God for forty days and forty nights. Our church seeks to strengthen its ministry, not only among those already committed to the journey with Christ, but to our neighbors and friends. Our giving is a symbol of our willingness to invest our time and best efforts to bring God's vision for humanity to life.

OFFERTORY PRAYER

God of clouds and devouring fire, we are amazed by the experiences of Moses and the disciples of Jesus. They point us beyond our everyday attempts to be faithful to you. Enrich our lives in the season we are entering, that we may see the lamp of your love shining amid the shadows. Let your new day dawn among us as we invest ourselves in your purposes for humanity. May we sense the morning star rising in our hearts, giving hope to a world reclaiming the values of your reign among us. Amen.

COMMISSION AND BLESSING

We have been to the mountaintop with Moses.
We know that God's established order brings life.
God is our refuge and our inspiration.
Prayer empowers our thinking and our doing.
We have caught the vision of the disciples.
We will know life abundant as followers of Jesus.
Christ expands our horizons day by day.
We are amazed at the possibilities Christ offers.
Days of waiting and watching bring revelation.
Times of loving service bring fulfillment and joy.
The Spirit sends us into the world to serve.
We share the message: We are beloved by God.
Amen. **Amen.**

(See hymn 28.)

THE LENTEN SEASON

Joel 2:1–2, 12–17 or Isaiah 58:1–12   2 Corinthians 5:20b–6:10
Psalm 51:1–17   Matthew 6:1–6, 16–21

CALL TO WORSHIP

We have left many important pursuits to gather here.
In these moments, worship is of first importance.
> *Together, we begin a season of self-examination.*
> *We begin a humble walk with God through Lent.*

This is a time for building spiritual disciplines.
Those disciplined by Christ become disciples.
> *We seek to follow in the steps of Jesus.*
> *We want to walk in the paths where Christ leads.*

May God empower us here with genuine righteousness.
Let patience, kindness, and truthful speech prevail.
> *We seek knowledge and the will to live by it.*
> *We seek community and the capacity to share it.*

INVOCATION

Send your Holy Spirit on this gathering of seeking people, O God of our salvation. Open our hearts to receive your gifts. Open our minds to think new thoughts. Open our hands in generous sharing. Open our lips to declare your praise. Keep us from pious pretension, that we may approach you with genuine yearning to please you, not to impress others. We hear you calling us: Now is the acceptable time; now is the day of salvation. Here we are, God. We seek your healing touch. Amen.

CALL TO CONFESSION

The prophet Joel warned that the day of God's coming would be full of clouds and gloom. Yet, God would be merciful to all who turned back with their whole being to worship and walk in God's way. As we gather in this solemn assembly in response to God's invitation, we ask God to spare us, to make us whole and to restore us to faithful service in Christ's name.

PRAYER OF CONFESSION

Have mercy on us, O God, according to your steadfast love. According to your abundant mercy, blot out our transgressions. Wash us thoroughly from our iniquity and cleanse us from our sin. We confess before you the sins we recognize in our individual lives and in this faith community, your church. Hear us as we recall them in silent communion with you . . . Help us, O God, to be truthful with ourselves and with one another, and with you. Spare your people, and guide us through our difficult walk with Christ amid the challenges we face on the way to the cross. Amen.

ASSURANCE OF FORGIVENESS

In steadfast love, God welcomes and forgives us, restoring to us the joy of salvation. Our contrite hearts and willing spirits can receive God's reconciling gifts. In secret, quiet times with God every day, we will know that in Christ we possess everything we need.

COLLECT

Merciful God, whose grace is poured out in extravagant abundance on all who open themselves to receive it, guide our Lenten journey that our prayers may be frequent and genuine, our speech truthful and kind, our mourning healing and hopeful, our fasting thoughtful and full of praise. In all things, help us to endure, that our lives may enrich the journey for all who come in contact with us. Amen.

OFFERTORY INVITATION

We give, not to impress others or to reap rewards for ourselves, but to share the joy we know in loving God and serving as disciples of Jesus Christ. Our sacrifices of thanksgiving go beyond what we place on the altar. God asks us to give ourselves fully in faithful, loving service to humanity.

OFFERTORY PRAYER

Receive, O God, our broken and contrite hearts, our restored and committed spirits, our renewed dedication of all we possess and all we are. Thank you for this day of salvation. Thank you for the daily presence of the Holy Spirit in our lives. Thank you for your promise to teach us the ways of steadfast love, purity, holiness, truthfulness, and power to accomplish the tasks you set before us. Amen.

COMMISSION AND BLESSING

Go out as reconciled, forgiven saints of God.
You are empowered to live as disciples of Jesus.
> *We will use this season as a time of learning.*
> *We commit ourselves to study and service.*
The grace of God will empower you daily.
The love of God will transform your outlook.
> *We anticipate each day with joy.*
> *Every moment becomes an exciting opportunity.*
Your prayers will be answered.
You will grow in wisdom and graciousness.
> *Thank God for mercy and steadfast love.*
> *Praise be to Christ throughout this Lenten journey.*
Amen. **Amen.**

(See hymn 29.)

Genesis 2:15–17; 3:1–7   Romans 5:12–19
Psalm 32   Matthew 4:1–11

CALL TO WORSHIP

We have entered into the season of Lent.
Sundays, however, are not a part of Lent.
> *We have entered a wilderness time.*
> *Yet this day of worship is an oasis in the desert.*
We are here to worship the God of all creation.
We gather to remember God's revelation in Jesus.
> *Today we revisit the garden of Eden.*
> *We remember God's overflowing generosity.*
We worship God, who gives us choices and limits.
Are we open to God's counsel and instruction?
> *Today we remember the temptations Jesus faced.*
> *We want to learn to make good choices.*

INVOCATION

We listen for your voice, holy God, amid the clamor of a world that scarcely notices this season of self-examination and instruction. Too long we have heeded the serpents among us whose craftiness beckons us away from faith and faithfulness. We delight in forbidden fruits and complain when they turn sour. Lead us, faithful Spirit, through the wilderness of our own creation, that we may once more find our way to you. Instruct us in the way we should go, and counsel us day by day. Help us rediscover your steadfast love. Amen.

CALL TO CONFESSION

Too long we have heeded the seductive voice of the serpent. How easy it is to seek the good life apart from God, to trust in our possessions and revel in beguiling attractions that focus only on our own pleasure. Then we blame God when we reap the fruits of our own unfaithfulness. Surely it is time to cry out for help!

PRAYER OF CONFESSION

Holy God, we confess our transgressions before you. We resent limits on our freedom to follow the impulses of the moment. We want life to revolve around us. We want other people to fit into the patterns that serve us best. Like a horse or a mule, we resent the bit and bridle that make us useful participants in the community you seek to create. We have tried to live apart from you. We sense that something is missing from our lives. Will you walk with us in this season and help us become all we are created to be?

ASSURANCE OF FORGIVENESS

God's grace comes to us as a gift. We cannot earn it, but we can reject it. When we are responsive to God's leading, when we open our lives to God in prayer, when we turn from our relentless pursuit of personal gain, when we embrace the obedience of Christ, we may recognize the abiding gifts of the Spirit. Happy are those who accept God's forgiveness!

COLLECT

Life-sustaining God, with us through all our trials and temptations, bear us up through this season of self-examination, that we might feed on the bread of your word, open ourselves to your presence without demanding proof and signs, and let go of all the idols that surround us to worship and serve you with joy and delight, in uprightness of heart, through the grace of Jesus Christ. Amen.

OFFERTORY INVITATION

As with Adam and Eve, our greed and pretensions are exposed before God. It is so tempting to want more of everything for ourselves. Yet, it is strangely true that only in generous sharing do we finally realize that we have enough, that God has blessed us richly beyond anything we could ever deserve. We give with gladness.

OFFERTORY PRAYER

By your surprising grace, O God, our eyes are opened, our ears unstopped, our hearts attuned to the needs of others. We give so more people may know your acceptance and forgiveness. We support the ministry of preaching, teaching, and healing among us and through the outreach of the church. Expand our horizons, we pray, and tear down the limits of our caring. Amen.

COMMISSION AND BLESSING

Let the worship of God be a part of all you do.
Serve with praise and joy every day this week.
> **God alone is the one we will worship.**
> **We will not put our God to the test.**
Know that it is not easy to keep our focus on God.
Many distractions will vie for our attention.
> **We pray that God will be present amid temptations.**
> **We seek strength and courage to be faithful.**
Be open each day to God's counsel and instruction.
Learn from Christ to make difficult choices.
> **God sends us out into the wilderness.**
> **But we know the oasis is here to refresh us.**
Amen. **Amen.**

(See hymn 30.)

Genesis 12:1–4a   Romans 4:1–5, 13–17
Psalm 121   John 3:1–17 or Matthew 17:1–9

CALL TO WORSHIP

People of God, where do we put our trust?
Where do we find wholeness and meaning?
> *We lift up our eyes to the hills.*
> *Our help comes from the Creator of heaven and earth.*
We are sons and daughters of Abraham and Sarah.
We trust in God, who neither slumbers nor sleeps.
> *We are followers of Jesus, who proclaimed God's realm.*
> *We are born of the Spirit, born from above.*
Our lives are a gift from God, who loves us.
By the grace of God, we are born anew each day.
> *God loved the world in the gift of Jesus Christ.*
> *Through faith in Christ, we receive eternal life.*

INVOCATION

Let the winds of the Spirit blow in our midst today, loving God. Let us hear the sound and feel the power. Open our hearts in new ways to the promise of your healing grace so we may be a blessing to one another and to your world. We need courage to face the challenges and struggles of life. We seek reassurance that you will be with us in our going out and our coming in. Strengthen our faith to withstand the trials and temptations that lead us away from a faithful journey with Christ. Amen.

CALL TO CONFESSION

Spiritual ancestors, like Abraham, sensed God's call to leave behind the security of the familiar to venture forward to new places God would show them. Others, like Nicodemus, were astonished by Jesus' call to rebirth in the Spirit. Reminded that both calls come also to us, we bow before God to confess our unfaithfulness.

PRAYER OF CONFESSION

O God, we confess that we have been far more ready to say we believe than to trust you to lead us to new ventures of faithfulness. We are afraid of the evil that surrounds us. We fear rejection, failure, and ridicule. We admire Jesus, but it is difficult to follow in footsteps that lead to a cross. In the midst of life as we know it here, how can we catch glimpses of eternity? Save us, we pray, from our timidity, and use our doubts as an entry to deeper faith. Amen.

Assurance of Forgiveness

Our lives are in God's hands. We can only glimpse the mystery of the Source of love, "who gives life to the dead and calls into existence the things that do not exist." Yet, as we look up in trust, there comes to us an abiding assurance that we are not alone. Receive, with humility and joy, the rebirth God offers this day and for all eternity.

Collect

Renewing Spirit, present in the waters of baptism, in the gentle breeze, and in the roaring winds, speak to us where we are and expand our vision beyond the immediate scene, that we may be equipped to follow where Christ leads, bearing witness to our faith and serving with joy wherever you send us. Amen.

Offertory Invitation

The faith that sustains us is not a commodity to be hoarded and protected. Rather, faith is an active, dynamic relationship which God calls us to share with one another, not just in the church, but with everyone. Our offerings make possible faithful ministries within the church and our outreach in the world.

Offertory Prayer

Thank you, God, for glimpses of eternity in the daily experiences of life. We are grateful for encounters that lift the horizons of our vision. We rejoice in the teaching and care you have provided to us. Bless now the gifts we return to you for the programs and outreach of the church. We want to share our faith with the world. We pray for trustful relationships among all your children. We rejoice together in the saving ministry of Jesus that inspires us to give our best. Amen.

Commission and Blessing

We rejoice that God has gathered us for worship.
Now we depart to go where God sends us.
> *We are God's messengers wherever we go.*
> *We are called to be Christian in all our dealings.*
In our work and in our leisure, may we serve faithfully.
By God's grace, we are empowered so to do.
> *Winds of the Spirit will daily refresh us.*
> *Faith finds new birth in us every day.*
God promises to be our helper whenever we call.
God's love surrounds us even when we do not ask for it.
> *With joy, we will go where God sends us.*
> *With confidence, we will share our faith with others.*
Amen. **Amen.**

(See hymns 31, 32.)

Exodus 17:1–7   Romans 5:1–11
Psalm 95   John 4:5–42

CALL TO WORSHIP

Come, let us sing a new song to our God.
Make a joyful noise to the rock of our salvation!
> **Let us enter God's presence with thanksgiving.**
> **Make a joyful noise with songs of praise!**
God is a great ruler, above all other gods.
The depths of the earth are in God's hands.
> **The highest mountains belong to God.**
> **The farthest reaches of the universe are God's own.**
O come, let us worship and bow down.
Let us kneel before God our Maker.
> **We are the people of God's pasture.**
> **Today we will listen to God with open hearts.**

INVOCATION

We come to you, God, because we are thirsty. Our spirits need the refreshing water of your word, just as our bodies need the refreshment of a cool drink. We worship you with joy, for we can already feel the gift of your presence all around us. Now open our ears that we may hear all that you expect of us. Open our lives to your truth and prepare us to follow Jesus in accepting the unacceptable, challenging the conventional, and joining together in a harvest for your realm. Amen.

CALL TO CONFESSION

Just as our ancestors in the faith quarreled and complained and tested God, we are tempted to do the same. We have hardened our hearts and turned away from the Source of Life. Yet God comes to us with reconciling grace. Are we ready to return to the relationship God intends with us?

PRAYER OF CONFESSION

What will you do with us, God? We are never satisfied with our lot. We rebel and complain when things don't go our way. Our hearts chase after things that become gods to us and consume our time, energy, and attention. We spend little time in communion with you and then begin to doubt your presence. You seem far away and unavailable. We create barriers among ourselves that separate us from one another and from you. Send your living water to cleanse us, O God. Empower us to worship in spirit and in truth. Amen.

Assurance of Forgiveness

Christ died for us, demonstrating the vastness of God's love for us, bringing reconciliation and the assurance of salvation. We are offered a new quality of life in which faithfulness is valued more highly than security. Rise up, all who have been drifting through life. Christ has come to lead us through the shadowed valleys. Let us respond in spirit and truth.

Collect

God of all worlds, whose care for us also includes concern for neighbors who differ from us, and whose love embraces all of humanity without distinction, we reach out for the water of life that you offer. Fill us with your Spirit that we may live your truth, share the story of Jesus, and lead others into discipleship, that your realm may be realized among us. Amen.

Offertory Invitation

When we stop to consider the amazing riches God has provided on this planet, how thankful we should be. Good soil and water give us food in abundance. Gifts of the Spirit grant life with eternity in it. Let us express our wonder and gratitude through our offering of tithes and lives.

Offertory Prayer

Thank you, God, for all the ways we have benefited from the labor of others. We here offer our best for the sake of brothers and sisters who need the love and encouragement you are eager to share through us. Keep us from being ungrateful as we continue to receive so much more than we stop to realize. When life is difficult, help us to endure and to hope because your love is sure and certain, ours to receive and to give, in Christ's name. Amen.

Commission and Blessing

The peace of God goes with us and dwells with us.
By God's grace, we share in the hope of glory.
> *While we were yet sinners, Christ died for us.*
> *Through this love, we are reconciled to God.*
Go, therefore, to tell your friends and neighbors.
God has done great things for us.
> *God is to be worshiped in spirit and truth.*
> *Every moment of every day is a time for praise.*
We scatter, singing songs of thanksgiving.
We will make a joyful noise, in praise to God.
> *We will also listen for messages God sends.*
> *God is among us and goes with us every day.*
Amen. **Amen.**

(See hymn 33.)

I Samuel 16:1–13   Ephesians 5:8–14
Psalm 23   John 9:1–41

CALL TO WORSHIP

God summons us to wake up and see.
Light has come to lead us to all that is good.
> **Our eyes have been opened to God's goodness.**
> **We seek to live as children of light.**

God sees beyond our outward appearance.
God knows the intent of our hearts.
> **We are here to find out what is pleasing to God.**
> **We want to know what is right and true.**

God listens to all who worship sincerely.
Praise God with openness and obedience.
> **We seek to know and follow God's will.**
> **This is a day to do the works of God.**

INVOCATION

Holy God, we sense your involvement in our lives. Like a shepherd, you watch over us and provide abundantly beyond our needs. You lead us in right paths when we are tempted to go astray. You refresh us with living water that overflows with your generosity. Let your light shine on us now to reveal truth we have not seen and open our eyes to possibilities we may not have realized. May we be receptive to learn from you and from one another. Amen.

CALL TO CONFESSION

With our limited insight, we often misjudge people and situations. Our view of things may be far from the way God sees the circumstances of our lives and our relationships. Individually and together, we are involved in sin that cuts us off from what God expects of us. Let us admit our need for forgiveness.

PRAYER OF CONFESSION

Great Shepherd, we thank you for finding us and bringing us to this time of prayer. We have wandered far from the paths of integrity, justice, and peace that you have set before us. We are ashamed of some things we do when we think no one will find out. We are quick to judge others and to excuse ourselves. We want to decide who is acceptable to you and who is not. Surely, we persuade ourselves, you prefer people like us and not those who appear, believe, or act differently. Even as we say those words, we know we are not in tune with your way. Forgive us, we pray, and help us to change. Amen.

Assurance of Forgiveness

The goodness and mercy of God are always available to us. We can receive these gifts when we are truly sorry for our sin and open to the richness of God's grace. When we let God touch our unseeing eyes, we gain new insights and can begin to view others with the compassion of Christ. Let us accept with joy the healing we are offered right here, right now.

Collect

God of mercy, whose thoughts are not our thoughts and whose ways are not our ways, thank you for reaching out to heal us even when we have not asked, for your touch is transforming, enabling us to witness to your truth and walk in your ways. May we do so today, that others may be drawn into the circle of discipleship. Amen.

Offertory Invitation

God has given us all that is good and right and true. What a joy to share these gifts with one another in the life of this community and far beyond our own reach. In this offering, we return to God with eager response to all we have received.

Offertory Prayer

Loving God, as you illuminate our lives with fascinating insights and possibilities, we reach out to share your love through our tithes and offerings and our investment of time and energy in tasks to which you call us. All this we offer now for your blessing, for apart from you, the light goes out of our lives and we slip into meaningless existence. Let us, rather, dwell with you and serve you wherever we go. Amen.

Commission and Blessing

God has drawn us out of the shadows of shame.
In the brightness of God's love, we are transformed.
>   *We see much that we had not seen before.*
>   *We have glimpsed others from God's point of view.*
God has challenged the way we label others.
We are invited to learn from them, not judge them.
>   *Not all disciples of Jesus are like us.*
>   *Yet all of us are welcomed by God.*
God will lead us daily by still waters.
We will be guided along the right paths.
>   *God restores our souls and keeps us from evil.*
>   *We can count on God's goodness and mercy.*
Amen. **Amen.**

(See hymn 34.)

Ezekiel 37:1–14   Romans 8:6–11
Psalm 130   John 11:1–45

CALL TO WORSHIP

God calls us from the valley of dry bones.
Come, listen for a word from our God.
> *We hear God calling us in a far distant voice.*
> *We had nearly forgotten God's care for us.*
The Spirit breathes life into our dry bones.
God offers hope when we have lost our way.
> *Our souls wait for the refreshment God offers.*
> *Our spirits are filled with great expectation.*
Christ came as a light to all the world.
Christ comes among us today to light our way.
> *We hear the teacher calling for us.*
> *Christ unbinds us that we may see and believe.*

INVOCATION

God of steadfast love, bring new life to this community of your people. We are eager to hear your voice and be filled with your Spirit. Come from the four winds, O Breath, and bring vitality and purpose to our gathering, that we might be energized and encouraged. Hear our voices, lifted in praise and crying out from our need. Be attentive to our supplications, lest we die apart from you. Only you can unbind us and set us free. Amen.

CALL TO CONFESSION

To set the mind on the flesh is death. Focused only on our own interests, we cannot see God. The law of God is foreign to us, and we are hostile to its demands. To live in sin—separation from God—is death. Come now to the promise of life as we confess our sin.

PRAYER OF CONFESSION

Out of the depths we cry to you, O God. Hear our prayers, the confession of our neglect, the admission of our desire to rule in your place. Like the house of Israel in Ezekiel's time, we are cut off from communion with you. We are like dead people, going through the motions of living. We cry out for forgiveness and a new start. We long to know you and to live in reverence before you. By your steadfast love, redeem us from our iniquities and raise us up to serve you, in Jesus' name. Amen.

ASSURANCE OF FORGIVENESS

Jesus says to us, "Did I not tell you that if you believed, you would see the glory of God?" Arise, in faith and trust, knowing that God will give life to our mortal bodies through the spirit who dwells in us and among us. We are not slaves to the flesh. God has made us to be instruments of self-giving love, who find life by giving it away. As God has invested in us, we are free to invest ourselves in ministry to others. Praise God!

COLLECT

Father of all worlds, Mother to all of earth's children, we cannot live apart from you. Send Christ to live among us and within us so we may be righteous in all our dealings and responsive to you wherever we go, that we may know the life abundant which you offer and be empowered to share it, with compassion and courage, with all whom we meet and with all whom you have called us to love. Amen.

OFFERTORY INVITATION

God invites us to view the valleys of dry bones that fill our world. Prophesy to these bones and say to them: O dry bones, hear the word of God. We here offer ourselves and our resources that the winds of God might blow through our world with life-giving energy.

OFFERTORY PRAYER

Lift us up, O God, from the graves of our self-interest as we invest ourselves in sharing the good news with the world. Increase our gifts of time and treasure, that all who are drained of hope might have their minds set on the Spirit. May the Spirit raise them to new life as we celebrate the resurrection Jesus promised to Lazarus and to all who trust and follow where God leads. Amen.

COMMISSION AND BLESSING

We are freed from all that has bound us.
The Spirit sends us out in trust and joy.
The Spirit dwells in us and empowers us.
The light of Christ will show us the way.
As you walk in the light, you will not stumble.
With trust in God, you will live, even in death.
God is attentive to our prayers.
We are assured of God's forgiveness and grace.
Go out to proclaim God's freeing love.
Spread a word of hope to all who are in distress.
With God, there is great power to redeem.
We eagerly share God's steadfast love.
Amen. **Amen.**

(See hymn 35.)

Fifth Sunday in Lent   65

Sixth Sunday in Lent
(Palm Sunday)

LITURGY OF THE PALMS
Psalm 118:1–2, 19–29   Matthew 21:1–11

LITURGY OF THE PASSION
Isaiah 50:4–9a   Philippians 2:5–11
Psalm 31:9–16   Matthew 26:14–27:66

CALL TO WORSHIP

This is a day of joyous welcome.
Yet joy is tempered by impending doom.
> *We welcome Christ with waving branches.*
> *We wait with Christ through hours of agony.*

Our leader comes humbly, riding a donkey.
Blessed is the one who comes in God's name.
> *Jesus rides into the tumult of our times.*
> *People still oppose the way of love.*

Yet love prevails in spite of opposition.
Give thanks that God's steadfast love endures forever.
> *Open to us the gates of righteousness.*
> *Let us enter in the light God offers.*

INVOCATION

Be gracious to us, O God, in our moments of grief and fear. Be with us as we rejoice in the day you have made. Our times are in your hands, both when we mourn and when we celebrate. Guide our thoughts and actions so we may appreciate the possibilities in every day. We trust in you, O God. Let your face shine on your servants. Amen.

CALL TO CONFESSION

In the garden, Jesus directed the disciples to watch and pray. But they failed in their support. Have we not also fallen asleep? How constant and persistent is our prayer life? How eager are we to take the risks of trusting in Christ's leading? Will we betray rather than follow? God is waiting to hear our plea for mercy.

PRAYER OF CONFESSION

Holy God, we have blamed you when the hosannas die and the parade turns into a mob scene. We heap our doubts on you even though our inaction adds power to those who shout, "Crucify." We rebel against the risks of discipleship. Why raise our voices against the evil we see? One voice simply becomes one more victim. O God, we protest, but we know down deep that the victim of our silence is the way of love, the way of life. Forgive our cowardice, and help us to stand with Christ in a world that has forgotten humility and obedience to you. O God, we want to be faithful. Why does it cost so much? Amen.

ASSURANCE OF FORGIVENESS

God does not forsake us. In times of terror and suffering we are not alone. In Christ, we are strengthened as we watch and pray. We receive courage to love in the face of ridicule and to act for truth amid the oppressive forces of deceit. Love is at the heart of creation, bringing us to new beginnings, to resurrection life in all its fullness.

COLLECT

Holy God, whose steadfast love offers direction and purpose to our lives, help us to be faithful in the small things you ask of us day by day, that we may see all that you reveal to us, give thanks in all circumstances, and grow toward the mind of Christ. In obedient trust, we enter this holy week, eager to participate in a world transformed by love. Amen.

OFFERTORY INVITATION

For thirty pieces of silver, Jesus Christ was betrayed. And still today he is denied in the way we use the resources entrusted to us. God does not ask of us a token of support. We are called to give our all, of which our offering here is but a symbol. Will our gifts shout good news to the world?

OFFERTORY PRAYER

May these offerings bring life-changing good news, both to those who give and to all who are reached by the caring ministries of the church. May they help to restore relationships of trust among us and outpourings of generosity that echo your steadfast love around the world. May your saints be raised to new life that cuts through the deceptions of society to bring your new order among us, O God of all times and places. Amen.

COMMISSION AND BLESSING

Lift high the branches that honor Jesus Christ.
Lift high the cross that proclaims love's sacrifice.
We will wave our greeting with joyous praise.
We will risk the commitment that led to a cross.
We are under oath before the living God.
May we have no reason to weep when the cock crows.
The promises we have made excite and challenge us.
We seek to be loyal and courageous in Christ's service.
God keeps covenant with us in all circumstances.
The cup of blessing is extended to us every day.
May our flesh be strengthened to match our willing spirits.
May love prevail in all our dealings this week.
Amen. **Amen.**

(See hymns 36, 37. Separate Passion Sunday and Palm Sunday liturgies are offered in *Fresh Winds of the Spirit*, pp. 50–53, and *Fresh Winds, Book 2*, pp. 64–67.)

Isaiah 42:1–9
Psalm 36:5–11

Hebrews 9:11–15
John 12:1–11

CALL TO WORSHIP

Children of the Living God, gather for worship.
Come to receive the blessing God offers.
We are not fit to come before the Holy One.
We have not paid attention to God's word.
We are God's chosen ones in spite of ourselves.
God is at our side, to offer justice to all people.
How amazing is God's steadfast love!
We have been arrogant in ignoring God's light.
God's righteousness is like the mighty mountains.
God's judgments are deeper than the deepest sea.
We have come to hear the new things God declares.
We want to respond to the Spirit's guidance.

INVOCATION

Your steadfast love, O God, extends to the heavens, your faithfulness to the clouds.
Your righteousness is like the mighty mountains, your judgments are like the great
deep. We come together, amazing God, to take refuge in the shadow of your wings.
We gather to feast on the abundance of your house and to drink from the river of
your delights. You bring light to our unseeing eyes. You free us from the prisons
we have created for ourselves through our poor choices. May your salvation be real
to us in this hour. Amen.

CALL TO CONFESSION

In this holy week, all the values by which we live are called into question. We are
reminded of our covenant with God, whose love for us has been constant, even
when we have strayed. In these moments, we accept the offer of God's hand to
lead us and restore us to faithfulness.

PRAYER OF CONFESSION

O God, we have wandered far from your intention for us. We have lived for our
own momentary pleasure, forgetting our kinship with your hurting children. You
call us to be a justice-seeking people, bringing light to the nations. Instead, we have
tolerated injustice because we benefit from the world's inequities. Your light is ex-
tinguished because we do not want to see what it reveals. We become prisoners of
our own deceits. O God, redeem us, purify us, redirect us in your new and living
way. Amen.

ASSURANCE OF FORGIVENESS

Christ, the mediator of a new covenant, invites us to accept the forgiveness God offers. The dead works we have substituted for a living faith are purified and transformed. We are being equipped with Christ's care and compassion that we might reach out to others from honest motives, with unselfish delight. How precious is God's steadfast love!

COLLECT

Eternal Spirit, by whose inspiration the friends of Jesus ministered to him in the closing days of his earthly life, help us now to stand with Christ during this fateful week, taking up the mandate of justice for all and giving ourselves unselfishly in the proclamation of your steadfast love, that our common life may be transformed and your people set free to live as you have planned. Amen.

OFFERTORY INVITATION

Mary, Martha, and Lazarus gave a dinner to honor Jesus. They gave their best to identify with the way of life he proclaimed. Now we are called to give our best. Our offerings and our lives will testify to the steadfast love of God revealed in the drama of this holy week.

OFFERTORY PRAYER

O God, we want to know the joy so many have found when they give their best to you. We want to share the good news of life's fullness in the company of Christ's disciples. Grant new light to us, even as you illuminate the lives of all who are helped by these gifts we dedicate in your service. Amen.

COMMISSION AND BLESSING

Like Christ, we are servants in whom God delights.
God's spirit is at work in and through us.
> *We take our dimly burning wicks into the world.*
> *We trust that God's light will shine through us.*
God's steadfast love will uphold and strengthen us.
God's truth will guide our work and witness.
> *We will worship God wherever we go.*
> *No idols will receive attention that belongs to God.*
Go out to share the gifts we have received.
Let good news be proclaimed in troubled times.
> *In God's light, we see the light.*
> *We go out to invite others into the light.*
Amen. **Amen.**

(See hymn 38.)

Isaiah 49:1–7   I Corinthians 1:18–31
Psalm 71:1–14   John 12:20–36

CALL TO WORSHIP

We have answered God's call and served faithfully.
Again, we gather before the One who has named us.
> **God is our strength and the source of glory.**
> **Yet it often seems we have labored in vain.**

God calls us as lights to shine in the world.
We carry good news of salvation for the whole earth.
> **Why, then, are we despised and ignored?**
> **Why is Christ, our Savior, brought to shame?**

The message of the cross is foolish to the perishing.
Yet it is the power of God to those being saved.
> **Amid cruelty and injustice, we hope in Christ.**
> **We seek to become children of light.**

INVOCATION

Come, O God, to lift us from hopelessness and despair as the cross looms ever larger on the horizon. Be to us a rock of refuge, a strong fortress. Rescue us from the grasp of the unjust and cruel. Save us from the foolishness of the world's wisdom so that we may find our true strength in you. Encounter us here that we may know you are working in spite of the wickedness that surrounds us. There is reason to praise you even when events seem so unreasonable. Fill us with hope as we walk with Jesus in this time of tension and anxiety. Amen.

CALL TO CONFESSION

Come, as God's chosen ones, to this time of renewal and healing. It is not easy to be faithful when the life of faithfulness runs counter to the ways of the world. God invites us to face our failures and to move beyond them as we confess our sin.

PRAYER OF CONFESSION

O God, you know how we have pretended to be strong as we follow the ways of the world. We have put our trust in "wisdom" that has no lasting value. We invest our energies for things that delight us today but are obsolete tomorrow. We neglect relationships with you and one another that have enduring quality. We are so busy with our busyness that we devote little time to you. So your way has appeared foolish to us, the cross is a stumbling block, and sacrifice is to be avoided. Save us, O God, from our fear-filled ways. Amen.

Assurance of Forgiveness

God has decided to save those who believe, who live by trust even when the road ahead is clouded by uncertainty and loss. God is the source of our life in Christ Jesus, who became for us wisdom from God, and righteousness and sanctification and redemption. As we walk in the light of Christ, we become children of light, bringing wisdom from God to illuminate the shadowy corridors of life.

Collect

Creator of all worlds, you have honored us in the life and witness of Jesus, who shared our humanity and faced death to demonstrate the power of love. We who seek to follow and to serve you in Jesus' name are the fruit of his sacrifice. We are drawn to the cross, even as we are repelled by it, for we see light for our way and the opportunity to make a difference for good in our world. Equip us as faithful witnesses. Amen.

Offertory Invitation

"The message about the cross is foolishness to those who are perishing, but to us who are being saved, it is the power of God." We share God's foolishness with the world because we have met that presence that changes our priorities and gives meaning to our lives. We give that others might live.

Offertory Prayer

God, we do not understand your economy. We only know that when we give, we have more. When we love, we sense your love in greater abundance. When we are faithful, we realize your greater faithfulness. Bless our offering of these tangible gifts and the rededication of our lives. May they bear fruit and bring closer to all of us the realization of your realm. Reign within and among us today. Amen.

Commission and Blessing

God is the ruler of all worlds.
Christ has come to reign in our lives.
> *Our mouths will be full of praise every day.*
> *Our voices will ring out with good news.*
Walk in the light, as children of light.
Dare to follow where Christ leads.
> *We proclaim Christ crucified as Savior of the world.*
> *Christ is the power of God and the wisdom of God.*
God is never far from us, and always available.
God will make haste to help us in times of need.
> *We will hope continually.*
> *We will praise God yet more and more.*
Amen. **Amen.**

(See hymn 39.)

WEDNESDAY OF HOLY WEEK— A, B, C

Isaiah 50:4–9a   Hebrews 12:1–3
Psalm 70   John 13:21–32

CALL TO WORSHIP

As we assemble, we are surrounded by a cloud of witnesses.
We join people of many generations as followers of Jesus.
    We lay aside the weight of sin that clings so closely.
    Let us run with perseverance the race set before us.
Jesus is the pioneer and perfecter of our faith.
He endured the cross, disregarding its shame.
    Jesus found joy in faithfulness to God's inclusiveness.
    We rejoice in Christ, our help and our deliverer.
Let us not grow weary or lose heart.
Let us stand up together with God's help.
    Surely God overcomes life's shame and confusion.
    We will put our trust in God's greatness.

INVOCATION

Sustain us, O God, in these troubled days. Waken our attention to all that Jesus lived and taught. Open our eyes to see, our ears to hear, and our hearts to feel the drama of this week. May we stand with Jesus in the face of insults and brutality. May we honor the cross as a symbol of salvation—a place where the power of your love overcomes the hostility of our pretensions. Meet us here to equip us as faithful disciples, that our words and deeds may glorify Christ, in whose name we pray. Amen.

CALL TO CONFESSION

"Jesus was troubled in spirit, and declared, 'Very truly, I tell you, one of you will betray me.'" Sometimes we wonder if we are the betrayers. At other times, we recognize our guilt immediately. We are invited to confess the ways we deny the pioneer and perfecter of our faith.

PRAYER OF CONFESSION

O God, there are times when we rebel against the claims you make on us. We live without gratitude for the gifts you have given us, and we resent the mandate to help those who seem less responsible than we. We receive the bread from your hand and then betray your purposes. O God, we are poor and needy. We have not lived as the body of Christ in today's world. Deliver your church and help each one of us to live as faithful disciples. Amen.

Assurance of Forgiveness

Consider the hostility Christ endured on our behalf, that you may not grow weary or lose heart. As Jesus forgave those who plotted against him, we, too, are forgiven. Let us lay aside every weight and the sin that clings so closely, and let us run with perseverance the race that is set before us, looking to Jesus, the pioneer and perfecter of our faith, who for the sake of the joy that was set before him endured the cross.

Collect

Holy God, who has given us tongues that we might teach and sustain the weary with a word, let us this night learn from Christ to live for others, to find joy in service, and to continue faithful amid insults and hostility, that our witness may reveal the mind of Christ and bring glory to your name. Amen.

Offertory Invitation

Our church and the offerings we bring are dedicated to helping us and our fellow human beings run the race of life with gratitude and joy. Together, we probe the mysteries of God, revealed in Jesus Christ, reaching out in ministry to one another and to a needy world. Our gifts are an expression of our worship.

Offertory Prayer

Thank you, God, for the message we receive from you each time we gather, and for tongues to share it. Sometimes it is our voices and our actions that communicate good news. Sometimes we send others to do the work beyond our reach. In the name of Jesus, the pioneer and perfecter of our faith, who expressed your love so eloquently, we dedicate our time, talent, and treasure. Amen.

Commission and Blessing

With Jesus, our spirits are troubled this day.
We, too, see denial and betrayal of God's way.
>   *Yet Jesus faced each day with joyous faith.*
>   *We want to walk with him, even toward the cross.*
Let us go forward together.
It is God who helps us live with confidence.
>   *We will not grow weary or lose heart.*
>   *Confusion and treachery cannot have the last word.*
We are surrounded by a great cloud of witnesses.
The faith we carry has been passed on to us.
>   *This heritage of faith is ours to share.*
>   *We want to pass it on to generations yet to come.*
Amen. **Amen.**

(See hymn 40.)

Exodus 12:1–4 (5–10), 11–14

I Corinthians 11:23–26

Psalm 116:1–2, 12–19

John 13:1–17, 31b–35

CALL TO WORSHIP

We have received through Jesus Christ a new covenant.
With broken bread and shared cup, we celebrate it.
> *This is a night of remembrance and celebration.*
> *It is also a time of fear and betrayal.*
At table with Christ, we receive a new commandment.
We are called to love one another as Christ loves us.
> *We are disciples of Jesus when we love one another.*
> *Through love, we thank God for the gift of Jesus.*
In thanks to God, we become a servant to others.
By Jesus' example, we become foot-washers.
> *We have come to learn from Jesus Christ.*
> *We are ready to follow where Christ leads.*

INVOCATION

Holy God, we need your help to face the challenges of this night. Our intentions are good. We want to share in the heritage of our faith, to remember the saving drama of Passover and to celebrate Jesus' last meal with close friends. We want to be disciples, but we also count the cost, and tremble. Incline your ear to us and hear our supplications. We gather as your servant people, knowing we are precious in your sight, yet afraid to take the risk of trusting you completely. Lead us this night into deeper commitment. Amen.

CALL TO CONFESSION

Before we come, in awe, to the table of Jesus Christ, we take these moments to prepare ourselves for that encounter. We are invited, as disciples, to share a last meal with Jesus before we go with our Savior to the cross. Let us confess how unready we are.

PRAYER OF CONFESSION

Deliver us, O God, from the grip of our fears. It is so costly to follow Jesus. We do not want to risk our lives. We do not want to sacrifice our advantages. There are people we find it difficult to love. There are places we do not want to go. We find it hard to speak of our faith. Yet we are attracted to Jesus and want to be disciples. Help us develop the self-discipline we need to follow Jesus, that we may not grow weary or lose heart. Amen.

ASSURANCE OF FORGIVENESS

Jesus welcomed imperfect people to the table and broke bread with persons of questionable reputation. We are welcomed at the table, not because we are worthy but because we are valued and forgiven. God, who created us, knows our potential. God provides for us this opportunity to grow in trust, commitment, and faithfulness.

COLLECT

God of judgment and mercy, whose ways are not our ways, we seek your protection and a double measure of courage, that we may dare to stand against principalities and powers that deny the humanity of our sisters and brothers, to the end that all people may live in a loving environment in which needs are met and all of us reach out in caring ways to one another. Amen.

OFFERTORY INVITATION

What will we return to God for all the bounty we have received? There is no perfect sacrifice that we can make. Nothing we give can match the outpouring of God's love in Jesus Christ. Yet there is much we can do and much that our tithes and offerings can accomplish.

OFFERTORY PRAYER

Loving God, we would offer you nothing less than our best, the firstfruits of our labors, a generous portion of all we have received from your hand. We here express our thanks for the salvation you have extended to us. You are our help and our deliverer. We rejoice in the opportunity to serve in Christ's name. Amen.

COMMISSION AND BLESSING

Fed at Christ's table, we have been strengthened.
We go with Christ to face life's tough realities.
> **The broken bread has refreshed us.**
> **The cup of blessing has filled us with God's peace.**
As disciples, much will be expected of us.
We cannot avoid the challenge of the cross.
> **Jesus is the pioneer and perfecter of our faith.**
> **He saw God's glory beyond the cross.**
Rejoice and be glad; death does not have the last word.
What is good and right and true prevails.
> **God's glory will be seen in the risen Christ.**
> **We go out in confidence, upheld by God's love.**
Amen. **Amen.**

(See hymn 41.)

Isaiah 52:13–53:12   Hebrews 10:16–25 or Hebrews 4:14–16; 5:7–9
Psalm 22   John 18:1–19:42

CALL TO WORSHIP

We huddle together on this day of gloom and fear.
Who can understand such a perversion of justice?
    Why does God seem so far away from our groaning?
    We cry out, but God does not hear or answer us.
Why do people despise and reject Jesus of Nazareth?
He announced and demonstrated God's inclusive love.
    Surely God could have prevented Jesus' suffering.
    Why does God fail to intervene when we pray?
Some say that Jesus was made perfect through suffering.
They see the cross as a sign of obedience and true worship.
    How can we see any light in this anguish?
    What can it mean that Jesus was wounded for us?

INVOCATION

Puzzling God, how can we deal with a day that denies the love Jesus lived and proclaimed? We see the evil of Good Friday repeated again and again in the suffering of innocent people. How can you let this happen? How can we find your will amid all this pain and loss? How can we know you care when everything goes wrong? We need you now, but you seem to have forsaken us. You seem so far away, so silent. Do you feel our anguish? Do you suffer with us? Is it your tears that we feel welling up inside us? O God, let us know you are here. Amen.

CALL TO CONFESSION

Isaiah wrote: "All we like sheep have gone astray; we have turned to our own way, and God has laid on him the iniquity of us all." The early church saw in Jesus one without sin who in some way "was wounded for our transgressions, crushed for our iniquities," as the prophet had proclaimed. We come now, seeking to turn away from the deeds and attitudes and omissions that keep us from the wholeness God intends for us.

PRAYER OF CONFESSION

O God, we see ourselves in the stories of this day. We see ourselves undisciplined in prayer, unable to stay awake to commune with you. We see ourselves reacting violently, as did Peter. We betray your trust in us and deny our commitment to you. We participate in the evil of Good Friday and the evil of our own day. This is not our intent, God. Save us from ourselves, we pray. Amen.

Assurance of Forgiveness

God says to us: I will remember your sins no more. I will put my laws in your hearts and write them on your minds. Your consciences will be cleansed and your bodies washed with pure water. Hold fast to hope without wavering. God is faithful and opens up to us a new and living way through Christ.

Collect

God of our beginnings and all our days, whose love is with us in our times of deepest loss and pain, we put our trust in you today as pictures flash through our minds—a garden, soldiers, swords, a fire in the courtyard of the high priest, Pilate's headquarters, flogging, a crown of thorns, the Place of the Skull, the thud of a hammer, soldiers casting lots . . . Open our emotions and strengthen our commitment that our discipleship may help some other traveler on life's way. Amen.

Offertory Invitation

Our offering is an act of faith on a day when our faith is shaken. It is an expression of trust in God when we find it hard to see beyond the agony of suffering and loss. We live by hope, with a profound sense that there is abundant reason to give thanks.

Offertory Prayer

O God, we trust your faithfulness, and so we seek to respond faithfully. May our giving encourage others and inspire in them good deeds that express your love. Amid the deceit and violence of our day, we seek to make a difference. Keep us from being drawn into a quagmire of cynicism and despair that can paralyze us. We place ourselves in your hands. Amen.

Commission and Blessing

God has not forsaken us in our time of grief.
Let us commit our course to God who delivers us.
> **God keeps us safe in the face of trouble.**
> **We can look to God for help in our need.**

Praise and glorify God in the great congregation.
Stand in awe to worship the Source of all life.
> **God opens up for us a new and living way.**
> **We are equipped for the challenges of each day.**

Let us look to one another for support and encouragement.
Let us hold fast to our confession of hope.
> **Evil will not have the last word.**
> **The threat of death cannot stop the reign of love.**

Amen. **Amen.**

(See hymn 42.)

Job 14:1–14 or Lamentations 3:1–9, 19–24   1 Peter 4:1–8
Psalm 31:1–4, 15–16   Matthew 27:57–66 or John 19:38–42

CALL TO WORSHIP

Gather together on this day of sadness and grief.
We need one another as we bear the absence of light.
> *Where is God amid this tragedy and suffering?*
> *Does God listen to our cries for help?*

God was present in the life and death of Jesus.
God mourns with us now in this time of trouble.
> *Is there really a God who understands our sorrow?*
> *Why doesn't God act to prevent all this pain?*

We are bewildered by so much we do not understand.
Where but to God can we turn for refuge?
> *Is this the end of all our hopes and dreams?*
> *If mortals die, will they live again?*

INVOCATION

Incline your ear to us, God. You have been a rock of refuge for us, a strong fortress to save us. But now it feels as if you have built a fence around us that we cannot climb over. We are penned in by our despair. There is no light here, and you do not seem to listen to our pleas. If such caring goodness can be nailed to a cross, what hope is there for us? If you abandon us, what is left? This is the end of everything. O God, are you with us, or not? How can we even say . . . Amen?

CALL TO CONFESSION

Certainly we feel separated from God on this day of treachery. Separation from God is a major definition of sin. Have we, indeed, caused the separation we feel so keenly? Has Jesus died because of our idolatry? What do we need to confess today?

PRAYER OF CONFESSION

O God, your tears fall as a judgment on us. We did not recognize Jesus in the poor wretch we ignored on the street. We did not know that the child who died of starvation in the arms of his grieving mother was Jesus. We did not realize that the angry words we hurled pierced the heart of our Savior. We did not comprehend the damage we inflicted on Jesus with our little deceits, our self-centered passions, our violations of trust. O Christ, you have borne our grief and carried our sorrows. How can you forgive? Amen.

ASSURANCE OF FORGIVENESS

That's what this day is all about. The One we grieve, the One we killed, died for us. The One who loves us with a perfect love risked everything to bring us to a realization of God's love for us. God, who judges the living and the dead, wants us to live in the Spirit, to give care and compassion to everyone we encounter, to share forgiveness and grace. God calls us to maintain constant love for one another. It is in that love that we are forgiven, by the grace of God.

COLLECT

Amazing God, whose love sustains us even when we feel your absence, lead us and guide us, for your name's sake, through our valleys of despair, that we might yet do what needs to be done to show love, to represent Jesus Christ and to proclaim the gospel, living by the hope that we shall rise again. Amen.

OFFERTORY INVITATION

What should we offer in the name of One who poured out life itself for us? No gift we bring can express adequate thanks. Yet there is joy in doing all we can to honor Jesus and proclaim Christ to the world. May our response be generous.

OFFERTORY PRAYER

With love, we offer our best for the body of Christ. As Nicodemus and Joseph ministered to the body of Jesus with tenderness and generosity, we bring our gifts, intending that the church, representing Christ today, might be raised up in new vitality and wholeness. Lift us up as a serving people to minister to the world in Jesus' name. May this offering assist our care for one another and our sharing of good news in word and deed to all who have not yet experienced it. Amen.

COMMISSION AND BLESSING

Now all is still. Time holds its breath.
We dare to live by a flicker of hope.
> *We continue in service to God and one another.*
> *We wait for the release we hope will come.*
Live that Christ's suffering may not be in vain.
Carry the light of God's love to the world.
> *We would not live by human desires.*
> *We commit ourselves anew to the will of God.*
Maintain constant love for one another.
Love covers a multitude of sins.
> *May God's face shine on all of Christ's servants.*
> *May we be saved by God's steadfast love.*
Amen. **Amen.**

(See hymn 43.)

The Easter Season

Acts 10:34–43

Colossians 3:1–4

Psalm 118:1–2, 14–24

John 20:1–18

CALL TO WORSHIP

Day has dawned and shadows are left behind.

The stone is rolled away and hope is reborn.

> *This is the day that our God has made.*
> *We will rejoice and be glad in it.*

God opens to us the gates of righteousness.

We enter to give thanks to our God.

> *We give thanks, for our God is good.*
> *God's steadfast love endures forever.*

Set your mind on things that are above.

Look up and welcome Christ's appearing.

> *We have been raised with Christ.*
> *Glory is being revealed to us on this holy day.*

INVOCATION

God of amazing surprises, the story of Easter is ever new. Suddenly we are aware of your presence with us. We had lost touch with you. Our minds were full of worries and distractions, set on things of this earth. Our spirits felt the grip of death. Jesus seemed a legend from the past, not a real person who shared our common lot. But today, you awaken something new within us. We hear the cry, Christ is risen, and we want to respond. Dry our tears and call our name. We need the good news of Easter. Amen.

CALL TO CONFESSION

Amid our Easter celebrations, it is well to pause for moments of reflection. How can we share the joy of new life if we have not taken time to examine old ways that lead to death? How will we recognize the risen Christ if we have not walked with the earthly Jesus?

PRAYER OF CONFESSION

O God, the message of Easter has come again before we were ready to receive it. The Palm Sunday parade demanded very little of us. We could join in the hosannas. But the betrayal and denial, the suffering and shame, the agony and death, have left us fearful and shaken. We have become enemies of Jesus without intending to be disloyal. We have left him in the tomb, lest he upset our daily lives. The Jesus of long ago seems more comfortable to us than the Christ who is risen today in our midst. We confess our reluctance to let Christ claim us and change us. O God, we need forgiveness! Amen.

ASSURANCE OF FORGIVENESS

God raised Jesus from death. Disciples who had deserted Jesus felt the embrace of forgiveness. The spirit of Christ has come among us today, claiming us for our new life together. God wants to forgive us. God intends that we move from death to life. All of us are invited to share in the promise of the Easter season.

COLLECT

God of empty tombs and empty hearts, fill us today with the joy of trusting and believing, that we might rise from the graves of our misplaced loyalties to live with Christ and serve wherever good news is needed. May gladness flow through us to bring inspiration and hope to sisters and brothers locked in prisons of despair, that all of us might have the courage to love as you have loved us in Jesus Christ. Amen.

OFFERTORY INVITATION

We have come together today to give thanks for God's steadfast love. Each one of us is an expression of that love. By the way we live and the way we give, that love is carried into the lives of others who have had little experience of God's care. May our offerings represent an outpouring of thanksgiving.

OFFERTORY PRAYER

By your hand, O God, we have been blessed with life, with food, with refreshment, with hope. Day by day you are saving us, healing our brokenness, calling forth our gifts, granting us strength to serve with Christ as a part of your revelation to the world. Thank you, God, for times of resurrection. Thank you for this day of celebration. We dedicate ourselves anew with our offering. Amen.

COMMISSION AND BLESSING

With hope reborn, we go out to proclaim good news.
The brightness of this day is meant to be shared.
> *We have seen the Lord Jesus Christ.*
> *This is the one we have been seeking.*
Run to tell others that Christ is alive.
Spread the message through the land.
> *Beyond the cross is a message of peace.*
> *Beyond death is the promise of new life.*
God is our strength and our might.
God answers our prayers and equips us for living.
> *We have been raised with Christ to fuller life.*
> *May God's reign be evident in us!*
Amen. **Amen.**

(See hymn 44.)

EASTER SUNDAY (ALTERNATE)

Jeremiah 31:1–6

Psalm 118:1–2, 14–24

Acts 10:34–43

Matthew 28:1–10

CALL TO WORSHIP

God promises: someday you will again be my people.

I will be your God and will give you peace.

O God, come today to claim us.

Take away the sting of death.

God has been patient and kind with us.

We are precious to God, who loves us.

God answers our prayers and offers salvation.

The rejected one has become the chief cornerstone.

This is the day that God has made.

Let us rejoice and be glad in it.

We rejoice to know that Christ is alive.

God has chosen us to witness to good news.

INVOCATION

Through earthquake and terror, appear to us, holy God, and roll away the stones that separate us from you. Turn our fear to faith, our doubts to delight, as Jesus, who was crucified, becomes for us an abiding presence. Raise us with Christ to seek the things that are above. Anoint us with the Spirit's healing power, that we may reach out with good deeds in the name of Christ. We raise our glad songs, giving thanks that you have opened for us the gates of righteousness. Amen.

CALL TO CONFESSION

On this day of resurrection, we remember the high expectations God has of us. We are called away from our frantic distractions to recognize the Creator of all things. God, who shows no partiality, invites us to be witnesses to the good news of Jesus Christ among all whom we meet.

PRAYER OF CONFESSION

God, we have lost our awe of you in the busyness of our days. We have forgotten to look for Christ in the people we meet. We have ignored your mandate to live as Christ in relation to our neighbors. On this day of resurrection, we ask you to raise us up and restore in us a commitment to our risen Savior. May we die to all that is selfish in order that Christ may live in us. Amen.

ASSURANCE OF FORGIVENESS

Punishment is meant to correct us, that we might not die but live to recount God's compassionate deeds. God answers our prayers and offers us salvation. In following Christ, we find wholeness and joy. We set our minds on God's gracious intention for us. Give thanks to God, whose steadfast love endures forever. Rejoice that Christ sends us out to tell others that they, too, may know resurrection.

COLLECT

Ever-present God, whom we worship with joy on this resurrection day, show us the places of death where you grieve for your children, that we might reflect the spirit of Christ, whose love risked all for others. Take away our fear so we may grow in discipleship and devote ourselves in service, in Christ's name. Amen.

OFFERTORY INVITATION

The message for us, on this day of celebration, is that Jesus goes ahead of us into all the challenges we face. In the midst of every difficulty, Christ meets us with a presence that gives strength and confidence. In that trust, we give ourselves as disciples, learning and serving in Christ's name. Our tithes and offerings, given today, are one part of that service.

OFFERTORY PRAYER

Thank you, God, for accepting us in ways that we had not even accepted ourselves. We want to do what is right and good. Receive our time and effort as well as our money, that your message of peace might be spread throughout our community and nation, and into the whole world. Inspire all of us to seek, above all else, to do your will and accomplish your purposes. Amen.

COMMISSION AND BLESSING

We have witnessed an earthshaking event.
Christ has been raised! Christ is alive.
> *We have been raised with Christ to new life.*
> *Our lives have been filled with new meaning.*
Gates of righteousness have been opened for us.
Give thanks for the new life we have entered.
> *God is our strength and our might.*
> *Christ has become our salvation.*
Continue to celebrate this first day of Easter.
There are many more to come as we grow in Christ.
> *God anointed Jesus with spirit and power.*
> *We carry with us new empowerment for living.*
Amen. **Amen.**

(See hymn 45.)

Isaiah 25:6–9   I Corinthians 5:6b–8
Psalm 114   Luke 24:13–49

CALL TO WORSHIP

Christ has been sacrificed to malice and evil.
Let us lay aside all that is hateful and wicked.
> *We are here to be cleansed of our old ways.*
> *We seek to be filled with sincerity and truth.*

God prepares a feast for us to eat.
Christ will be known to us in the breaking of bread.
> *God takes away our disgrace and wipes our tears.*
> *We rejoice in the salvation Christ brings.*

Let us celebrate the festival of resurrection.
Christ is alive and opens the Scriptures to us.
> *Peace comes amid our terror and fear.*
> *We are touched by the Spirit that makes us whole.*

INVOCATION

Appear to us again, O Christ, as you appeared to Simon and to unnamed disciples
in their home. Take away the shroud that covers over our doubts that we might be
exposed to your healing, assuring presence. The surprising news of life overcom-
ing death has left us wondering and amazed. We do not know what to think. Our
minds want answers, but our hearts want to feel you near, no explanations needed.
Let the mountains once again skip like rams at the good news of your abiding love.
Amen.

CALL TO CONFESSION

We celebrate resurrection, but what does this mean to us? Have our lives changed,
our priorities been redirected, our loyalties rekindled? How are we yet living in
the grip of death? This is a time to examine ourselves with honest intent to let
God redirect our energies.

PRAYER OF CONFESSION

God of our times, we confess that we often try to keep the story of Easter in the
past. We can marvel at the empty tomb, but it is hard for us to welcome Christ to
our own tables. We want to fit in to our skeptical age rather than bear strange tales
that might mark us as peculiar or fanatical. Can't we just change a little, take off a
few rough edges? Why must we challenge the ways of the world? What will happen if we rise to new life?

ASSURANCE OF FORGIVENESS

God hears our honest confession and offers us far more than we dare to ask. Our disgrace is taken away. Salvation comes to us as a gift. We are cleansed and healed and emboldened to live as disciples and apostles. Hope is restored, courage is given, trust is strengthened. We are an Easter people. We will be clothed with power from on high. Praise God!

COLLECT

God of faithful women and men, whose revelations are often unexpected and surprising, we seek to be open to your word and responsive to your call. Melt our hearts, taking away the defenses that keep us from recognizing your voice or following your way. May we be faithful witnesses to the good news of this day, for the sake of those who need a resurrection experience to know life in all its fullness. Amen.

OFFERTORY INVITATION

God has made known to us the ways of life. Giving is one of the privileges made possible by God's gracious gifts to us. We have good news for all who are disbelieving and wondering. Let us rededicate ourselves and our resources to the proclamation of our resurrection faith.

OFFERTORY PRAYER

Our hearts are burning with amazement, O God, because of all the ways you have blessed us. May the astonishing news of Easter inspire our witness, filling our offerings with love for all your people. Let our way of life be so attractive that many will be moved to join us at Christ's table to experience the mystery of broken bread and shared cup, in Jesus' name. Amen.

COMMISSION AND BLESSING

Peace be with you as you celebrate resurrection.
Let this season fill you with new life.
> **Christ is bringing fresh leaven to our lives.**
> **We rejoice in the salvation we are experiencing.**
Let us not be slow of heart to believe.
We trust God to lift our vision.
> **Christ joins us as a guest at every meal.**
> **We are also guests of Jesus at a common table.**
Listen for the assurance of God's gift of peace.
Let the Scriptures speak to you of God's love.
> **Our hearts burn within as the Scriptures come alive.**
> **We will witness to all we have experienced.**
Amen. **Amen.**

(See hymn 46.)

Acts 2:14a, 22–32　　　　　　　　　　　　　　　　　I Peter 1:3–9

Psalm 16　　　　　　　　　　　　　　　　　　　　John 20:19–31

CALL TO WORSHIP

We come again to celebrate resurrection.

God gives us new birth into a living hope.

> **Death has no power over us.**
> **Christ goes before us in the new life God offers.**

Blessed be the God of our Savior Jesus Christ!

Our faith, tested by fire, is renewed.

> **Our hearts are glad, our souls rejoice.**
> **God shows us the path of life.**

Again, Jesus says to us: Peace be with you.

Come to receive life in Christ's name.

> **We rejoice in God's amazing good news.**
> **In God's presence, we find fullness of joy.**

INVOCATION

Your Easter people gather to praise you, amazing God. Continue to make your ways known to us. Fill us with your presence. We cannot live apart from you. Your counsel and instruction are with us day and night. We have only to open ourselves to your direction. Inspire in us fullness of joy, we pray, as we respond in faith to the risen Christ and embrace the tasks you set before us. Build up our sense of community that we may truly care for one another through all life's trials. Amen.

CALL TO CONFESSION

How quickly we forget that we are an Easter people, raised up out of the ways of death into fullness of life. The power of death leaves us shaken and afraid, but God in Christ calls us out of our fear to experience a presence that embraces us with eternal hope. We confess now all that keeps us from accepting the gift of the Holy Spirit.

PRAYER OF CONFESSION

Forgive us, God, for seeking to limit your truth to what we can understand. Forgive us for chasing after gods of our own making. We are so busy with them that we forget to open ourselves to your larger reality. We reduce the circles of connection and caring that Jesus demonstrated. Goodness is crucified by our narrow prejudices, and our doubts plunge us into despair. Be to us a refuge, granting us courage to face the questions that haunt us until they lead to deeper understanding. Amen.

ASSURANCE OF FORGIVENESS

God never abandons us, no matter how far we stray. We have a goodly heritage which is ours to claim. God shows us the path of life and offers us fullness of joy. Let our hearts be glad and our tongues rejoice. The Living Christ is in our midst. We are granted new birth into a living hope.

COLLECT

God of peace, by whose breath the Holy Spirit enters our lives and transforms our community of faith, come to us now, whether we have opened or locked our doors. Lead us to faith beyond sight, trust beyond doubt, deeds beyond words, that we may live as your forgiven and forgiving children, leading the way for realization of your peace among us and in all the world. Amen.

OFFERTORY INVITATION

The boundary lines have fallen for us in pleasant places. We are blessed beyond all deserving. How marvelous is the opportunity placed before us to share what we have received. Let us express our thanks to God for all that is more precious than gold, as we pass on God's gifts to us.

OFFERTORY PRAYER

We rejoice in the inheritance you have given us, O God, and delight in sharing it with others. You have given us new birth into a living hope through the resurrection of Jesus Christ. You have touched our lives with eternity, with indescribable and glorious joy. We want others to experience what we have begun to realize in company with one another and with you. To that end, bless all the offerings of this day. Amen.

COMMISSION AND BLESSING

Jesus says to us again: Peace be with you.
As God has sent me, so I send you.
> *We receive God's peace into our lives.*
> *We will go where Christ sends us.*
Feel the wind, the breath of God.
Receive the gift of the Holy Spirit.
> *We are empowered as disciples and apostles.*
> *We will learn and serve in Jesus' name.*
Blessed are all who trust and obey.
God will give you counsel and instruction.
> *Our hearts are glad and our souls rejoice.*
> *We are learning the way of life God intends.*
Amen. **Amen.**

(See hymn 47.)

Acts 2:14a, 36–41   I Peter 1:17–23
Psalm 116:1–4, 12–19   Luke 24:13–35

CALL TO WORSHIP

God has called us together for this time of worship.
God is listening to our thoughts and to our speaking.
> **God inclines an ear to us and hears us.**
> **God knows us better than we know ourselves.**

Let us open our hearts to the One who gives us life.
Let us set our faith and hope in God.
> **In one another's presence, we renew our vows.**
> **Together we offer our thanksgiving sacrifice.**

God's promises to us are ancient and ever new.
God is with us here and on all the roads we travel.
> **Together we lift our voices in songs of praise.**
> **Together we recognize we are precious in God's sight.**

INVOCATION

Wondrous God, present with us when we do not know it, valuing us when we do not care for ourselves, planting in us the seed of your word even when the soil of our hearts is hard and unyielding, open our eyes to recognize you here. May we sense your presence next to us. May we hear your voice. May we know your touch. May we see you in one another and in the beauty all around us. May your reality emerge deep inside each life, transforming our thoughts and deeds and our relationship with one another. Amen.

CALL TO CONFESSION

Peter preached: "Save yourselves from this crooked generation. Repent . . . so your sins may be forgiven." We participate in our society's alienation from God. We have joined the "me" generation in putting our own interests before all else. We have much to confess before we can claim the wholeness God offers.

PRAYER OF CONFESSION

O God, we confess that we rush through our days without recognizing your presence with us. We follow our busy diversions without reference to your will for us. We strive for financial success and personal recognition, while you call for obedience to truth and genuine mutual love. Purify our souls, we pray, and redirect our priorities. May we be born anew through your living and enduring word. Amen.

ASSURANCE OF FORGIVENESS

The promise of forgiveness is for us and for our children, for everyone whom God calls. The gift of the Holy Spirit is ours to receive. Lift up the cup of salvation every day, and call on God's name. Give thanks for the words and deeds of Jesus, who revealed God's love for us and enlists us as disciples and apostles.

COLLECT

God of love and judgment, who made Jesus both Sovereign and Messiah, and who welcomed us into your family through the waters of baptism, we seek once again to know the risen Christ in our midst and to receive the gift of the Holy Spirit, that we might be obedient to your truth and genuine in our love for one another. May the new birth provided by your living and enduring word send us forth today as deeply committed messengers of good news. Amen.

OFFERTORY INVITATION

Our offerings are a sacrifice of thanksgiving in the spirit of Jesus, who gave everything, even life itself, to proclaim God's inclusive love. God calls all people to become children of the promise, and to this end we dedicate our gifts.

OFFERTORY PRAYER

Thank you, God, for the privilege of joining with Christ in the proclamation of your love for all people. May the ministries we support serve to unite people across all differences, building up the body of Christ and reaching out to the world with healing energy. Bless these gifts and all who give in any way to make your love known. Amen.

COMMISSION AND BLESSING

We have been called away from a corrupt generation.
We have been ransomed from our futile ways.
> *Life's meaning is not to be found in silver or gold.*
> *We have found new life in trusting God.*
We have been born anew through God's enduring word.
We embrace a living faith and hope.
> *We purify our souls through obedience to truth.*
> *We love one another deeply from the heart.*
Christ is alive in our midst.
Christ goes with us along all life's roads.
> *We go out to serve in Christ's name.*
> *May the love of Christ find expression in us.*
Amen. **Amen.**

(See hymns 46, 48.)

Acts 2:42–47   1 Peter 2:19–25
Psalm 23   John 10:1–10

CALL TO WORSHIP

How awesome to gather before God!
We are here to celebrate with wide-eyed wonder.
> *The God of all worlds is with us.*
> *Praise God for this season of Easter.*

Praise God for all the signs of new life.
Praise God for all we can do together.
> *Praise God for the life and ministry of Jesus.*
> *Praise God for all who share that ministry today.*

Christ came to offer us abundant life.
We are here today to reclaim that gift.
> *We gather in the name of Jesus Christ.*
> *We want to follow in the steps of Jesus.*

INVOCATION

Let us hear your voice today, O Shepherd. Call our names and claim us as your own. Lead us beside still waters and restore our souls. Comfort those who suffer pain and loss. Assure all who are afraid. Lead us in right paths for your name's sake. We have known your goodness and mercy in so many times and places. We open ourselves now to receive these gifts again. Unlock within us the barriers that keep us from recognizing and appreciating all the evidence of your love that surrounds us. Amen.

CALL TO CONFESSION

The Scriptures compare us to sheep who have gone astray. As sheep seem not to see beyond the next tuft of grass, we seem to be attracted to the immediate temptation. We become ravenous consumers rather than good stewards of God's abundance. Christ calls us to respond to the Shepherd's voice.

PRAYER OF CONFESSION

O God, we do not want to admit that our possessions possess us. Yet we do seem captive to all the things we have acquired and all the things we want. We are reluctant to share too much, lest we be deprived of the comforts we cherish. We do not want to suffer for our faith. There are limits to our willingness to follow Jesus. O God, help us trust you beyond these limits. Amen.

Assurance of Forgiveness

God provides for us as a good shepherd provides for a flock of sheep, seeking green pastures and still waters for us even in periods of famine and drought. In fearful times, amid loss, the Shepherd's care is always available. Surely God's goodness and mercy will restore all who give up their own pretensions in order to live in community, with glad and generous hearts.

Collect

God, beyond our knowing, yet revealed so personally in Jesus Christ, help us to embrace the abundant life you have offered us. May we follow the example of Jesus, risking abuse and suffering for the sake of your children, trusting in your abiding care for each one of us until all join in praising you with mutual goodwill and joy. Amen.

Offertory Invitation

Our cups overflow with the abundance of God's mercy. There is more than enough for all when we who break bread together are willing to share ourselves and our possessions. We offer Christ's healing example to a world shattered by selfishness, strangers to God and one another.

Offertory Prayer

Thank you, God, for the abundant life we enjoy, not in the things we possess but in the relationships you offer and the opportunities for sharing that you provide. May all that we here dedicate to you be distributed in ways that meet human need and offer praise to you. Extend our outreach beyond our vision, that we may live in awe and wonder before you, marveling before your goodness and mercy. Amen.

Commission and Blessing

You have been claimed by God, our Good Shepherd.
Know God, not as stranger, but as friend.
> **God is our shepherd; we shall not want.**
> **God leads us daily and restores our souls.**
Easter continues, for Christ lives in us.
Jesus came that we might have abundant life.
> **Daily we receive God's goodness and mercy.**
> **Our cups overflow with God's generosity.**
Let us devote ourselves to the apostles' teaching.
Let us pray and break bread together.
> **We find our lives in giving them to others.**
> **In Christ, we discover the joy of service.**
Amen. **Amen.**

(See hymn 49.)

Acts 7:55–60   I Peter 2:2–10
Psalm 31:1–5, 15–16   John 14:1–14

CALL TO WORSHIP

Gaze into heaven and see the glory of God.
Lift up your eyes to behold the risen Christ.
> **God is our rock of refuge, a strong fortress.**
> **Christ leads us and guides us every day.**

Indeed, you have tasted the goodness of God.
You have known the presence of Christ, God's chosen one.
> **Every day we long for pure spiritual milk.**
> **Each day, we are inspired by the living Christ.**

Then let us lay our troubles at Christ's feet.
Let us enter the sanctuary God prepares for us.
> **We have come to find the way, the truth, and the life.**
> **We are here to ask and to receive and to serve.**

INVOCATION

Open your heavens to us, God of all worlds. We long for the pure spiritual milk
you provide so we may grow into salvation. We are your people, sisters and brothers of your Chosen One. Let us this day be built into a spiritual house, a community of your faithful people. Keep us from judging those whose views differ from
our own, or from throwing stones at those with whom we disagree. Incline your
ear to us and rescue us from ourselves, we pray in Jesus' name. Amen.

CALL TO CONFESSION

We, who use our doubts and questions as excuses for irresponsibility, are called to
account. We have disobeyed God's word and rejected the One who revealed God's
love. Because we do not believe, we cannot see the goodness of God. Let us seek
God's mercy and forgiveness.

PRAYER OF CONFESSION

We confess that sometimes we have covered our ears so we cannot hear your word
of judgment, holy God. We seek to isolate ourselves from a world in pain. We become enemies and persecutors of Christ, who identified with poor, needy, and oppressed people. We reject the One you sent as the way, the truth, and the life. We
do not pray, as Jesus prayed, trusting that you hear and respond. O God, deliver us
from ourselves. Amen.

Assurance of Forgiveness

Let not your hearts be troubled. Whoever believes in God will not be put to shame. If you truly believe, you will show care for others. When you care, you will join in doing the things Jesus did to help all the people God loves. You are chosen to proclaim the mighty acts of One who called you out of the shadows into God's marvelous light. Rejoice! You have received the mercy of God.

Collect

Creator, Parent of all humankind, whose love for all of us was revealed in Jesus Christ, draw us into a relationship of trust in you that will help us day by day to discern more clearly the way, the truth, and the life you intend for us. Help us, in all humility, to follow Jesus, to do the works of Christ without calling attention to ourselves. We long to become that spiritual household of mutually caring people that Jesus sought to model among us. Amen.

Offertory Invitation

There are moments when the heavens seem to open to us, and we sense the vast possibilities for life that God offers. We long to reach our God-given potential and to offer that opportunity to others. The tithes and offerings we bring are devoted to that purpose.

Offertory Prayer

We commit ourselves to you, gracious God, as we dedicate material gifts that represent our labor. When we ponder the amazing wonder of life, we are filled with awe. When we remember Jesus as the cornerstone of the spiritual house you are seeking to build in our midst, we are eager to help. Let your face shine on us and on this offering that your mighty acts may be proclaimed to all the world. Amen.

Commission and Blessing

Jesus sends us out into paths of service.
We are summoned to greater works than Jesus did.
> *How is it possible for us to do more than Jesus did?*
> *Can we preach and pray and heal as Jesus did?*
We are chosen as Christ's representatives.
We are the church, the body of Christ on earth.
> *Together we can make a difference.*
> *God is at work in us to heal our world.*
Christ has gone ahead to prepare a place for us.
Following in Christ's way, we know fullness of life.
> *We believe God dwells in us and among us.*
> *God's mighty acts are revealed through us.*
Amen. **Amen.**

(See hymn 50.)

Acts 17:22–31   I Peter 3:13–22
Psalm 66:8–20   John 14:15–21

CALL TO WORSHIP

The God of heaven and earth calls us together.
We come to explore matters of the Spirit.
> *There is so much we do not know or understand.*
> *So much of God is unknown to us.*
Let us look carefully at the objects of our worship.
Our attention is easily diverted from God.
> *We want to worship the One who gives us breath.*
> *We reach for the Reality beyond our knowing.*
In God we live and move and have our being.
All that we have and are comes from God.
> *God is not limited to shrines made by us.*
> *God is everywhere present in the whole universe.*

INVOCATION

Let the sound of praising you be heard among us today, and in all the places of
your dominion, O God. We believe you are present with us even when we cannot feel or see or hear you as we would like. We thank you for the times when you
have caught our attention. We ask for one of those times today. Shake us out of
our complacency and our cherished iniquities. Hold us in your steadfast love
and call forth within us an awareness of all your blessings. Stimulate among us an
eagerness to live as you intend. Amen.

CALL TO CONFESSION

We have been baptized and claimed in the name of Jesus Christ for a lifetime of
service. Yet we are often intimidated by our fears and seduced by our fantasies. We
worship autonomy and deny community. We ignore the commandments God has
given us. We need to face our guilt. God demands our repentance.

PRAYER OF CONFESSION

O God, we confess that we have loved our own way more than we love you. The
Spirit of truth does not abide in us, for our actions belie the words of praise we
utter in worship. We neglect the spiritual disciplines that would draw us close to
you and the caring outreach that would link us with sisters and brothers who need
to know of your love. We have not witnessed to our faith in ways powerful enough
to evoke opposition or cause us to suffer. O God, it is hard to follow Jesus! Forgive us, teach us, help us! Amen.

Assurance of Forgiveness

You are not left to struggle alone. You have an Advocate who is always with you. You are not rejected. God hears your prayers and offers you steadfast love in all circumstances. Do not be afraid to hope, and to share that hope with others around you. Claim God's gifts of reverence and gentleness as you testify to the resurrection. Who will harm you if you are eager to do what is good?

Collect

Abiding God, who does not leave us orphaned, reclaim us now as we experience the Scriptures, that we might renew our commitment and be empowered for faithful service. Use our hands to do the work you have called us to do. Use our caring to build community. Use our witness to overcome ignorance of your way of love for all people. Amen.

Offertory Invitation

Our spiritual ancestors brought sacrifices as offerings to God. We are invited to join them in bringing our best to proclaim God's rule over all things. God claims our labors and the fruit of our labors. In response, we offer them gladly.

Offertory Prayer

May all that we give today be used to express your love among us and beyond us, God of all people. We are thankful for your gift to us in Christ Jesus, who was so committed to sharing your love that he risked rejection and death. We are grateful that even though his suffering resulted in death in the flesh you made him alive in the spirit. May Christ live today in us, in our caring, in our giving, in our speaking, in our doing. We rededicate ourselves to your service. Amen.

Commission and Blessing

God has listened to our prayers and abides with us.
God's blessing rests on us as we scatter to serve.
The Spirit lives within us and among us.
We seek to live as resurrection people.
Daily God will add to your understanding if you ask.
Do not fear to seek after the truth God will reveal.
Every day can be an adventure in faith.
All our encounters can link us more closely with God.
Our Creator draws us into community.
Our spiritual journey is linked to others' stories.
Together we will seek to know God more fully.
We will remember one another in prayer.
Amen. **Amen.**

(See hymns 51, 52.)

ASCENSION (OR SEVENTH SUNDAY AFTER EASTER)—A, B, C

Acts 1:1–11   Ephesians 1:15–23
Psalm 47 or Psalm 93   Luke 24:44–53

CALL TO WORSHIP

In awe and wonder, we lift our eyes to the heavens.
We raise our songs of joy to the Ruler of all time and space.
> *Sing praises to God, sing praises;*
> *Shout to God with loud songs of joy.*
We gather to remember the One who shared our common lot.
Jesus Christ, who visited this earth, dwells in heaven.
> *We celebrate the life and ministry of Jesus.*
> *We rejoice in the hope to which Christ has called us.*
We open ourselves to baptism with the Holy Spirit.
We expect to be empowered as witnesses in today's world.
> *We seek a spirit of wisdom and revelation.*
> *We are here to be filled with power from on high.*

INVOCATION

As Christ ascended to heaven, our spirits are lifted to you this day, O God. Your Spirit fills all the universe. We dwell within your embrace and cannot escape from your watchful care. You are with us here, choosing us as apostles and instructing us in the way we should go. Focus our limited understanding on the person of Jesus, that all he did and taught might come alive in us during this hour. Grant to us convincing proof of your promises as we welcome your winds of change in our lives. Amen.

CALL TO CONFESSION

On this day of mystery and wonder, we reflect on our record as an Easter people. Is there evidence that Christ is alive within us and among us? Is the work of the Spirit obvious to any who observe our words and deeds? Let us admit how things are with us, as we seek God's forgiveness.

PRAYER OF CONFESSION

Hear us, God, our hope, for we have too easily denied our heritage amid the competing claims all around us. We declare ownership of what is only lent to us for a time. We strive for knowledge and control beyond our capacity, wanting power on our own terms rather than through the unpredictable empowerment of your Spirit. Sometimes we stand on tiptoe to view what is out of sight, then arrogantly conclude that there is nothing to see. O God, open our eyes and our hearts that we might be forgiven and find true life in you. Amen.

Assurance of Forgiveness

Repentance and forgiveness of sin are proclaimed to all people in the name of Jesus Christ. Forgiveness is God's gift to us, one we can never earn but are welcome to accept. When we agree to God's freeing offer, we are also agreeing to let God's love change us. We are blessed by this opportunity for newness of life.

Collect

God of all times and places, whose promise of the Holy Spirit is for us as well as for generations past, let your blessing fall on us while we are together, clothing us with the resources to be your witnesses through the church, Christ's body. May the glorious inheritance that is ours be shared that our communities may be enlightened and transformed. Amen.

Offertory Invitation

Our giving expresses our faith in Jesus Christ and our love for all the saints. In the church, we depend on our prayers for one another and the generosity of our support for the programs that help us all to grow in wisdom and capacity to serve.

Offertory Prayer

May our offerings express our care for one another and our commitment to serve the world in the name of Christ. Help us to use well all the resources you entrust to us. Equip us, as forgiven and forgiving people, to carry the good news to people we meet every day as well as to unknown sisters and brothers who live in desperate circumstances we can scarcely imagine. May our gifts and our lives praise you. Amen.

Commission and Blessing

The risen Jesus appeared to friends in many ways.
Christ is seen by persons today in people like us.
> *The life and teachings of Jesus point us to God's reign.*
> *God promises to empower our witness.*
We will be baptized with the Holy Spirit.
This is the promise Jesus made to us.
> *Through revelation, we will know more of Christ.*
> *Through the work God gives us, we will grow.*
Our worship sends us out to work and witness.
We scatter to continue our worship through service.
> *God sends us out with love for all the saints.*
> *We commit ourselves to care for all God's children.*
Amen. **Amen.**

(See hymn 53.)

Acts 1:6–14   I Peter 4:12–14; 5:6–11
Psalm 68:1–10, 32–35   John 17:1–11

CALL TO WORSHIP

Sing to God; sing praises to God's name.
Let all the nations bow down to worship God.
> **God is ruler over all creation.**
> **God reigns over earth and the farthest heavens.**
Ascribe power to God, whose majesty is over all.
Listen to hear God's mighty voice.
> **This sanctuary is filled with God's presence.**
> **Here we receive power and strength from God.**
Here we pray together for God's guidance.
The Holy Spirit empowers us to witness.
> **God draws us together as one people.**
> **We can experience eternity in the midst of time.**

INVOCATION

We worship you with joy, awesome God. Through times of trial and suffering, your love has sustained us. You have restored our self-confidence when we floundered in doubt and fear. You have been our protector through the wilderness. Meet us now in the particular situations each of us faces. Pour out your presence that we may be resources to one another, finding our oneness and our prime vocation in Jesus Christ. May our worship honor you and equip us to serve you. Amen.

CALL TO CONFESSION

We who have promised our loyalty to Jesus Christ pause now to examine our faithfulness to the way he showed us. We who have been gifted with the Holy Spirit within and among us ask ourselves whether others can see that gift in us. Is God reigning among us, or have we chosen to pursue other gods, chosen to devote our time and energy and attention to lesser matters?

PRAYER OF CONFESSION

O God, if we suffer, it is usually not because of our loyalty to Christ. When we are glad and shout for joy, it is seldom because we want to celebrate your presence with us. We even forget to say thank-you when, by the power and strength you give us, we accomplish some cherished goal. Our lives are not focused on realizing your rule of love on earth, as in heaven. O God, receive our confession and help us to discipline ourselves in caring discipleship, in Jesus' name. Amen.

Assurance of Forgiveness

Let the righteous be joyful! The God of all grace cares about you and wants the very best for you, in company with all God's children. God restores, supports, and strengthens you. God establishes you as a person of worth and as a community of faithful, loving people. Individually and together, we are called to eternal glory in Christ, whose love we share.

Collect

O God, who in Jesus Christ has called us into one body and invited us to share our lives and all we have with one another, let our time together this day provide a glimpse of eternal life. Let us know you, the only true God, and Jesus Christ, whom you have sent, that we may resist evil, discipline ourselves, and be alert to opportunities you give us to witness and serve and extend your reign among us. Amen.

Offertory Invitation

As Christians, we are often called to stand against the practices being followed by our government or in our workplace. We are challenged to live by a standard that insists on justice and fairness; no one is to be exploited for our gain. We support our church as a beacon of hope for all people. We give ourselves and our offering that God's will might be realized among us.

Offertory Prayer

Thank you, God, for empowering our prayers and multiplying our gifts. You provide for the needy through us. What a privilege! Widows and orphans and prisoners find hope in you because we join you in caring for them. You gives homes to the desolate when we share. Your power is working in us. Blessed be your name, O God! Amen.

Commission and Blessing

The reign of God is being restored among us.
The Holy Spirit is coming to empower us.
We are together in awe before God.
Now we carry our worship into our work.
God cares for us and supports us day by day.
In all we do and say, God is present.
We see God's power in the skies.
We realize the power of God's love within.
Go now to share that love to strengthen others.
Trust God and be alert to life's possibilities.
God dwells among us and unites us in Christ.
In this faith is our deepest joy.
Amen. **Amen.**

(See hymn 54.)

PENTECOST AND THE SEASON

FOLLOWING

Acts 2:1–21   1 Corinthians 12:3b–13
Psalm 104:24–34, 35b   John 20:19–23

CALL TO WORSHIP

The peace of God be with you today.
Receive with joy the gift of the Holy Spirit.
    We feel the winds of God blowing among us.
    We sense the tongues of fire empowering us.
How amazing is the power God gives us.
How manifold are the works of our Creator.
    The breath of God fills us with confidence.
    The Spirit creates new life within and among us.
God calls us to be dreamers and prophets.
God gives us a vision for a world of peace.
    May the glory of God endure forever.
    We will sing praise to God as long as we live.

INVOCATION

Powerful God, whose ways are beyond our knowing, we long to grow spiritually. We are thirsty for the living water you have promised to those who seek. We are eager to catch the Spirit, to be set on fire with confidence and trust to use the gifts you have given. Let Pentecost happen again in this gathering of your people. Inspire us to witness to your love and prophesy in your name. Give us courage to speak of your deeds of power, and to take the risks of daring discipleship. Amen.

CALL TO CONFESSION

We can say the words that come with Pentecost: spirit, wind, fire. We can claim an interest in knowing the God of all creation. But how much time have we devoted to this quest? How open are we to God's unpredictable summons and direction?

PRAYER OF CONFESSION

O God, we are frightened by strange tongues and people out of control. We want to manage our own lives and assure our own safety. We are afraid that you will ask more of us than we are willing to risk. We do not want others to consider us strange or fanatical. We are skeptical of dreams and visions. We cannot trust some people you ask us to love. We want to believe, but how can we know that you are more than our collective imagination, a hope we cling to in our despair? Help us, God. Amen.

Assurance of Forgiveness

God comes unexpectedly to those willing to wait and listen and trust. The Spirit amazes and astonishes even those who wait expectantly. There is more to life than the things we can see—and more in the things we see than our eyes can discern. So, too, God is more than we can know or think. Even now, the Holy Spirit is resting on you and on this family of God's people. Do not be afraid.

Collect

All-knowing God, whose gifts to us evoke a variety of activities and services for the common good, guide us to use all the resources you grant us to build up the body of Christ and empower the church's ministry, extending the good news to those who suffer, who ignore, who doubt and deny, that all may be drawn together by the one Spirit to the peace you give and the high purpose to which you call us, in Jesus' name. Amen.

Offertory Invitation

Your gift is needed for the church to be complete. Your gift is expressed through your personal investment of time and talents, but also through the money you received for using your gifts day by day in your work. What we invest in the church's work is an expression of our thanks to God for all the gifts we have received.

Offertory Prayer

Thank you, God, for filling our lives with good things. The abundance of your gifts to us is beyond our counting. Bless all that we return to you for the work of ministry among us and beyond us. Let your Spirit enliven our caring and add effectiveness to all our doing. Make us one in Christ Jesus our Savior, in whose name we pray. Amen.

Commission and Blessing

May God's glory endure forever.
May God take pleasure in works done through us.
> *We have found renewal in our time together.*
> *Now God sends us forth to serve in Jesus' name.*
May the empowerment of Pentecost continue with us.
May the Spirit lead and guide us every day.
> *We have acknowledged our many gifts.*
> *Now we seek to use them for the common good.*
We are one body with many members.
When we work together, much good is accomplished.
> *We commit ourselves as people of vision and action.*
> *The peace of God equips us to serve.*
Amen. **Amen.**

(See hymn 55.)

PENTECOST (ALTERNATE)

Numbers 11:24–30   Acts 2:1–21
Psalm 104; 24–34, 35b   John 7:37–39

CALL TO WORSHIP

Let anyone who thirsts come to Christ.
Let all who dare to believe drink deeply.
> **The Spirit comes like a flowing stream.**
> **We receive living water that quenches our thirst.**

God's Spirit is for young and old, rich and poor.
Men and women, slave and free, receive God's gift.
> **Our sons and daughters shall prophesy.**
> **We will see visions and dream dreams.**

This is the day for a new Pentecost.
We hear the message all can understand.
> **How amazing are all the works of God!**
> **May our meditations please our Creator!**

INVOCATION

Come to us out of the clouds of our doubt and inattention, Holy God. Speak to us in ways that reach deep into our consciousness. Let your Spirit rest on us, creating excitement and anticipation, empowering us to speak and act as your representatives. Make us all, in some way, prophets who observe the larger picture and help one another sense your truth. We look to you today for all we need. May your glory fill this place. Amen.

CALL TO CONFESSION

Pentecost, in the book of Acts, was a time of sudden, dramatic surprises and change. People were transformed and empowered. They took great risks for their faith and suffered for it. Are we today open to God's surprises and willing to risk our security to live as followers of Christ?

PRAYER OF CONFESSION

Eternal God, we admit that we are seldom amazed and astonished. We take for granted much that was once thought to be impossible. We are confident consumers of human ingenuity. Sometimes we think we have no need of you. Matters of the spirit are far down on our list of concerns. We are even suspicious of those who claim to see visions and skeptical of those who seem carried away in their devotion to the faith. Yet we long for something more than our daily routines. O Spirit, come to save us from ourselves. Amen.

Assurance of Forgiveness

Would that all God's people were prophets, welcoming the Holy Spirit's gifts! It is God who fills our life with good things, and renews us day after day. Accept the promise that everyone who calls on God's name will be saved. Dare to believe that God has a mission for you and will supply all that you need.

Collect

Holy One, whose great and glorious day is yet to come, and whose promises are sure, pour out your Spirit on all flesh today, and especially on those gathered here to sing your praise. Let all the earth tremble in anticipation of your transforming power that evokes visions and dreams and great accomplishments. Let today's good news come alive in us to make this a better world. Amen.

Offertory Invitation

As God has filled our lives with good things, let us open our hands to help others. Our gifts may provide for some the basic physical necessities, for others the depth of meaning to be found in a trusting relationship with God. Even more, we will know the joy of giving.

Offertory Prayer

God of wind and fire, blow through our sharing a sense of empowerment, both for us and for all who are reached through our offerings. Set us ablaze with eagerness to hear and respond to the message you want us to carry into all the world. May many lives be touched and renewed today and throughout this season. Let us see the signs of your presence and the direction of your leading—and inspire our following. Amen.

Commission and Blessing

This is the great and glorious day of God's coming.
Every day the Spirit waits to bless us.
>   *We are open to God's gifts and eager to share them.*
>   *We have rivers of living water to pass on to others.*

Join the company of Christ's living disciples.
Take time for meditation and prayer.
>   *We join the devout of all ages to learn from Jesus.*
>   *We seek to support one another's ministries.*

Notice all around you the signs of God's care.
Let them amaze and astonish you.
>   *May God's glory endure forever!*
>   *I will sing praise to God as long as I live!*

Amen. **Amen.**

(See hymn 56.)

TRINITY SUNDAY
(FIRST SUNDAY AFTER PENTECOST)

Genesis 1:1–2:4a　　　　　　　　　　　2 Corinthians 13:11–13
Psalm 8　　　　　　　　　　　　　　　Matthew 28:16–20

CALL TO WORSHIP

How majestic is God's name in all the earth!
We see God's glory in the expanse of the heavens.
> *All plants and animals are God's creation.*
> *All that God has made reflects God's goodness.*

We are created in God's image, to relate to God.
We receive great abundance and care from our Creator.
> *God blesses us day by day with good things.*
> *We are given dominion over the works of God.*

Gather to praise God and greet one another.
Celebrate all the ways God is revealed to us.
> *We worship the Creator and Sustainer of all things.*
> *We rejoice in Christ's promise of the Holy Spirit.*

INVOCATION

Triune God, known to us in more ways than we can count, we marvel at the mystery of life, and wonder at your attention to our lives. As we ponder the vast expanse of space, we are fascinated by distances too extensive to understand. The times we have measured are a tiny ripple in your eternity. Yet you have honored this planet by revealing yourself in the life and ministry of Jesus and the empowerment of your Holy Spirit. Let us experience your presence in this time of worship. Amen.

CALL TO CONFESSION

All that God has created is labeled "very good." Life in all its forms is complex and interrelated. Human life is precious and marvelously linked. Let us confess our neglect and irresponsibility in relation to all creation and to one another.

PRAYER OF CONFESSION

Amazing God, the more we learn of your creation, the more we are filled with awe and wonder. Yet, our vision narrows to our limited concerns, and we forget the immense reaches of the stewardship to which you appoint us. We have not taken good care of this tiny spaceship, Earth, which is our home. We have not cared well for one another as sisters and brothers. Our doubts outweigh our obedience. O God, help us fulfill our baptism and claim our discipleship, as forgiven and forgiving sinners. Amen.

ASSURANCE OF FORGIVENESS

We are created in the image of God and are blessed with the capacity to reflect God's will in our daily lives. God cares for us and invests us with responsibility. Thus God honors us with high expectations and confidence in our willingness to seek out life's best for all people. We are loved. We are forgiven. Our baptism is renewed.

COLLECT

God of all creation, whose attention focused on the earth in the life, death, and resurrection of Jesus, and whose gift of the Holy Spirit has empowered Christ's disciples through the years, may our worship unite the saints in mutual caring, that our witness to the world may reflect the grace of Jesus Christ, your love for all humankind, and the communion of the Holy Spirit. Amen.

OFFERTORY INVITATION

What will we return to God for all the bounty of the universe we have been given to enjoy? We cannot count the blessings of life which God supplies to us. The mandate of Christ is clear: "Go and make disciples of all nations." That means we must, first of all, accept our own discipleship in wholehearted obedience and self-giving service. God expects no less than all we have and all we are.

OFFERTORY PRAYER

Amid our doubts and the temptation to grab life's blessings for our own personal use, we come to dedicate our time, talent, and treasure to realize your reign on earth, majestic God. As we enjoy your bounty, we give that all our sisters and brothers might also come to appreciate the amazing gifts you entrust to us. Thank you for life and all its wonders. Amen.

COMMISSION AND BLESSING

Go out to tell the world that God cares.
Celebrate the gift of life and all its possibilities.
> *We are awed by God's vast creation.*
> *We are amazed at how God honors us.*
God has given us stewardship over creation.
We are given the care of every living thing.
> *Land, sea, and air are ours to enjoy.*
> *All are entrusted to our careful watch.*
Generations before us have passed on God's gifts.
Generations to follow depend on our faithfulness.
> *We pray for insight and generosity to save this legacy.*
> *We seek to live in peace and love with everyone.*
Amen. **Amen.**

(See hymn 57.)

PROPER 4

Genesis 6:9–22; 7:24; 8:14–19	(or Deuteronomy 11:18–21, 26–28	Romans 1:16–17; 3:22b–28 (29–31)
Psalm 46	Psalm 31:1–5, 19–24)	Matthew 7:21–29

CALL TO WORSHIP

Come, walk with God in these moments of worship.
Celebrate God's covenant with us and all humankind.
> **Surely God is in this place today.**
> **We find refuge and strength as we gather.**

Be still and know that God is God.
All our names for God are limited metaphors.
> **The Most High lives in us and among us.**
> **The whole universe is God's dwelling place.**

All people on earth are God's concern.
Those who do the will of God will experience God's realm.
> **We have come to hear what God would have us do.**
> **We seek the courage to do what God intends.**

INVOCATION

Teach us your word in this hour, faithful God, for we want to communicate your truth to our children and their children. We want to follow your commandments, to love you with all our hearts. We intend to walk in the ways you set before us. Preserve us, we pray, and grant us courage to face each day's challenges. Help us to live by faith and to serve with abiding trust. Amen.

CALL TO CONFESSION

There is no distinction: all have sinned and fall short of the glory of God. No matter how close is our relationship with God, we always fall short of God's expectations. We fail the One who gave us life. Confession removes our attempts to cover up our failure and gives us the opportunity of new beginnings.

PRAYER OF CONFESSION

We admit, O God, that we have seldom claimed the full power of the gospel. Rather we have been ashamed to speak of the good news in various settings of our lives. We join ourselves to the earth's corruption, rather than risking a protest. We battle one another rather than daring to be peacemakers. We give little thought to your laws and fail to teach them to our children. False pride keeps us from complete trust in you. Help us find release from the limits we place on ourselves. Amen.

ASSURANCE OF FORGIVENESS

Amid vicious gossip, God is our protection. God is a shelter and refuge, a very present help in trouble. We need not fear the changes all around us, for God is in the midst of them. We are in covenant with the One whose grace is sufficient for all our needs. Jesus Christ draws us into oneness with God. We are justified by faith, and good works will follow.

COLLECT

God of law and grace, who shared our common lot in Jesus Christ, we are drawn to your righteousness, believing that you will justify us and lead us to a wholeness that is freeing to us and attractive to others who need the good news of the gospel. Unite us in love for you and one another, that your will might find life in us and in all we meet. Amen.

OFFERTORY INVITATION

We have been given stewardship over the earth and over every living thing. All that we do has consequences. The way we use resources entrusted to us has implications not only for ourselves but also for many other people. An important channel of our stewardship is our collective efforts as a church to work for a more just, peaceful, and caring world. To this end, we dedicate our tithes and offerings.

OFFERTORY PRAYER

As Christ sacrificed all personal gain for the sake of others, we venture little sacrifices to support the ministries of the church. O God, we have experienced your blessing when we give, so our most generous efforts do not seem a sacrifice. We give that your will might be done, and when it is, all of us benefit. Multiply, we pray, the power of these gifts to do the good you intend. Accept our effort to be faithful disciples of Jesus Christ. Amen.

COMMISSION AND BLESSING

Commit to memory the laws and promises of God.
Share them with your children and your neighbors.
> **God has richly blessed us.**
> **Our God has high expectations of us.**
God listens to our prayers and saves us.
God seeks this relationship with all our friends.
> **We want the gospel to come alive in us.**
> **We will share the good news in some new way.**
Build lives of faithfulness to God's will.
Then the storms of life will not destroy you.
> **The authority of Christ is our foundation.**
> **We trust God's revelation in Jesus Christ.**
Amen. **Amen.**

(See hymns 27, 58.)

PROPER 5

Sunday between June 5 and June 11
(if after Trinity Sunday)

| Genesis 12:1–9 | *(or Hosea 5:15–6:6* | Romans 4:13–25 |
| Psalm 33:1–12 | *Psalm 50:7–15)* | Matthew 9:9–13, 18–26 |

CALL TO WORSHIP

God calls us out of places known and secure.
God invites us into a living, trusting relationship.
> **Happy are those whom God chooses as a heritage.**
> **God's counsel to every generation comes to us.**

God continues to bring new worlds into being.
God is constantly offering new opportunities to us.
> **We are called away from empty pursuits.**
> **God wants to employ our talents for the common good.**

Let us worship God with our whole being.
Let us use all our talents to praise our Creator.
> **Praise God with instruments we have made.**
> **Sing praises with voices God has given.**

INVOCATION

God Most High, it is hard to hear you calling us, for there are many competing voices vying for our attention. It is difficult to believe your promises because we have been misled by so many empty commitments. We are hesitant to hope for healing and fulfillment amid the living death so many experience in our times. Yet, as we gather here to touch the Unseen Presence, we are moved to rejoice. We stand in awe before you, eager to live by faith, anticipating your mercy, giving thanks for your word. Amen.

CALL TO CONFESSION

How tempted we are to resist the idea that we are numbered among the sinners who need periods of confession. We deplore such thinking as negative, ignoring the positive value of self-examination and penitence. We are more ready to trust our own judgments than to rely on God's direction. Thus we pray:

PRAYER OF CONFESSION

God of justice and righteousness, we come to you as tax collectors and sinners flocked to Jesus long ago. We have wavered in distrust of your promises, yet cling to their truth. We believe that your ways are far more fulfilling than any we can devise, yet we shrink from following where Christ leads. Forgive our pursuit of lesser gods we create, and wean us away from our fascination with the false values that tempt us. Draw us closer to you, we pray. Amen.

ASSURANCE OF FORGIVENESS

Rejoice, for God gives life to the dead and calls into existence possibilities we could not imagine. Christ died for our sins and rose to new life that we might be justified. Let us explore together what that means in the assurance that God is able and willing to fulfill all the promises made to us. God takes us by the hand and lifts us up to abundant life. Praise God!

COLLECT

God of all nations, by whose word the heavens were made and in whose dominion the universe continues to expand, stretch our thinking in this time of reflection, refresh us as your rain waters the earth, and restore our strength that we might live faithfully according to your promises. Give us courage to trust even when the odds seem against us and to live truthfully even when challenged and attacked, that our witness might be helpful to others on life's journey. In Christ's name we pray. Amen.

OFFERTORY INVITATION

Through our giving to the church, we build altars for the worship of God, not just in sanctuaries made with hands, but in lives enriched by caring and sharing. We bring our offerings in thanksgiving to God, remembering that we are but temporary stewards over all we possess.

OFFERTORY PRAYER

Thank you, God, for hearing our prayers and restoring our strength. Thank you for drawing us apart from our selfish ways and self-serving pursuits. Let our offering today fulfill your purposes, not ours. Let these gifts summon others to follow Christ. Let them know the joy of breaking bread with the Great Physician who offers healing to all who dare to trust your mercy. Amen.

COMMISSION AND BLESSING

Happy are the people whom God has chosen.
We are inheritors of God's grace and mercy.
> ***God's counsel is available to us every day.***
> ***By faith we receive God's gracious promises.***
God sends us to places unknown and full of risk.
The Spirit provides the resources we need.
> ***We live by hope, even when the way is unclear.***
> ***We seek to be faithful to God's intention for us.***
Jesus says to us, "Follow me," and we respond.
Christ answers our needs with a healing touch.
> ***We are inheritors of God's grace.***
> ***Rejoice with us in the blessings God provides.***
Amen. **Amen.**

(See hymn 59.)

Genesis 18:1–15 (21:1–7)   (or Exodus 19:2–8a   Romans 5:1–8
Psalm 116:1–2, 12–19   Psalm 100)   Matthew 9:35–10:8 (9–23)

CALL TO WORSHIP

This is a time of God's appearing; let us worship!
Let us recognize that God is within and among us.
> **God's ear is inclined toward us.**
> **We know that God listens and hears our prayers**

We are here to offer our thanks to God.
We will pay our vows to God in the presence of others.
> **We are grateful for the grace in which we stand.**
> **We praise God with great joy and gladness.**

God bears us up on eagles' wings.
God draws us into covenant community.
> **We will listen for God's commandments.**
> **We will seek to do all that God requires.**

INVOCATION

God of all creation, help us to recognize your presence among us. May we greet
one another as your precious children and as messengers of your care. Help us offer such hospitality to one another that even the most skeptical among us will be
touched by love. You are love; in you we find hope amid our weakness and doubt.
Let your glory shine in this place today as we lift up the cup of salvation and call
on your name. Amen.

CALL TO CONFESSION

Meeting God can be a very disturbing experience, for God may require of us
changes that we fear. We may hear challenges that push us beyond our comfort
zones. In our prayers of confession, we seek to overcome our resistance to God's
direction and open ourselves to greater possibilities.

PRAYER OF CONFESSION

God, we often fail to recognize that you are always with us. We are the ungodly
ones who deny your love by our failure to love. We deny your law by our failure
to live by it. We laugh at your promises. We appear more burdened than joyful in
the midst of the wondrous gift of life. We seldom pause to give thanks. The compassion of Christ finds little echo in us, who claim to be Christians. We need your
forgiveness, O God, and a new vision. Amen.

Assurance of Forgiveness

God's favor rests on us. Sincere confession is met with caring acceptance. God hears the prayers of our hearts and grants us peace the world cannot give. While we were yet sinners, Christ died for us, that we might have access to the grace in which we stand. Lift up the cup of salvation and offer sacrifices of thanksgiving. God has loosed our bonds and freed us to share God's glory.

Collect

Shepherd of the flock, whose compassion reaches out to all who are harassed and helpless, teach us and empower us to proclaim the good news of your dominion, that healing may be offered, new life received, and demons overcome. May your love tend all of us day by day, transforming us in the image of Christ. Amen.

Offertory Invitation

What shall we return to God for all the bounty we have received? Everything we have comes from God and is but lent to us for a time. Let us offer a thanksgiving sacrifice, rejoicing in the opportunity to share in bringing in the harvest for God.

Offertory Prayer

We repeat our vows of commitment to you, gracious God, as we dedicate this offering. We are disciples of Jesus Christ, commissioned to share the good news. May all that we dedicate here—our abilities, the fleeting moments of our days, the resources entrusted to our management—announce your reign and the nearness of your dominion. We give with joy and serve with delight, thanking you for this opportunity to share what you have given. Amen.

Commission and Blessing

Go out, prepared each day for God's appearing.
Recognize the Christ within and among us.
> **Surely God is present wherever we go.**
> **God listens and responds to our prayers.**
The harvest is plentiful but laborers are few.
Ask God to send the laborers who are needed.
> **As we are able, we will serve.**
> **God will empower our witness and ministry.**
We have peace with God through Jesus Christ.
God's love has been poured into our hearts.
> **We have received the gift of the Holy Spirit.**
> **We carry God's grace into the world.**
Amen. **Amen.**

(See hymns 60, 61.)

PROPER 7

Genesis 21:8–21	(or Jeremiah 20:7–13	Romans 6:1b–11
Psalm 86:1–10, 1–17	Psalm 69:7–10 (11–15), 16–18)	Matthew 10:24–39

CALL TO WORSHIP

Come, nations of the earth, to bow before God.
Distant galaxies proclaim the Creator of all things.
We are humbled by the wonders of creation.
We are amazed by God's mighty works.
This infinite God cares for each one of us.
God hears our cries and responds to our needs.
In our days of trouble, we call on our God.
We are confident that God listens and answers.
Let us also call on God with our prayers of thanks.
Let us celebrate the wondrous things God provides.
God cares for us, even when others reject us.
We gather to glorify God's name.

INVOCATION

Holy God, come to us in our distress. We are weary of conflict and long for your
healing waters of forgiveness and renewal. You have sent us a teacher to draw us
into discipleship, and we have found fulfillment when we are faithful to Christ's
call. We long to find peace as we serve, but more often we encounter a sword. Our
disagreements are many, and our capacity to forgive is strained. Send your light that
we might not falter in our caring and in the proclamation of your good news.
Amen.

CALL TO CONFESSION

God's grace has been poured out among us that we might die to sin. Yet, we are
persistent in our disobedience, as if we thereby give to God more opportunities to
be gracious. Let us bring to God all the brokenness of our lives, our alienation from
our Creator, from persons we are called to love, and even from our own best selves.

PRAYER OF CONFESSION

God, we are poor and needy in matters of the spirit. You have offered us newness
of life, but we are fearful of its cost. Your gifts place us in debts so vast that we can
never repay. We are not worthy of your love and cannot earn your forgiveness.
How is it that when we accept your grace we sense a freedom we have never before enjoyed? O God, we want to be dead to sin and alive to you. Help us! Amen.

ASSURANCE OF FORGIVENESS

As Christ was raised from the dead by the glory of God, we are lifted up to walk in newness of life, accepted and forgiven. You can never be your old self again, for Christ has set you free. Old divisions and misunderstandings are overcome in the steadfast love of God. All who give up their self-occupied ways for Christ's sake find abundant life. This is God's gift to you today.

COLLECT

Gracious God, in whose eyes every sparrow has value, and in whose love even the hairs of our heads are counted, lead us to the light, that we might proclaim your love from the housetops and put you first in our lives. May our discipleship reflect the witness of our teacher, Jesus Christ, that all nations may bow down before you and glorify your name. Amen.

OFFERTORY INVITATION

We have received God's help and comfort. Let us express our thanks. We have been called into the community of disciples. Let us offer the witness of our sharing. We have been assured of our own worth and value. Let us dedicate our offerings to building up others in God's love.

OFFERTORY PRAYER

For all the great and wondrous things you have done for us, O God, we are grateful. You give us strength to go on when we are troubled and discouraged. You grant newness of life as we share in Christ's resurrection. We want to pass on the good news through this offering and by the way we live each day. Lead us and guide us in your steadfast love, that we might channel your gift to all we meet. Amen.

COMMISSION AND BLESSING

The Teacher has called you as disciples.
Learn from Christ to serve without fear.
> *We expect to learn daily from our Teacher.*
> *We commit ourselves anew to Christ's service.*

You have been baptized into Christ's death.
Live, with Christ, your resurrection faith.
> *We are not afraid of the cross.*
> *It calls us to fullness of life, spent for others.*

Let God's love be your first awareness each day.
Let that love flow through every activity.
> *We bow down to glorify God's name.*
> *We rejoice that God makes a place for our witness.*

Amen. **Amen.**

(See hymns 62, 63.)

PROPER 8

Genesis 22:1–14	(or Jeremiah 28:5–9	Romans 6:12–23
Psalm 13	Psalm 89:1–4, 15–18)	Matthew 10:40–42

CALL TO WORSHIP

Early in the morning, our thoughts turn toward God.
We have been led to this mountaintop of worship.
> *We come, trusting in God's steadfast love.*
> *We gather, seeking the way of salvation and peace.*

God has made an everlasting covenant with us.
Let us proclaim God's faithfulness to all generations.
> *Sometimes we think God has forgotten us.*
> *Often we do not understand what God expects of us.*

God deals bountifully with us in much that we take for granted.
God shows us the value of life and helps us celebrate it.
> *We bring our sorrow and pain to this healing time.*
> *May God provide what we need to grow in Christ.*

INVOCATION

Have you forgotten us, God? Will you remain hidden from us forever? We speak of you, but we do not know you. We often distrust those who speak glibly of your intervention in their lives. We marvel at the amazing variety of life on this planet. All that we see with our eyes is but a small hint of all that is revealed through microscopes and telescopes—other worlds of form and beauty so amazing beyond any telling. Yet our spiritual ancestors have known you not only as Creator of all things but as one who knows and loves each one of us. Help us to know you here, today. Amen.

CALL TO CONFESSION

Was it God who tested Abraham? Does God put us to the test? Do we believe that God will provide what we most need? Are we willing to trust God, or would the apostle Paul describe us as "slaves of sin"? This time of confession is not meant to weigh us down with guilt, but to free us to respond to God's love.

PRAYER OF CONFESSION

Free us, O God, from such absorption in our own concerns that we forget your loving intention for us. We find it hard to view what is happening around us through any eyes but our own. We obey our own passions rather than joining your intention for the good of all. It is hard for us, who so value our autonomy, to speak of obedience. Yet we are ashamed of things we have done and things we have failed to do. We want to claim your free gift of eternal life through Jesus Christ. We sense that you intend for us to accept and live within that gift here and now. Help us, loving God. Amen.

Assurance of Forgiveness
We are not under law but under grace. We are being given God's great bounty as we receive the teaching of Jesus, the witness of our spiritual forebears, and the exultation of the psalmist. God comes to us, not only from the past, but in every moment when we welcome another with even a cup of water in Christ's name. We are forgiven and renewed!

Collect
Eternal God, whose provision for us is generous and compassionate, and whose will for us is total commitment in love of you, of neighbor, and of self, keep us from withholding any part of ourselves from obedience and loyalty to you, so we may be free to give genuine welcome to all people, to your honor and glory. Amen.

Offertory Invitation
We can offer to God only what we have been given. God may require our dearest treasure, for it is only lent to us for a time. What God has provided, we are now invited to invest in the disciple-making business of the church.

Offertory Prayer
We bring our offering, not with thought of reward, but because we are grateful. We give, not from guilt over having so much, but because it is such a privilege and joy to share. We dedicate these gifts, not to pay bills, but to enable a ministry that meets basic human needs with the good news of the gospel. May your people be empowered to give the service each moment requires, in even a deed as simple as giving a cup of cold water to quench another's thirst. Amen.

Commission and Blessing
Scatter into the world, believing God will provide.
Our service in Christ's name will be blessed.
> *We present ourselves for service in the world.*
> *We seek to be instruments of righteousness.*

Extend Christ's welcome to your friends.
Dare to share that welcome with strangers.
> *We will honor all people as God's own.*
> *We will reach out to bless all God's children.*

God's grace will be with you wherever you go.
There is delightful freedom in serving God.
> *We rejoice in the light we have received.*
> *We accept with joy the tasks of discipleship.*

Amen. **Amen.**

(See hymns 64, 65.)

PROPER 9

Genesis 24:34–38, 42–49,   *(or Zechariah 9:9–12*   Romans 7:15–25a
   58–67   *Psalm 145:8–14)*
Psalm 45:10–17   Matthew 11:16–19, 25–30
   or Song of Solomon 2:8–13

CALL TO WORSHIP

Come with joy and gladness to praise and honor God.
Come to the refreshing waters that God provides.
> *God is gracious and merciful and full of compassion.*
> *All creation joins us in giving thanks.*

Give ear, all people, to the law of God.
Give thanks for all the guidance God gives us.
> *God upholds all who are falling.*
> *God raises us up when we are bowed down.*

Come, all who are weary and carrying heavy burdens.
Come, for Christ has promised rest.
> *The gentle spirit of Christ invites us.*
> *We have come to find rest for our souls.*

INVOCATION

We come together, gracious God, because we have heard your invitation. We sense that you alone know the burdens we carry. You understand our weariness. Sometimes our journey seems long and without respite. We long for the refreshment you provide as we come to worship you. The anticipation of this hour of rest and nourishment fills us with renewed joy and gladness. We thank you, God, that your revelation comes to us, not because we are worthy, but because we are open to your word. Open our hearts to receive all you offer. Amen.

CALL TO CONFESSION

We live in a generation of complainers, rich in things but poor in spirit. Increasingly isolated in our abundance, we have denied the community of mutual caring into which God has called us. It is easier for us to find fault with others than to celebrate their goodness. Let us seek God's mercy.

PRAYER OF CONFESSION

God, we do not understand our own actions. We turn away from the good we are intent on doing. Yet, we find wisdom in your law. We delight in the idea of mutual caring and celebrating life together, but we get bogged down in our own concerns. We are too busy to seek community and too preoccupied to ponder your will for us. We go our own way, cutting ourselves off from you and one another. O God, help us to put away this sin. Amen.

Assurance of Forgiveness

God's forgiveness is realized most profoundly by those who understand their own emptiness and seek the refreshment God alone can provide. We are drawn to God and to one another by the Eternal Spirit who wills our unity, who offers help with the burdens we carry and invites us to find rest for our souls. Christ assures us: "My yoke is easy, and my burden is light."

Collect

Holy God, in whose service we find joyous delight, may we learn from Christ to share one another's burdens, to let others care for us in our time of need and extend to them our help and comfort in their distress, that we might be united across time and space in the community of mutual caring where you reign. Amen.

Offertory Invitation

God has greatly blessed us with many kinds of wealth. Let our joy and gladness overflow as we express gratitude to God with our offerings. As we support the ministries of the church, let us consider those whose lives are grievously burdened, reaching out to them in practical acts of mercy.

Offertory Prayer

With all the gifts of creation, you have blessed us, gracious God. We give thanks for all your works. Gratitude is our first impulse for giving. Accept our grateful hearts, along with our gifts. We ask for wisdom as our church determines priorities for the use of resources. May we be as concerned about outreach and mission as we are about programs for ourselves. As you are faithful to us, O God, may we be faithful in all things, seeking always to live by your gracious will. Amen.

Commission and Blessing

Carry with you, in your innermost selves, delight in God's law.
Meditate day by day on God's purpose for your lives.
> *We rejoice that God dwells with us every day.*
> *We want to know and do God's will for us.*

We encounter God in unexpected places.
God surprises us in the life and witness of people.
> *We learn from the youngest in our midst.*
> *Simple and humble persons have much to teach us.*

Take Christ's yoke upon you, for that yoke is easy.
It imparts confidence that lightens our burdens.
> *We will find rest and renewal through Christ.*
> *We seek to express the same humility and gentleness.*

Amen. **Amen.**

(See hymn 66.)

PROPER 10

Genesis 25:19–34	(or Isaiah 55:10–13	Romans 8:1–11
Psalm 119:105–112	Psalm 65:(1–8), 9–13)	Matthew 13:1–9, 18–23

CALL TO WORSHIP

God's Word is a lamp to our feet and a light to our path.
Open yourselves this day to receive the Word.
We have committed ourselves to follow the light.
We come now to be instructed by God's law.
Minds set on the flesh are hostile to God.
Let us, therefore, open ourselves to the Spirit.
We reach out for more than we can see and hear.
We long to know Love's embrace deep within.
The Spirit of God raised Jesus from the dead.
That Spirit dwells in you and offers you new life.
We praise God, who saves us and gives us hope.
God cares for the earth and for each one of us.

INVOCATION

All-powerful God, we celebrate the freedom you give us to make our own response
to all the possibilities you lay out before us. We are grateful for the revelation you
provide through the witness of many in the Scriptures. Through their words, help
us to discern your Word. Come to us in the midst of our diversity to bring understanding and mutual caring. Open us to a new appreciation of our birthright
as your children. Beyond all our clamor for the things of this world, we long for
the richness of spirit you alone can provide. Feed us here, we pray. Amen.

CALL TO CONFESSION

We have gathered to find release from the cares of life which sap our energy and
depress our spirits. We have come seeking deeper roots for our faith and the ability to survive and thrive amid life's thorny pathways. We open all the hidden places
of our lives to the light of God's forgiving love, that we might be cleansed, healed,
and set free from sin. God knows our need for this time of confession.

PRAYER OF CONFESSION

All-knowing God, we know you understand us more deeply than we understand
ourselves. You know how much the cares of this life weigh us down. Our thoughts
and actions are often very shortsighted. We take so much for granted, failing to
value the wonder of life all around us, the gift of family and friends, the amazing
reality of your Spirit dwelling in us. We want to be like good soil, receiving the
seed of your word with understanding that nourishes roots of trust and joy. Free
us from all that keeps us from bearing fruit for you. Amen.

ASSURANCE OF FORGIVENESS

There is no condemnation for those who are in Christ Jesus. As disciples of Jesus, we have the opportunity to grow in understanding and in the joy of serving others in Christ's name. The Spirit of life sets us free from our narrow concerns to celebrate the good within and around us. Life is transformed by our new attitude of gratitude.

COLLECT

Spirit of Life, whose care for us is constant through low times of despair and high moments of hope, teach us your ordinances that we might not forget your law or stray from your precepts. May your decrees be our joy as you incline our hearts to perform your statutes, that we may bear fruit in our realm, even a hundredfold. Amen.

OFFERTORY INVITATION

God's Word has been sown among us. We are the soils, receiving seeds of truth. The harvest depends on our accepting the Word, letting it take root and getting rid of the weeds. What we offer to God is a small return on God's investment in us. Let us give with joy.

OFFERTORY PRAYER

Accept our offering of praise and our offering of ourselves, O God, along with our tithes and contributions toward our church's mission. You have given us life and guidance for living. You have made us partakers of your own Spirit. We rejoice in the opportunity to receive and share your Word. May the ministry in which all of us have a share bear much fruit, bringing in an abundant harvest for your realm. Amen.

COMMISSION AND BLESSING

Carry the lamp of God's Word into the week ahead.
Share its light with all you meet.
> **God's Word lights our path and guides our feet.**
> **The heritage we have received is ours to pass on.**
Do not be bound by concerns of the flesh.
Set your minds on matters of the Spirit.
> **The Spirit of Christ dwells in us.**
> **God gives us gifts of life and peace.**
Share in daily offerings of praise to God.
Pass on the joy of living in the Spirit.
> **Our hearts are inclined to God's statutes.**
> **Your ways, O God, bring joy to our hearts.**
Amen. **Amen.**

(See hymns 67, 68.)

Proper 11

| Genesis 28:10–19a | (Isaiah 44:6–8 | Romans 8:12–25 |
| Psalm 139:1–12, 23–24 | Psalm 86:11–17) | Matthew 13:24–30, 36–43 |

Call to Worship

God has searched us and knows us.
God knows when we sit down and when we rise up.
> **God searches out our path and our lying down.**
> **God is acquainted with all our ways.**

Before a word is on our tongues, God knows it.
God's hand is ever available to guide us.
> **Such knowledge is a wonder to us.**
> **It is beyond anything we can attain.**

We cannot escape from God's spirit.
There is nowhere to flee from God's presence.
> **Darkness is as light to our God.**
> **God illuminates the way before us.**

Invocation

Search us, O God, and know our hearts. Test us and know our thoughts. We gather with eager longing to know you, ever-present God, and to be known by you. We want to live as your beloved children. Assure us in these moments that you hear our prayers, even as your will is revealed to us. Fill our dreams and our waking hours with radiant hope. May every time of encounter move us to awe and fervent worship. Lead us in your way everlasting. Amen.

Call to Confession

When we run away from our problems, we discover that we cannot run away from ourselves. Yet God is present with us to hear our confession and offer forgiveness. God brings us back to face what we have left behind in order that we may claim the promise of reconciliation and wholeness.

Prayer of Confession

Search us and test us, that all wickedness may be purged from us, O Creator. Save us from our futile striving after our own advantage. Reshape our will to conform with your intentions for us. We confess that we have allowed weeds to grow in our lives. Our focus has drifted from the harvest you intend to the fears and greed that hold us hostage. Release us from bondage to decay that we may grow in likeness to Jesus Christ. We want to bear fruit for you. Turn us to the brightness of a new day. Amen.

ASSURANCE OF FORGIVENESS

If by the Spirit we put to death the misuse of our bodies, we will live. We are set free from bondage to death to claim the freedom of the glory of the children of God. Live in the hope God offers, waiting with patience for all that God will yet reveal. You will shine like the sun in the realm of God, who leads us in the way everlasting.

COLLECT

Ever-present God, to whom each of us is fully known, and before whom we bow in awe, grant that we may live as children of your realm, listening for your word, responding to your call, and following the way of Christ. Inspire us to witness to your glory, bear fruit to benefit all your children, and grow together in light and love, that all the world may come to know you and honor your reign. Amen.

OFFERTORY INVITATION

We are debtors to God, who has given us the precious gift of life. We were created of good seed in God's own image that we might bear fruit for God's realm. We have the capacity to dream and envision a better world, free of the sin that so often seems to choke out the good. Through our offerings we give support to our common mission.

OFFERTORY PRAYER

Thank you, God, for the rich heritage of faith we have received from our ancestors. We are grateful that your Spirit is ever with us, assuring us of your acceptance and love. May our offerings share this good news with other children of God who have not yet discovered their identity. May all of us grow in righteousness that we might together experience the reality of your realm in our daily lives, here and now and for all eternity. Amen.

COMMISSION AND BLESSING

Scatter to serve, listening for God's direction.
Let your faces shine with the good news you have received.
> *The Spirit of God will lead us day by day.*
> *God claims us and is with us every moment.*
God promises to be with us wherever we go.
We can say, "Surely God is in this place."
> *God searches us and knows us.*
> *All our thoughts and actions are discerned by God.*
Let us live, then, according to the Spirit.
Let us show forth the firstfruits of the Spirit.
> *With eager longing, we seek to live in the Spirit.*
> *We look up with hope and patience and joy.*
Amen. **Amen.**

(See hymns 69, 70.)

Genesis 29:15–28   (or 1 Kings 3:5–12   Romans 8:26–39
Psalm 105:1–11, 45b   Psalm 119:129–136)   Matthew 13:31–33, 44–52
  or Psalm 128

CALL TO WORSHIP

Let us call on our God and give thanks.
Let hearts rejoice as we sing God's praise.
> *Glory be to God in whose covenant we find life.*
> *Let all the people tell of God's wonderful works.*
Let us open ourselves continually to God's presence.
Let us seek the strength that God alone provides.
> *Surely the Spirit helps us in our weakness.*
> *The Spirit searches our hearts and enlarges our prayers.*
Who can separate us from the love of God?
Will hardship, distress, or peril overcome us?
> *Nothing can separate us from God's love.*
> *We can face all things, knowing God's care.*

INVOCATION

Meet us here, holy God, to search our hearts and strengthen our spirits. Plant your
Word among us that it may spring up in nurturing, inviting ways for the sake of
all your creatures. May we find in these moments of worship the assurance we need
to live triumphantly in the face of loss, discouragement, and suffering. Lead us, by
the teaching and example of Jesus Christ, to trust you and your will for us. We believe that whatever happens, you can bring some good from it. Show us, O God,
the good you intend. Amen.

CALL TO CONFESSION

We who profess our faith are challenged to be honest about our doubts. Our pretense of concern for others is tainted by our self-interest. Our great plans are com-
promised by little deceits. God judges as well as upholds. Surely all of us need to
seek forgiveness.

PRAYER OF CONFESSION

You know us, God, better than we know ourselves. You know the ways we scheme
and manipulate for our own advantage. You are aware of how often our deeds fail
to match the faith we claim. Help us to face ourselves with honesty. Give us the
will and courage to change our ways. We give thanks for Christ's intercession for
us. We rejoice as the Spirit gives voice to all we cannot express. Save us, O God,
that our lives might give expression to your reign. Amen.

ASSURANCE OF FORGIVENESS

Praise our God who forgives and restores. Give thanks for the inheritance that is ours in Christ Jesus. We have received a pearl of great value, a treasure undeserved, a pardon unmerited. Nothing can separate us from the love of God—not death or life, not angels or rulers, not things present or things to come, not heights or depths; no earthly power or anything in all creation can take away God's abiding concern and care for each one of us. Praise God!

COLLECT

Loving God, whose realm is like treasure hidden in a field, like a pearl of great value, like a tree with many branches that emerges from a tiny seed, focus our attention on your will for us, for our community, for our world, that we might experience your reign among us, yearn for its fulfillment, and give our best efforts toward full realization of the community of faith on earth as in heaven. Amen.

OFFERTORY INVITATION

We gather an offering, not so much to support an institution as to follow our passion to share the good news of the realm of God with one another and with many who have never heard it. Amid an atmosphere of deceit and distrust in the world, where community is so seldom realized in our day, we aspire to discover and live God's will for us. Let us give generously.

OFFERTORY PRAYER

The gift of your realm is precious to us, O God. It is worth our greatest efforts and our caring sacrifice. As we search for the best in life, we also want to share our faith discoveries with friends and neighbors. We do that personally and with our giving. May our outreach proclaim to all that nothing can separate us from your love. We give you thanks that you have entrusted to us all that we are privileged to share. Amen.

COMMISSION AND BLESSING

God remembers the covenant made with humanity.
May we remember our part of that covenant.
> *We will praise our God wherever we go.*
> *We will tell of God's wonderful works.*
God brings good from the worst of circumstances.
Those who trust God live with confidence.
> *We believe nothing can separate us from God's love.*
> *In Christ, we are assured of God's care.*
We are invited to make God's realm our first priority.
Living as God intends is life's greatest fulfillment.
> *May our mustard-seed faith grow strong.*
> *We treasure God's realm in our midst.*
Amen. **Amen.**

(See hymns 71, 72.)

PROPER 13

Genesis 32:22–31   (or Isaiah 55:1–5   Romans 9:1–5
Psalm 17:1–7, 15   Psalm 145:8–9, 14–21)   Matthew 14:13–21

CALL TO WORSHIP
Come into the presence of God to be fed.
Come to call on God, who is eager to answer.
  We gather to seek God's face.
  Let our eyes see all that is right and true.
Incline your ears to hear all God would teach.
Seek to experience God's steadfast love.
  We are here to receive God's blessing.
  God is our refuge in a frightening world.
God is near to all who call and seek.
Come to praise God and receive a blessing.
  Open all our senses to pay close attention, O God.
  We want to renew our covenant with the living God.

INVOCATION
We are in awe before you, O God, for you have provided for us in rich abundance.
The earth is full of your provisions. There is beauty all around us from the work
of your hands. You have surrounded us with people who care about us with the
love of Christ. Help us, O God, to count our blessings. Point us beyond our cries
and complaints that we might realize our capacity to act in your name for the sake
of others. As we wrestle with issues of faith and trust, help us to risk our false security for the venture of feeding others in the spirit of Christ. Amen.

CALL TO CONFESSION
All of us need times of wrestling with God over issues in our lives. These moments
of confession offer us one such opportunity. Bring your own distress to this time
of confessing the sin in which all of us have a part.

PRAYER OF CONFESSION
God of justice and righteousness, whose compassion for humankind was expressed
so vividly in Jesus of Nazareth, we bring to you our sorrow and anguish that we
have not followed faithfully in the footsteps of Christ. Unkindness and deceit are
all around us, and we have sometimes joined in their destructive ways. We waste
resources you have entrusted to us. We cause others to stumble and fall. Take away
our wickedness, O God, and restore your covenant among us, we pray in Jesus'
name. Amen.

ASSURANCE OF FORGIVENESS

God is merciful, patient, kind, and loving. All creation is subject to God's care and concern. God attends to our cries and frees our lips from deceit. In Christ, our brokenness finds healing, and relationships are mended and strengthened. God feeds us in ways beyond our knowing and prompts our generosity. Know the glory of God surrounding us here as we worship. Celebrate the refreshment God offers.

COLLECT

God, whose law is perfect and whose covenant with us is sure, teach us today as Jesus taught the crowds long ago. May we hear the voice of compassion and sense the healing touch which we need as much as they did. Multiply among us the food of your Word, that as we are fed, we may be eager to pass on your gifts to us with a transforming generosity of spirit, in Jesus' name. Amen.

OFFERTORY INVITATION

God has created a world of abundance for everyone. Yet many do not share in the bounty. Christ calls us to find sufficiency among us and to make sure that all are fed. We give as we have been blessed.

OFFERTORY PRAYER

Thank you, God, for all you have given to satisfy our needs. You quench our thirst and alleviate our hungers when we turn to you. You turn scarcity into plenty and give us the opportunity to help others. May our offerings proclaim your goodness and mercy. May they be devoted to extending the beloved community of your people. Keep our words and actions attuned to your will, that we may offer to all what they need from your hand. Amen.

COMMISSION AND BLESSING

Go out to wrestle with God and the world this week.
Know that God intends that you will feel blessed.
>   *We believe that God preserves our lives.*
>   *All we have is a gift to us from our Creator.*
God bids us welcome others into the faith community.
Christ commands: Give them something to eat.
>   *As God has fed us, we want to share God's bounty.*
>   *We want to pass on God's steadfast love.*
Call on God in your times of need.
Listen for the answers God supplies.
>   *God keeps covenant with us at all times.*
>   *We will seek to keep our promises to God.*
Amen. **Amen.**

(See hymns 73, 74.)

PROPER 14

Sunday between August 7 and August 13

Genesis 37:1–4, 12–28 (or 1 Kings 19:9–18 Romans 10:5–15
Psalm 105:1–6, 16–22, 45b Psalm 85:8–13) Matthew 14:22–33

CALL TO WORSHIP

Over the wind and waves, Christ comes to us.
Do not fear to meet Christ here.
> **We have heard the invitation.**
> **Our hopes have brought us together.**

The storms of life do not have the last word.
Our faith keeps us from sinking.
> **Our doubts lead to greater faith.**
> **Our losses open us to greater possibilities.**

Let us call on God's name and give thanks.
Let the hearts of all who seek God rejoice.
> **We will sing of God's wonderful works.**
> **We will share with others God's marvelous deeds.**

INVOCATION

We seek your presence, holy God. Break through all our pretenses that we might sense the vibrant energy embracing the whole universe yet know ourselves to be personally loved within the vast expanse of space and time. How amazing are all the miracles of life that surround us! We praise you. We thank you. We bow in awe before you. In this hour, we pray that our faith may be enlivened, our trust deepened, our commitment expanded to meet the challenges of our times. Amen.

CALL TO CONFESSION

We profess our faith in God, yet we rely more heavily on our own ingenuity. We say we believe, but our lives seldom show confident trust. We want to care as Jesus did, but we're often ready, as were Joseph's brothers, to sell off those with whom we disagree. Who can save us from ourselves?

PRAYER OF CONFESSION

God, we confess that we are dreamers more intent on our own importance than on your vision for us. We like our favored position on this earth, and we are jealous of those who have even more than we. We want to walk on water before we have even learned to stand upright on the land. We want to rise above others rather than reaching out with helping hands, that all might be uplifted by you. We pray for pardon, for greater insight, for another chance to live and serve with faithfulness. Amen.

Assurance of Forgiveness

O you of little faith, why do you doubt? Take heart. Do not be afraid. The harsh winds will abate. The seas will not overwhelm. The treachery of some will not wipe out the good God intends. Everyone who calls on God's name will be saved. Remember God's wonderful works and share the good news. Let all humankind praise God. Praise God!

Collect

Glorious God, whose word took on flesh in Jesus, and whose saving grace can be known by all who believe in Christ, open our hearts and minds to encounter your word personally, that the church may more fully express our identity as the body of Christ, carrying on the mission Jesus began, assuring a frightened world of the power of love. Amen.

Offertory Invitation

Like Joseph, we have been entrusted with our ruler's possessions. We are stewards of all that God places in our hands—our time, our talents, our accumulated treasures—life itself. Our offering is not just about tithes and gifts for the church's mission; it is about rededication of all of life in Christ's service.

Offertory Prayer

God, we cannot deceive you with the appearance of generosity. You know how we manage the wealth entrusted to our care. Help us to know the joy of sharing from the abundance you provide. Help us to trust when we feel we do not have enough. We give thanks that you enable us to be givers, not just receivers. May what we offer here provide a helpful ministry to many. May what we offer to our families, friends, and co-laborers tomorrow also be blessed as ministry. Amen.

Commission and Blessing

Go out to share the good news, without favoritism.
Meet both friend and enemy with forgiveness and grace.
> **God's word is on our lips and in our hearts.**
> **We face a dangerous world with assurance and trust.**
Take heart; do not be afraid.
God is with you wherever you go.
> **We are assured of God's presence and protection.**
> **We believe God's help is always available.**
Let faith grow as doubts are explored.
Christ invites us to follow new pathways.
> **We will listen for Christ's invitation.**
> **We will follow where God leads us.**
Amen. **Amen.**

(See hymns 75, 76.)

PROPER 15

Genesis 45:1–15   *(or Isaiah 56:1, 6–8*   Romans 11:1–2a, 29–32
Psalm 133   *Psalm 67)*   Matthew 15:(10–20), 21–28

CALL TO WORSHIP

This is a Sabbath dedicated to our God.
Let this gathering place be a home for all people.
> *May God be gracious to us and bless us.*
> *May God's face shine over all the earth's people.*

Let all the people praise the God of all nations.
Let us give thanks and enjoy the blessings God gives.
> *May God grant us understanding and courage.*
> *May faith grow beyond our doubts.*

The earth has yielded its blessing.
Let all the ends of the earth revere our Creator.
> *God brings us together in unity of purpose.*
> *May our circle grow as we welcome newcomers.*

INVOCATION

How good and pleasant it is, O God, when kindred live together in unity. Draw us now into the community you intend for all your people. Help us to listen and understand, both your word for us and our sharing with one another. Keep us from being misled by popular acclaim and the wisdom of the marketplace. May we not be unobservant guides to one another but rather be fully open to your gifts and obedient to your call. Come to us now with healing and blessing. Amen.

CALL TO CONFESSION

Both our speech and our actions call into question our faithfulness to God. In times of stress, we have made statements that we regret. Jealousy and anger have led to deceit, betrayal, and broken relationships. Our best intentions sometimes go astray. Rather than being distressed with ourselves, we bring the wounds of our common life to this time of confession, that we may receive God's healing.

PRAYER OF CONFESSION

Forgive us, O God, for the sin we recognize in ourselves and the wounds we do not see. Show us how we have hurt one another and grant us courage to seek forgiveness and reconciliation. Reveal to us our disobedience to you and keep us from leading others into our sin. We seek your mercy for the times we have willfully offended. Help us to put aside all actions and comments that defile. Cleanse us for new life in Christ. Amen.

ASSURANCE OF FORGIVENESS

God is merciful toward us and listens to our honest prayers. Our thoughts and deeds are fully known to God, who is eager to forgive and to lead us to new understandings. When we earnestly seek God's help, we are set free to discover new opportunities. Even in the worst of circumstances, God works with us to bring some good and to preserve life. May God be praised!

COLLECT

God of many blessings, whose gifts to us are more numerous than we can count, show us how to use these benefits according to your will and purpose, that opportunities may be opened for all your children and unity may become a reality among us. May we know a taste of eternal life in the quality of our mutual caring and our sharing with a needy world. Amen.

OFFERTORY INVITATION

For many in the world, famine is a constant reality. Millions lie down at night hungry and without shelter, with no better hope for tomorrow. There is no relief from illness for themselves or for their children. God is a distant unknown. Their betterment is a part of our mission.

OFFERTORY PRAYER

As you have blessed us, O God, we are eager to share. May we offer more than crumbs from your table. May none be sent away from the blessings you intend for all. We want our offerings to preserve and extend life to your children, here in this place and wherever our influence can reach. What is in the offering plates is only a part of what we dedicate ourselves to do and be that your reign of unity and peace may come. Amen.

COMMISSION AND BLESSING

God's call to service goes with you from this place.
We cannot escape from God's expectations.
We intend to be faithful to God's call.
We want to make sure no one is excluded.
God's bounty is meant for all to share.
Because we have received so much, we have much to give.
In giving, we also receive so much more.
We learn from those we seek to benefit.
May no evil intent enter hearts cleansed by God.
May the Spirit help us live in unity.
We have received God's abundant mercy.
We depart, intent on showing mercy to all.
Amen. **Amen.**

(See hymn 77.)

PROPER 16

Sunday between August 21 and August 27

Exodus 1:8–2:10   (or Isaiah 51:1–6   Romans 12:1–8
Psalm 124   Psalm 138)   Matthew 16:13–20

CALL TO WORSHIP
> Our help is from God, who made heaven and earth.
> Come to worship the One who answers our prayers.
>> **If God were not on our side, we could not live.**
>> **If God were not for us, we would be swept away.**
> God has gifted each one of us in unique ways.
> In our variety, we complement one another.
>> **We rejoice in God's love and faithfulness.**
>> **Blessed be our God, whose word is true.**
> In thankfulness, we bring our joyous songs.
> We are here to pay attention to God's instructions.
>> **We are here, seeking to discern God's will.**
>> **We are open to God's transforming Spirit.**

INVOCATION
God beyond our knowing, we believe that you care for humble people who seek to follow your Word more than for those who are pretentious and proud in places of power. You have protected your people when they were surrounded by trouble. You have provided a way of escape in the midst of oppression. Your love never fails. Come, Holy One, to transform us. Work within and among us to renew our minds and build community. Nurse us into the health you intend for all your children. You are our help and our hope. Amen.

CALL TO CONFESSION
We who look with horror at the oppression of the pharaohs of Egypt need to view our own privileged positions. We, like the ancient rulers, enjoy the fruits of others' hard labor, the benefits of their slave-like toil. We eat food picked by migrant laborers and wear clothing sewn in sweatshops. Our insensitivity separates us from God.

PRAYER OF CONFESSION
O God, we did not realize that we are among the rich oppressors of this world. We think we are poor when we cannot have everything we want. Keep us from misusing the power we have. We confess our fear of those who are unlike us. We set up barriers against them when we are afraid. Keep us from acting in ways that alienate and divide. When we are tempted to conform to the world's standards, set before us the higher model of sacrifice and service that is given to us in Jesus, in whose name we pray. Amen.

Assurance of Forgiveness

God gives us grace to think with sober judgment and to act with confident faith. By that grace, we have unique gifts to use within the body of Christ. God forgives and heals and empowers us with new insights and expanded capacity to serve. In humble obedience, we learn the joy of following Jesus and living for the highest good for all.

Collect

Holy God, who revealed to Peter the significance of Jesus' loving ministry, open our ears to hear your Word for us, and our eyes to see ways you are working among us today. We seek the keys to your realm where all are welcome and freedom is offered to become all we can be. May cheerfulness, generosity, and compassion abound among us. Amen.

Offertory Invitation

We are invited to give with generosity, to minister in caring ways, to lead with diligence, to teach with enthusiasm. We cannot be all things to all people. But we can tithe the many gifts God pours out on us and do our best to live up to God's trust in us.

Offertory Prayer

Receive our offering, gracious God, as an expression of our thankfulness. In your church, we are privileged to cultivate the dimensions of our lives that give meaning and purpose to all we do. Here we become aware that the greatest gifts we receive are not material, and we learn how best to use the particular gifts you give us. At the same time, you show us how our material advantages can help others. May many be blessed through our sharing of these offerings and our sharing of ourselves. Amen.

Commission and Blessing

Serve the world as people transformed by God.
Let others know God's mercy and forgiveness.
> **We seek to live as Jesus taught.**
> **We seek to embody trust in God and love of all.**
Daily God renews our energy and confirms our gifts.
In Christ we are drawn away from conformity to the world.
> **Our agenda is to discern and do God's will.**
> **We aim to use well the gifts God has given.**
Remember that God is on our side.
God calls us into community with one another.
> **In Christ, there are no enemies.**
> **We recognize all people as God's children.**
Amen. **Amen.**

(See hymn 78.)

Proper 17

Sunday between August 28 and September 3

Exodus 3:1–15	(or Jeremiah 15:15–21	Romans 12:9–21
Psalm 105:1–6, 23–26, 45c	Psalm 26:1–8)	Matthew 16:21–28

CALL TO WORSHIP

Why have we gathered on this holy day?
What has drawn us to this time and place?
> **We have been drawn to a flame burning here.**
> **We sense the glory of God in this place.**

God calls us to this time of worship.
The place where we are standing is holy ground.
> **Give thanks to God: sing praises.**
> **Give attention to the voice of God.**

Out of a burning bush, God spoke to Moses.
In the rhythms of worship, God speaks to us.
> **We will listen for God's message to us.**
> **Surely God's strength will supply our needs.**

INVOCATION

We tremble to think that the Source of all life, the Creator of all worlds, is in this place, observing our worship, knowing our innermost secrets, calling us by name. O God, we dare to call on you, to bow before you, to welcome your Word. We tremble to think what you might expect of us, for we remember what you expected of Moses. You sent him against the rulers of his people to win release from oppression. You sent him from the comfortable places he knew to plead for freedom amid threatening conditions. We dare to worship you, O God, knowing that you expect much of us. Amen.

CALL TO CONFESSION

So often we are complainers, not seekers. We proclaim our innocence and justify our anger when so much in life does not go the way we had hoped. We blame God for conditions entrusted to our stewardship. We become stumbling blocks, not facilitators, of God's design. Let us seek reconciliation with our God.

PRAYER OF CONFESSION

O God, we have wavered in our faith in the midst of suffering, and we have not persevered in prayer. We have claimed to be wiser than we are, and have even tried to correct you. We make excuses for ourselves rather than listening for your direction and heeding your call. Our days are so filled with the busyness of this world that we cannot see your reign among us. We are so weighed down by our own concerns that we have no energy to serve in your realm. Send your cleansing fire among us, forgiving God. Amen.

Assurance of Forgiveness

God is ever willing to grant us forgiveness, but we cannot receive it if we are unwilling to be changed by it. As long as we focus on preserving our own lives, protecting our advantages, we will be lost. If we want to be Christ's followers, we will deny ourselves and take up the cross, not as a burden, but as the joyous symbol of loving and giving for all the right reasons. We will overcome evil with good.

Collect

God of our ancestors, whose presence on the human scene in Jesus Christ continues to challenge us, grant strength and courage to deny ourselves, take up the cross, and follow. Increase among us empathy with all who suffer, identification with the lowly, and a spirit of hospitality for all. We would live with hope and patience that bridge differences, promote harmony, and contribute to the peace you intend for humankind. Amen.

Offertory Invitation

God invites us to observe the misery of our sisters and brothers who live in oppression and poverty. We have the resources to help make a difference in their lives. Beyond the limits of charity, we are challenged to invest our lives for the mutual benefit of all God's children. Let us give as God has blessed us, with joy.

Offertory Prayer

May our offerings be an expression of genuine love that reflects your love for us, O God. We seek to honor you as we serve one another in Christ's name. We reach out to overcome evil with good. Direct our use of the resources you entrust to us that we may not only contribute to the needs of the saints but also devote our lives to the building of a peaceable worldwide community in which all are valued. Amen.

Commission and Blessing

Seek every day the presence we have known here.
God offers strength for every challenge we face.
> *We will give thanks and call on God's name.*
> *We will open our eyes to see God's daily miracles.*
God promises life in all its fullness, not earthly riches.
Life is fruitful when lived for others.
> *With mutual affection, we honor one another.*
> *With hope and joy, we reach out helping hands.*
Let worship continue as we pray for one another.
May God's will be done as we overcome evil with good.
> *Praise God for all the wonders of this life.*
> *Praise God for opportunities to serve in Christ's name.*
Amen. **Amen.**

(See hymns 79, 80.)

Exodus 12:1–14　　　(or Ezekiel 33:7–11　　　Romans 13:8–14
Psalm 149　　　　　　Psalm 119:33–40)　　　Matthew 18:15–20

CALL TO WORSHIP

Tell the whole congregation of God's people:
This is a day for new beginnings.
> **This is a time of God's appearing.**
> **This is the moment for faithful response.**

Praise God in the assembly of the faithful.
Make melody to God and sing a new song.
> **Praise God for life enriched by love.**
> **Praise God for love that fulfills God's law.**

This is the hour to wake from our sleep.
The energy of God's love fills this place.
> **Here we claim our identity as Christians.**
> **Here we become the church of Jesus Christ.**

INVOCATION

This is a festival day, glorious God, a day of remembering your faithfulness through the centuries, a time for celebrating your vibrant presence with us, a pause of anticipation for the seasons yet to be. We rejoice at the assurance that you take pleasure in us, that we are known by you, called by you, empowered by you to live honorably and humbly, in the spirit of Christ. We would exalt your name and sing for joy, knowing that we can trust you for the guidance and direction we need. Amen.

CALL TO CONFESSION

Our ancestors in the faith sometimes sought vengeance on their enemies. Jesus challenged his friends to listen and reconcile those with whom they disagreed. Paul counseled followers to put away quarreling, jealousy, and harmful behavior. There is much in our lives that is harmful to ourselves and others, much that leads to brokenness and lasting pain. Let us confess our need for healing.

PRAYER OF CONFESSION

O God, we have not been faithful to your commands. We have been more ready to condemn than to console, more eager to justify ourselves than to work for understanding. We feed the flames of dissent instead of welcoming the freeing power of forgiveness. We gather as two or three, not to welcome your presence but to gossip about those who are absent. Our sins are destroying us, God. Turn us around to a new way of being. Amen.

ASSURANCE OF FORGIVENESS

Salvation is nearer to us now than when we became believers. God's healing presence has come among us and dwells within us. Our openness to God's transforming love releases in us the potential for wholeness. We will be amazed at what we can do and who we can be as humble, joyous followers of the One who is the way, the truth, and the life.

COLLECT

Eternal God, to whom we owe all we have and all we are, and whose law of love points to fulfillment in this life and beyond, show us how to live honorably and help us to make those choices that are pleasing to you, that your church may become a trusting community that leads many to lives of quality and realization, in Jesus' name. Amen.

OFFERTORY INVITATION

Our Hebrew ancestors offered the best of their flocks and crops to honor God. We bring symbols of our labor, dedicating them and ourselves to upholding the highest values of human life. May our offerings be a joyous expression of worship.

OFFERTORY PRAYER

May these offerings help to free your people, O God, from bondage to sin. Unite us in a community of mutual caring in which differences are resolved as we listen to one another and seek to offer understanding. May the light of your love shine through all our efforts to share your good news. Keep us in the light when we are tempted to ignore and violate your commandments. With these prayers, we dedicate our gifts. Amen.

COMMISSION AND BLESSING

We are God's servants, sent on a mission.
Let us make God's deeds known among the people.
> *We will ready ourselves to go where God sends us.*
> *High praises to God will be in our throats.*
Owe no one anything, except to love one another.
Keep the commandments God has given.
> *"Let us then lay aside the works of darkness*
> *and put on the armor of light."*
God grants victory over sin to the humble.
Rejoice, for God takes pleasure in us.
> *Where two or three gather, God is with us.*
> *We seek to live honorably in the spirit of Christ.*
Amen. **Amen.**

(See hymn 81.)

PROPER 19

Exodus 14:19–31   *(or Genesis 50:15–21*   Romans 14:1–12
Psalm 114 or   *Psalm 103:(1–7) 8–13)*   Matthew 18:21–35
  Exodus 15:1b–11, 20–21

CALL TO WORSHIP

Tremble, O earth, at the presence of God.
Let us remember God's marvelous works.
> **Surely God has saved us in difficult times.**
> **How can we forget God's guiding hand?**

When evil surrounds us and we have been wronged,
God helps us turn the evil to good.
> **We need not be afraid whatever happens.**
> **We are in God's care wherever we go.**

Sing the praises of God, our strength.
Know that God is majestic and holy.
> **How great is God's mercy for all who worship!**
> **We sense among us God's kindness and patience.**

INVOCATION

Majestic God, who led our spiritual ancestors with a pillar of cloud that hid them by day and protected them by night, lead us through the threatening times in which we live. Save us from the floods of our own misplaced trust, as you saved them from the waters of the sea and the weapons of their pursuers. On this day, grant strength to those who are weak and support for all who are stumbling. Let every tongue praise you as we give account to you of our deeds. Amen.

CALL TO CONFESSION

Why do we pass judgment on our brothers and sisters? Why do we quarrel with those whose ways are different from our own? How can we despise another who is also a child of God? How can we ignore the suffering of other human beings? Surely we have much to confess to our God.

PRAYER OF CONFESSION

We bow before your judgment seat, O God. We have ranked our sisters and brothers by the faulty standards of our society to decide who is worthy of our attention. We have rejected those whom we dislike and have been harsh with those we think do not measure up. We have been quite willing to overlook our own faults as we look down on other people. O God, you have shown us a better way. Save us from the pain we inflict and help us to discover the blessing of forgiveness. Amen.

ASSURANCE OF FORGIVENESS

God has pity on us and releases us from the debts we have accumulated. In the great design of the universe, we are equipped to receive this forgiveness only when we extend it to others. Jesus points us to unlimited willingness to forgive—seventy times seven. How amazing is God's love for us, and God's expectation of us!

COLLECT

Forgiving God, whose strength enables us to stand against the temptations we face and whose judgment discerns our deepest motives, empower us by your Word to embody the spirit of Christ in our relations with one another, and in our care for all people, that oppression may end, desperate needs be met, and mercy be extended to all your children. Amen.

OFFERTORY INVITATION

We are indebted to the Creator for all we have and for the precious gift of life itself. Nothing we can do will ever begin to repay this debt. Therefore, with gratitude, we extend to others the gracious acceptance and generosity we have experienced. Let us thank God with our offerings.

OFFERTORY PRAYER

We honor you, O God, as we give. We know we do not live or die to ourselves but are a part of a large community, linked in ways beyond our knowing with you and all generations of your children. We are accountable to you and share in responsibility for one another and for the care of this planet. Thus, we dedicate our resources and our lives to you for the work of your realm. Receive our gifts and draw us to yourself. Amen.

COMMISSION AND BLESSING

We have observed this day to honor God.
God's promises go with us as we depart.
> **God upholds us and helps us to stand.**
> **We are grateful that God strengthens our faith.**
We do not live or die to ourselves.
Christ has claimed us and offered us life.
> **From Christ, we have learned to forgive.**
> **We have been taught to value every person.**
Let every knee bow daily before our God.
Let every tongue give praise to the Almighty.
> **God helps us turn evil into good.**
> **Every day we can know God's loving presence.**
Amen. **Amen.**

(See hymn 82.)

PROPER 20

Exodus 16:2–15	*(or Jonah 3:10–4:11*	Philippians 1:21–30
Psalm 105:1–6, 37–45	*Psalm 145:1–8*	Matthew 20:1–16

CALL TO WORSHIP

Call on God with praise and thanksgiving.
Tell of God's wonderful works.
> *Today we open ourselves to God's presence.*
> *Let the hearts of all who seek God rejoice.*

When we eat, we are reminded of God's provision.
When we drink pure water, we give thanks.
> *Surely God has blessed us with food and drink.*
> *Daily we are strengthened for tasks we face.*

We are guided by God's laws and statutes.
We benefit from God's generosity.
> *Let all the people worship with joy!*
> *Let all whom God has chosen sing together!*

INVOCATION

Glory to your name, holy God. We rejoice in your wonderful works, in miracles you have caused among us, and in the wealth you have entrusted to our steward-ship. You have called us to important work in your vineyard. Wherever we go, we represent your church and interpret your ways to those who observe our words and deeds. Enfold us in your presence and give us strength and courage to pass on the light you have sent to illuminate our journey through life. We are eager to be fed by your Word today. Amen.

CALL TO CONFESSION

Like the Israelites in the wilderness, we have been heard to complain. God is of-ten blamed for calamities more than praised for the sustaining presence that works for our good. It is easier for us to be jealous of others than to rejoice in the op-portunities God gives them. Surely we need to repent.

PRAYER OF CONFESSION

O God, we are people of the flesh more than people of the spirit. Our lives are not worthy of the gospel of Christ. We admit our resentment when some people we deem unworthy benefit from your generosity. We confess our lack of attention to your laws, your living Word, your prompting Spirit. You alone are our salvation, our healing, our high opportunity to serve. We choose to belong to you. Accept and change us, we pray. Amen.

ASSURANCE OF FORGIVENESS

God has offered us a presence we have not recognized, bread we have ignored, and compassion we have not deserved. The food from heaven is offered to us daily, freely given to all who are open to receive it. Let us rejoice in this moment of God's amazing generosity, opening our lives to the gifts of God, that we might share them with others. Praise God!

COLLECT

Gracious God, whose attention to all your children amazes and surprises us, help us this day to hear your call to us, to accept your direction, and to follow your commands that the world may become more faithfully your realm, a place acknowledging your rule, a home for those who have been intimidated and afraid, a community in which all are valued and welcomed, whatever their contribution. Amen.

OFFERTORY INVITATION

God provides generously for all of us. We are blessed with pure water and nourishing food. We have found joy in the faith that sustains our spirits. Let us now expand the circle of opportunity as we share what God has promised.

OFFERTORY PRAYER

Receive our tithes and offerings to your honor and glory, loving God. May fruitful results occur through and beyond our sharing. Call us all into the vineyard of meaningful labor and constructive leisure, that your Word, living through us, may call our neighbors to joyous reunion with you. May we help one another to live in a manner worthy of the gospel of Christ, in whose name we pray. Amen.

COMMISSION AND BLESSING

May you know joy and progress in your faith.
May this be a week of spiritual growth for you.
> *May Christ dwell in us and among us.*
> *May the faith of the gospel empower us.*
In all your struggles, know that Christ is with you.
In all your labors, the love of God surrounds you.
> *Glory be to God's holy name.*
> *Let all who seek God be assured and rejoice.*
God surprises us and provides for us.
Trust and give thanks for God's wonderful works.
> *There is a song on our lips and joy in our hearts.*
> *In Christ our suffering finds meaning.*
Amen. **Amen.**

(See hymns 83, 84.)

PROPER 21

| Exodus 17:1–7 | (or Ezekiel 18:1–4, 25–32 | Philippians 2:1–13 |
| Psalm 78:1–4, 12–16 | Psalm 25:1–9) | Matthew 21:23–32 |

CALL TO WORSHIP

Come, let us remember God's presence with us.
Let us give ear to all that God would teach us.
> **Our ancestors have told us about God's might.**
> **They have celebrated God's wondrous deeds.**
In the wilderness of Sinai, God provided water.
Through the sea, God provided safe passage.
> **Yet the Israelites questioned God's presence.**
> **They needed assurance amid their doubts.**
Our doubts can lead to honest searching.
God welcomes questions that seek new truth.
> **We want to see God's larger picture.**
> **We are here to broaden the scope of our concern.**

INVOCATION

We marvel, O God, at the thought that you care about us. We are amazed that the Creator of the universe would take on human flesh to draw near to us in ways we could begin to understand. As Jesus emptied himself to serve, modeling your love even in the face of death, we seek in these moments to lay aside self-interest that we might take direction from you. Help us to humble ourselves in order to obey you, to listen in order to hear, to care in order to serve. Lead us day and night through the dangers of the wilderness of our times. Lead us in these moments to honest and fervent worship. Amen.

CALL TO CONFESSION

Like the chief priests and scribes of Jesus' day, we are tempted to confuse our ways for God's way. We trust our own authority and defend the way we live as if we have earned all that we claim as our own. We see the sins of others more readily than we see our own. Our church sometimes reflects our priorities more than the mind of Christ. We need to pray.

PRAYER OF CONFESSION

We fear to approach you with our confession, holy God, for you may require changes in us that are costly. You ask us to have the mind of Christ, a mind free of pretense and self-interest. You challenge us to lay aside our advantages to go where you send us. We fear loss of security if we are obedient. It is hard to see ourselves as exploiters when we pursue advantages for our families. It is difficult to consider others when we feel like victims. We confess our need for you and our desire to find your purpose for us. Amen.

Assurance of Forgiveness

God accepts us in the midst of our struggles. There is encouragement in Christ, there is consolation from love, there is compassion, sympathy, and the opportunity to share in the Spirit. God blesses us as we gather in community, calling us to find our common mind in Christ Jesus. May we not only agree to do the work God places before us as a ministry of love, but let us do all we can to share our faith with a faithfulness stripped of pretense and conceit. May our lives praise God.

Collect

Loving God, whose messengers have shown us the way of righteousness, and whose revelation in Jesus Christ has demonstrated humble obedience to your will, lead us this day to the joy they have known through serving you, that our witness may be as authentic as theirs and be influential in the lives of all we meet, adding to your realm in heaven and on earth. Amen.

Offertory Invitation

As Christ gave up selfish ambition and conceit for human beings like us, may we offer our best for sisters and brothers who need the message we can send and the practical help we can provide through our offerings.

Offertory Prayer

We empty our pockets, trusting you, O God. We empty our selfish ambitions, believing that the common good is of greater concern. We give because you have richly blessed us. We present ourselves in your service because you have gifted us in so many ways. We reach out helping hands because we care about all those you have called us to love. May every tongue confessing Christ as Savior share in that mind which so powerfully demonstrates your love. Amen.

Commission and Blessing

Go forth to serve in the spirit of Christ.
Dare to question false values that hold us captive.
> *We will seek the mind of Christ in all things.*
> *We will put aside selfish ambition and conceit.*
Look to the greatest interests of all people.
In humility, view each person as precious to God.
> *We count it a privilege to serve in Christ's name.*
> *We are grateful for the saving power of love.*
Remember always that God is at work in you.
With God's help, amazing good can be accomplished.
> *May we do what we have so boldly declared.*
> *May we follow and serve in joyous obedience.*
Amen. **Amen.**

(See hymns 85, 86.)

PROPER 22

Exodus 20:1–4, 7–9, 12–20	(or Isaiah 5:1–7	Philippians 3:4b–14
Psalm 19	Psalm 80:7–15)	Matthew 21:33–46

CALL TO WORSHIP

The God who frees us invites us to worship.
The God of law welcomes our loyal response.
> **The heavens are telling the glory of God.**
> **The firmament proclaims God's handiwork.**

God is present with us, eager to speak to us.
Our Creator is here to test us and to keep us from sin.
> **The law of God is perfect, reviving the soul.**
> **God's decrees are sure, making wise the simple.**

We tremble before God, yet are not afraid.
We are ready to listen to God's word.
> **May our awe before God be pure and enduring.**
> **May our thoughts and our words be acceptable to God.**

INVOCATION

O God, our rock and our redeemer, enlighten us today through the ancient witness of your faithful people. Lead us to desire the guidance of your word. Remind us of your ordinances that are true and righteous altogether. May they shape our living and warn us when we are in error. We seek to honor your name, to divest ourselves of idols, to keep this day of rest and worship. Work with us to develop right relationships in our families and with all your children near and far, we pray in Jesus' name. Amen.

CALL TO CONFESSION

We are tenants to whom God has leased some of the earth's wealth. God comes among us to collect what we have produced, to claim a portion of all that is God's own. Our Creator seeks an accounting of our faithfulness to the way of life designed for us. Let us seek forgiveness for our shortcomings.

PRAYER OF CONFESSION

O God, we have no righteousness of our own. We have bent and ignored your law. Your commandments inform us but do not transform. We give lip service to your law but seek to avoid its implication for our lives. We recognize some of our errors, but many are hidden from us We devote our energies to accumulating possessions that function as idols in our lives. We depend on them more than we honor you. Save us, we pray, from great transgressions and help us to reorder our days. Amen.

Assurance of Forgiveness

Moses said to the people, "Do not be afraid; for God has come only to test you and to put the fear of God upon you so that you do not sin." The One who orders all worlds seeks to bring order and joyous freedom into our lives. To fear God is to open our eyes to the amazing vastness of God's dominion and to the astonishing awareness that God knows each one of us, loves us, and has a purpose for us. Let God reign among us!

Collect

Amazing God, whose presence among us has been revealed so dramatically in Jesus of Nazareth, the One who became the cornerstone for your church, build each one of us into your household of faith, fitting us together by your great design into a beautiful witness to your truth, that resurrection power may energize us for service in your name and bring joyous transformation to all your children. Amen.

Offertory Invitation

God has planted a vineyard on this tiny planet we call home. The earth has been blessed with vast resources entrusted to our care. What is produced by our caretaking is not our own but is rightfully claimed by God for the benefit of all. It is the fruit of God's realm that we share today.

Offertory Prayer

Ruler of all space and time, we want to be faithful stewards in your vineyard. All that we have is yours. Our lives are in your hands. Help us to use well all that we here devote to the work of your church. Help us to manage well, to your honor and glory, all that we retain for ourselves. May we know heaven on earth because you hold first place in our priorities and our daily goal is to serve you. Amen.

Commission and Blessing

With eyes enlightened, go forth to serve with joy.
With hearts made pure, pass on God's love.
> **With souls revived, we go out rejoicing.**
> **God's law has revealed to us God's love and care.**
All that we have gained is a gift from God.
What is most important is not things, but Christ.
> **We seek to gain Christ within the church community.**
> **We dwell together in Christ's body, the church.**
Seek the growth of this body, for Christ's sake.
Bring others to dwell here, for their sakes.
> **We will press on toward our heavenly call.**
> **Our resurrection faith gives us hope.**
Amen. **Amen.**

(See hymn 87.)

Exodus 32:1–14   (or Isaiah 25:1–9   Philippians 4:1–9

Psalm 106:1–6, 19–23   Psalm 23)   Matthew 22:1–14

CALL TO WORSHIP

Come away from the valleys of misplaced loyalty.

Come, seeking to meet the God of all worlds.

> *We have come to praise God and give thanks.*
> *We believe God's steadfast love endures forever.*

We come together that our faith might be strengthened.

We seek the strength to live by all we profess.

> *God's awesome deeds saved our ancestors.*
> *Surely God's steadfast love continues with us.*

God continues to deliver us in times of distress.

God's steadfast love endures forever.

> *We rejoice that God is near and available to us.*
> *We hear God welcoming us to this time of prayer.*

INVOCATION

Gracious God, you have invited and welcomed us to this place of worship. You draw us away from the idols we create to take your place. When we come together, we sense that there is nothing in life that can substitute for a vital relationship with you. Yet we are only dimly aware of who you are. All the mysteries of the universe are in your hands, yet you have made yourself known among the people of this earth. We catch glimpses of your work among us and are amazed. We want to meet you again today, as for the first time. Touch us. Remake us. Help us to stand firm in the faith. Amen.

CALL TO CONFESSION

God is not fooled by our pious words of faith. God knows our fascination with golden calves—with pastimes and possessions that take our attention and resources every day. Like our ancestors before us, we have sinned and deserve God's wrath. As Moses implored God to spare the Hebrew people, we bring our petitions, seeking a fresh start.

PRAYER OF CONFESSION

God of all mercy, you have planted within us a desire to observe justice and do righteousness. We want to be fair and honorable, delighting in life shared openly and honestly with family, friends, and co-workers. Instead, we are often defensive, fearful, and distracted. We spend more time with our toys than with your truth. We seek temporary thrills rather than lasting meaning. Then we are disappointed when our "golden calves" bring no fulfillment. We return to you, loving God, intent on following the guidance we are receiving from you. Save us from ourselves. Amen.

ASSURANCE OF FORGIVENESS

Rejoice, knowing that God is always near. Our thanksgiving and our supplications are always heard. The peace of God, which surpasses all understanding, will guard your hearts and minds in Christ Jesus. Find joyous focus for life in all that is honorable, just, pure, and excellent. Know that your goodwill is pleasing to God. You are chosen by God to share in the mind of Christ.

COLLECT

Gracious God, whose banquet table, prepared for our enjoyment, offers all the best that life can hold, grant us in these moments we spend together such a taste of your bounty that we will be eager every day to meet you in prayer, meditation, and study of the Scriptures, and be confident of finding you in our relationships and in all we do, that our lives may honor you and bring joy to others. Amen.

OFFERTORY INVITATION

God invites us to invest our time and resources in ways that build rather than destroy, in work of lasting value rather than temporary distraction. Through the church, we seek to offer a quality of life focused on the worth of every individual, on justice for all and excellence in all things. May our offerings and our lives praise God.

OFFERTORY PRAYER

May our offerings help to prepare many to feast at your banquet table. May our generosity reflect the amazing abundance you entrust to our care. As we find joy in giving, may others be inspired to give their best, and may all of us realize your peace, dwelling within and among us as we serve in Christ's name. Amen.

COMMISSION AND BLESSING

God is opening our minds to what is true.
God is filling our lives with ways that are just.
> *We will honor God by respecting one another.*
> *We stand firm in the faith that God can be trusted.*
God calls us to daily self-examination.
God offers us choices that lead to wholeness.
> *We will seek what is pure and pleasing to God.*
> *We want to think and do what is worthy of praise.*
God's plan for us is not disaster but fulfillment.
God delivers us from evil and gives us peace.
> *We rejoice in God, who loves us.*
> *We are eager to live as Christ teaches us.*
Amen. **Amen.**

(See hymn 88.)

PROPER 24

Exodus 33:12–23   (or Isaiah 45:1–7   I Thessalonians 1:1–10
Psalm 99   Psalm 96:1–9 (10–13))   Matthew 22:15–22

CALL TO WORSHIP

We are drawn to worship by a Reality unseen.
The One we call God is beyond human description.
> **God is more than we can ever imagine.**
> **We sense God's presence as we meditate.**

We gather in awe to bring our songs of praise.
The Creator of all things has given us life.
> **We are amazed by the wonders around us.**
> **We feel God's presence as we sing together.**

We are summoned by One who is just and merciful.
The Ruler of all worlds expects us to respond.
> **How amazing that God chooses us as messengers.**
> **We know God is with us as we work for justice.**

INVOCATION

Appear to us here, God of all worlds, for we need your assurance and blessing. We seek the strength to do what is right and just. We long to see you, even though we sense that a god we could see would be only a tiny part of you whose Spirit fills all time and space. We want you to have a face like ours, so we find your face in Jesus, and occasionally in one another. We want to be certain that our decisions and actions are right, but often it is only long afterwards that we realize you were with us. O God, we want to be open to all you are revealing to us now. Amen.

CALL TO CONFESSION

We are invited to reflect on the wrongs we have done, the good we have neglected and the motives that underlie our behavior. What are the idols that attract us, the responsibilities we seek to avoid, the schemes by which we pursue selfish advantages? God knows, but we need to recognize and confess them.

PRAYER OF CONFESSION

Awesome God, how puny is our cleverness before the magnitude of your reality! How fleeting are our days measured against the far reaches of eternity! Yet we set our limited knowledge and restricted purposes against your will for us and presume to direct our own affairs and those of the whole world. O God, we are trapped in our pretensions. Turn us from our need for proof to extravagant praise. Turn us inside out so our self-interest becomes concern for all your neglected children. Suppress in us the sinful ways we find so difficult to manage on our own, that we may joyously render to you all that is already yours. Amen.

ASSURANCE OF FORGIVENESS

When we allow God to touch us, our malice is melted down, our fears are defeated, our failures are forgiven. God raises us from death to new life, from helplessness to hope, from arrogant self-seeking to humble service. Enter into the joy of true worship!

COLLECT

Great and awesome God, just and righteous beyond all our prejudices, valuing all people without partiality, allow us to sense your presence within and among us, that we may know we are your people. Call us by name and let your favor rest upon us, that we may have no need to feel superior or seek fame and fortune over others but may rather extend your grace to all we meet, imitating Christ and extolling you in all our words and deeds. Amen.

OFFERTORY INVITATION

We are partners with one another in this land and beyond, seeking to share the benefits of God's creation with all God's children. We support government efforts to lessen the inequities among us, but through the church we address spiritual problems that feed the prejudices and false pride that result in injustice within God's world. We join our offerings with our personal efforts to do God's will.

OFFERTORY PRAYER

O God, we sense that you are calling us to manage well all the things that belong to you. The empires of this world have no claim on the resources you have provided except as they are used for the common good. The offerings we receive as a church are not for our private benefit or to buy services for ourselves. Thus we here dedicate the gifts you have provided in our money and our abilities and our time to extend a helping hand and joyous welcome to every people on the face of the earth. May our efforts find favor with you. Amen.

COMMISSION AND BLESSING

We have gathered in community to worship God.
Now our service of praise continues in the world.
>   *We have been equipped with the gospel message.*
>   *God empowers our outreach wherever we go.*
God has forgiven and blessed us in this gathering.
Now we scatter to forgive and bless others.
>   *Here, the Holy Spirit has deepened our convictions.*
>   *Now God calls to let our faith be known in other places.*
We serve a true and living God, everywhere present.
We are blessed to be God's own people.
>   *We will spend ourselves this week for God's children.*
>   *Then we will return to strengthen one another.*
Amen. **Amen.**

(See hymn 89.)

PROPER 25

Deuteronomy 34:1–12   (or Leviticus 19:1–2, 15–18   I Thessalonians 2:1–8
Psalm 90:1–6, 13–17   Psalm 1)   Matthew 22:34–46

CALL TO WORSHIP
> Gather together to hear stories of faith and courage.
> Listen for the ways God has acted among us.
>> *Our ancestors in the faith listened for God's word.*
>> *They dared to believe God's promises.*
> Leaders like Moses and Paul saw evidence of God's work.
> They believed they were face-to-face with God's truth.
>> *They looked beyond the present moment.*
>> *They lived for dreams not yet realized.*
> Many felt God's love in knowing Jesus.
> They experienced a new relationship with neighbors.
>> *We have come seeking community centered in Christ.*
>> *We want to feel God's presence as we worship.*

INVOCATION
God, you have been our dwelling place in all generations. Before the earth was formed, long before there were people on this planet, you were fashioning life in its myriad forms. Out of the billions of years you have been creating, our lives have come to this moment of meeting. We stand in awe before you, amazed to discover that you care about us, tiny blips on the screen of eternity. O God, we want our lives to count for something. Show us how to fit into your plans. Amen.

CALL TO CONFESSION
The word of God comes to us through Moses: "You shall be holy, for I, your God, am holy." But we have taken little delight in holiness. We scoff at pretensions of saintliness, preferring the company of sinners. Wickedness seems more attractive than righteousness, not only for our entertainment but also to boost our success in the marketplace. Do we want to change our accommodation to today's world?

PRAYER OF CONFESSION
O God, we have missed your signs and wonders because we are so busy creating our own. Those around us who pretend to be your prophets offer little to which we aspire. Yet, we would pray with the psalmist, "Satisfy us in the morning with your steadfast love, so we may rejoice and be glad all our days." Where is the meaning we have missed in all our striving? Does Jesus hold the key when he says, "Love God with all your being," and "Love your neighbor as yourself"? O God, we long to make sense out of life. Help us to follow your way. Amen.

Assurance of Forgiveness

It takes courage to question the way things are, especially when present arrangements are to our benefit. We who are privileged seldom notice those who suffer and are shamefully mistreated. Yet we cannot ignore them. We can only suppress knowledge of the evil around us for a little while. God is even now nudging us gently, caring tenderly for us amid our confusion and inner turmoil. The favor of God is upon us, entrusting us with the gospel for our own lives and for the world. Receive forgiveness and blessing as good news.

Collect

Eternal God, whose wisdom defies our limited insights, and whose commandments are from everlasting to everlasting, open our hearts and souls and minds to your love that surrounds us and seeks a dwelling place in us, that we may regard ourselves as your valuable children and accord the same care and concern to others as we would, at our best, lavish on ourselves. May our lives honor you and display the power of your love to the world. Amen.

Offertory Invitation

We who have been entrusted with the message of the gospel have the means to make it known to the world. Our tithes and offerings are dedicated to that purpose. As we present them, we also submit ourselves to God's purposes and direction.

Offertory Prayer

As we give ourselves and our offerings, we pray, O God, that they may reveal your love in such a way that many will respond. Awaken in us a love for you and for one another that is contagious. Remove from us all apathy, pretension, and greed that we may grow in holiness and compassion, living joyously in communion with you. Amen.

Commission and Blessing

Brothers and sisters, our coming together is not in vain.
God is doing a new thing among us and beyond us.
> **We have sensed a vision of God's plan for us.**
> **God's sign and wonders await our discovery.**
God has compassion on all who seek to serve.
Steadfast love is with all who continue in faithfulness.
> **God's glorious power is manifested in humility.**
> **Surely God's favor rests upon us here.**
Now we go out with courage, entrusted with the gospel.
We carry good news of God's love to our neighbors.
> **We will be gentle with others as God is gentle with us.**
> **We offer tender care in the spirit of Jesus.**
Amen. **Amen.**

(See hymns 90, 91.)

Proper 25　　　153

PROPER 26

Joshua 3:7–17   (or Micah 3:5–12   I Thessalonians 2:9–13
Psalm 107:1–7, 33–37   Psalm 43)   Matthew 23:1–12

CALL TO WORSHIP

Come, all who are thirsty, whose souls are fainting.
Come, all whose troubles seem overwhelming.
> **The Source and Creator of all things welcomes us.**
> **God hears our cries and is ready to help us.**

Come, all who are pure, upright, and blameless.
Come, all who dwell day by day in God's realm.
> **The Messiah has more to teach us.**
> **Jesus turns us from seeking honor to humble service.**

Draw near and hear the word of our God.
Open your lives to the Spirit who fills all things.
> **We sense the presence of truth seeking to enter us.**
> **We feel the love of God eager to embrace us.**

INVOCATION

O God, our true home, we come together to unite our stories with those of our spiritual ancestors. Some of us have come from desert places, desperate for nourishment. Some of us come from places of abundant harvests and yet are not satisfied. You are among us all, a living God, present in ways we have not yet realized. We come to learn, to let what we learn mold and change us, to find courage and energy to live by your direction. We bring our joyous worship, confident of your welcome to us. Amen.

CALL TO CONFESSION

Let there be no pretense among us as we address our thoughts to God. We may fool one another, but God knows us as we really are. All that we try to hide from ourselves comes to light before the One who searches our hearts.

PRAYER OF CONFESSION

Gracious God, help us to be honest with ourselves, with one another, and with you. We have searched for life amid temporary attractions. We have sought excitement in places that turned out to be desert wastelands. We have burdened others with our mistakes. We have sought honors and made comparisons to look better than those around us. We have devoted little time to thanking and praising you, the Source of all things. Open us now, O God, to the Word we need from you. Amen.

ASSURANCE OF FORGIVENESS

God gathers us from the east and the west, the north and the south, drawing us into a caring community where burdens are shared, hope is renewed, and people are freed and equipped to use their God-given gifts. Springs of water emerge from parched lands as we alert one another to blessings we had overlooked. Let the redeemed of the Creator say so. Let us give thanks to God, whose steadfast love endures forever.

COLLECT

God of all worlds, who calls us into your own realm and glory, grant us truly to hear your word and follow it, that our hunger and thirst might be satisfied and our attention expanded beyond our own concerns. Lead all of us, your people, by the straight way of humble service that the world might realize the joy of life in your realm and honor you in all things. Amen.

OFFERTORY INVITATION

We bring the firstfruits of our labor and toil to honor our Creator and give thanks for the wonder of life. We want to share the steadfast love of God through the ministries of this church and through our mission for others near and far. Let us give with joy.

OFFERTORY PRAYER

Let your Word be at work in us, gracious God, and through the offerings we present for your blessing. We offer here our support for the work of teaching, preaching, and good counsel, our assistance for those who are burdened and hungry and lost, our encouragement for questioners, seekers, and risk-takers intent on leading a life worthy of your approval. We are all your students. Let us also be your humble servants, through the offering of our substance and ourselves. Amen.

COMMISSION AND BLESSING

Our hunger and thirst are being satisfied.
Our fainting souls have found refreshment here.
> **Surely God has been with us and helped us.**
> **Our cries have been heard in this place.**
God sends us out, purified, forgiven, and equipped.
We can be sure that God is with us every day.
> **We can be confident that God will teach us.**
> **Day by day we can learn as we serve.**
We commit ourselves anew to living God's word.
We ask God to bless and multiply our efforts.
> **God will provide a way for us through life's deserts.**
> **God will go with us to make life fruitful.**
Amen. **Amen.**

(See hymn 92.)

PROPER 27

Sunday between November 6 and November 12

Joshua 24:1–3a, 14–25   (or Amos 5:18–24   I Thessalonians 2:9–13
Psalm 78:1–7   Psalm 70)   Matthew 25:1–13

CALL TO WORSHIP

Put away the things you have substituted for God.
Let your worship of the one true God be genuine.
> *We seek to know God and to rejoice before our Creator.*
> *We know that God is beyond all our false images.*

God is not deceived by our solemn assemblies.
Our empty festivals do not impress our God.
> *We want to give joyous expression to a growing faith.*
> *We choose to serve the God whom Jesus revealed.*

Our hope is in God's grace beyond all judgment.
Our trust is in God's love, greater than our feeble imitation.
> *We welcome the light God promises us.*
> *We seek to respond with faithful service.*

INVOCATION

God of our ancestors, be our God today as we gather in sincerity and faithfulness to honor you. Attune our hearts to your commandments as we remember your mighty acts. Declare your Word to us so we may be inspired to obey. We know that we must decide today whether or not we will serve you. Not to decide is to reject you. O God, save us from the idols that appear so attractive to us, the toys that take so much of our attention and the pursuits that dominate our time. Make your dwelling place with us here. Amen.

CALL TO CONFESSION

How seriously do we regard the decrees of our spiritual ancestors? The psalmist commands the teaching of God's law to our children, that we and they might not forget all that God has done. Obedience to the way of life God sets before us makes hope real. Let us confess our need for help.

PRAYER OF CONFESSION

If sin means cutting ourselves off from you and being unprepared to respond to your presence, surely we have sinned. Our lamps are not trimmed; our lives are not ready for your trumpet call. We have not listened well or encouraged one another in the faith. The distraction of many things has kept us from meditation and prayer. We are witnesses against ourselves, for we have vowed our loyalty and then have gone our own way. Merciful God, we seek your forgiveness. Amen.

Assurance of Forgiveness

God brought our spiritual ancestors out of bondage and protected them along their way. We believe God is eager to free us from all that imprisons us. Our days on earth are a trust from God, and we serve God best by investing our time in learning and living God's intentions for us. It is God's will that we live in harmony with one another, that we learn to love all God's children. God extends full pardon to us. Praise God for forgiveness and a second chance.

Collect

Holy God, whose covenants we ignore at our peril and whose ways we dare not forsake lest we be consumed by our own folly, grant us courage to serve you well, to live always in the knowledge of your presence with us, and to share the story of faith with each new generation, that your realm may be realized among us and your love celebrated in all our relationships. Amen.

Offertory Invitation

How will our neighbors be prepared for times of crisis? Who will teach them where to find oil for their lamps? Who will help them discover spiritual riches more valuable than all their material possessions? Our church is a resource, and our ministry is for the whole world. Let us give our support.

Offertory Prayer

We set our hope in you, God of all ages, and seek to serve you through our offerings and our efforts to encourage and equip one another for ministry. Help us decide daily to live according to your will, preparing ourselves for the opportunities and challenges you give us. May your rule shape our lives in ways that introduce many to the joys of eternity in the midst of time. Amen.

Commission and Blessing

God expects our complete loyalty and devotion.
God's love frees us for joyous living.
>   ***We will serve the God we have met here.***
>   ***We know that God goes with us everywhere.***
May worship continue wherever we go.
May our service extend God's love to all we meet.
>   ***We will consult God in our daily choices.***
>   ***We will respond to others in the spirit of Christ.***
God is faithful in covenant with us.
The counsel of God is always available to us.
>   ***We will take time to rest in God's promises.***
>   ***We will listen for God's word of hope.***
Amen. **Amen.**

(See hymn 93.)

| Judges 4:1–7 | (or Zephaniah 1:7, 12–18 | I Thessalonians 5:1–11 |
| Psalm 123 | Psalm 90:1–8 (9–11), 12) | Matthew 25:14–30 |

CALL TO WORSHIP

Lift up your eyes, seeking to know your God.
Attune your spirit to the One in whom we dwell.
> *God's love surrounds us here today.*
> *God calls us to be children of light.*

We belong to the day when we have faith.
We live confidently in the hope of salvation.
> *We seek to be faithful to the best we know.*
> *We want to invest the talents God gives us.*

Faithfulness gives us a sense of greater abundance.
Doing justice adds to our sense of worth and dignity.
> *We are here to build up one another.*
> *May our worship encourage each of us today.*

INVOCATION

Fill us, gracious God, with a sense of your abiding presence. Awaken our spirits to realities unseen. Turn us from the dullness of our fear-filled grasping for security and help us to live with trust in you. Expand among us such mutual regard and encouragement as will build up community and lead all of us to live in the light. May faith and love dominate all our relationships as we enter into the joy of serving in the name of Jesus Christ. Amen.

CALL TO CONFESSION

Sometimes we are objects of scorn and contempt, but sometimes we are the ones at ease, filled with pride and thinking ourselves better than others. We cling to a false sense of peace and security amid injustice and oppression. The day of the Sovereign can surprise us like a thief in the night, and judgment is sure.

PRAYER OF CONFESSION

We are reluctant to face your judgment, all-knowing God. We know we have not fully invested the talents you have entrusted to us. We hide them and hoard them, retreating into a false sense of security. We live in the nighttime of self-protection rather than in the light of full participation in loving, faithful service. We seek to escape your wrath by shrinking from life rather than investing ourselves in the tasks to which you call us. Have mercy on us, O God. We want to be children of the day—your day. Help us! Amen.

Assurance of Forgiveness

God has not destined us for wrath but for obtaining salvation through Jesus Christ, who offers us life in all its fullness. Continue, then, to build up one another with encouragement and hope. Look to God each day for mercy and assurance, and be alert to hear God's commands. Live as children of light.

Collect

Amazing God, who entrusts to us the management of the earth, help us to appreciate and value the talents you have given us, using them for the benefit of all your children, that all of us may grow in faith, hope, and love to the end that all will dwell in your realm of light. Amen.

Offertory Invitation

God asks us for an accounting of what we have done with the wealth entrusted to us. All that we have and all that we are belongs to God. The climax of worship is an accounting of our stewardship. What are we doing with our time, talent, and treasure? It is not only what we offer to the church today but what we offer to God every day that is under judgment here. May we give with thankfulness.

Offertory Prayer

There is no escape from your judgment, O Spirit of Holiness, but neither can we flee beyond your limitless love. We offer an accounting of our stewardship in and beyond the offering of this day. Reshape our lives for joyous, responsive participation in work that builds up the body of Christ. Use what we offer here to bring encouragement and hope to many who have lost a sense of meaning for their lives. Bless us and our offerings. Amen.

Commission and Blessing

As another week unfolds, continue to look up.
Dare to invest yourself for the sake of others.
> **God will go with us to uplift our spirits.**
> **We will pass on to others the encouragement God gives.**

Live as children of the day, children of light.
Keep awake, sober, and full of faith and love.
> **God's saving grace is a healing force among us.**
> **God's trust in us helps us to trust others.**

Listen for God's commendation and affirmation:
"Well done, good and faithful servant."
> **We will seek to be worthy of that award.**
> **May God bless our worship and our service.**

Amen. **Amen.**

(See hymn 94.)

PROPER 29 (REIGN OF CHRIST)

Sunday between November 20 and November 26

Ezekiel 34:11–16, 20–24   *(or Ezekiel 34:11–16, 20–24*   Ephesians 1:15–23
Psalm 100   *Psalm 95:1–7a)*   Matthew 25:31–46

CALL TO WORSHIP

> Come, God is seeking to gather us together.
> Like a shepherd searching for lost sheep, God calls us.
> > **Something or someone has summoned us here.**
> > **Dare we believe that God knows and welcomes us?**
> God reaches out to rescue all who have strayed.
> Scattered, weak, and injured ones are drawn to God.
> > **We come, in need of healing, seeking a blessing.**
> > **Our faith draws us here, in spite of our doubts.**
> Come, above all else, to worship and give thanks.
> Make a joyful noise to the Creator of all worlds.
> > **God's steadfast love becomes real to us here.**
> > **We are reminded of God's immeasurable greatness.**

INVOCATION

We come with gladness, loving God, drawn by our need and by a desire to praise you and give thanks. Enlighten the eyes of our hearts that we may be full of hope. Enlarge the circle of our concern that we may see the stranger as next of kin, the hungry person as part of our own family, the one who is sick as a whole individual deserving of our care. Grant us the presence of Christ that we may learn more fully to follow in the footsteps of Jesus. Amen.

CALL TO CONFESSION

God both loves and judges us. High standards are held before us, and God expects much of us. Where we have grown fat and lazy, God calls us to a more disciplined life. When we are tempted to forget those less fortunate than ourselves, God alerts us to make radical changes. Let us begin by recognizing our sin.

PRAYER OF CONFESSION

All-knowing God, you are aware of our comfort-seeking weakness. We ignore strangers in need as if they were no concern of ours. We resist programs that might threaten our privileges. We do only enough good to keep us from feeling guilty. We give grudgingly of our time and resources, instead of overflowing with thanksgiving and joyous sharing. We treat the church as our possession rather than letting Christ rule as head of the body. O God, we pray we have not wandered beyond your reach. Amen.

ASSURANCE OF FORGIVENESS

God says, I will judge between the fat sheep and the lean sheep, between the sheep who respond to the needs of others with compassion, and the goats who pretend that everything is fine. God judges because God loves, and we are invited to share in loving acts that reveal God's care. God is good and is faithful in steadfast love to all generations.

COLLECT

Eternal God, whose empire promises abundance for all and mutual caring, turn us away from indifference to the inequalities that grant to us advantages we enjoy, that we may see and serve those who are hungry, thirsty, ill-clothed, sick, persecuted, or shut out. We seek to be faithful to your rule of love, that together we might experience your gift of eternal life. Amen.

OFFERTORY INVITATION

The riches we enjoy grant to us an exciting opportunity to be generous and work for good. Through our offerings, we seek to share the good news, to bind up the injured, strengthen the weak, secure justice for the oppressed, and bring back those who have strayed. Join in this venture as we present our gifts.

OFFERTORY PRAYER

God of steadfast love, receive these expressions of our thanks for the glorious inheritance entrusted to us. We hereby enlist ourselves and our resources toward the realization of your eternal purpose for all humanity. May this congregation become more and more a source of hope for each of us and for all we meet. Amen.

COMMISSION AND BLESSING

Go forth in faith, with love for all the saints.
Open your eyes to see the good in all you meet.
>   *We believe that God is empowering our ministry.*
>   *God's love enables us to love even in difficult times.*
Among God's gifts is a spirit of wisdom and revelation.
God grants insight and resources to be helpful to others.
>   *Reaching out to people in need is a service to Christ.*
>   *We want to treat others as part of God's family.*
We partake of eternal life through our caring.
We sense life's meaning in the midst of our sharing.
>   *God's steadfast love inspires our risk-taking service.*
>   *God's faithfulness to us evokes our generosity.*
Amen. **Amen.**

(See hymn 95.)

SPECIAL DAYS

ALL SAINTS' DAY

November 1 or First Sunday in November

Revelation 7:9–17	1 John 3:1–3
Psalm 34:1–10, 22	Matthew 5:1–12

CALL TO WORSHIP

Come, all who hunger and thirst for truth.
Come to experience God's presence in community.
> **We have been called together as children of God.**
> **What we may grow to become is not yet revealed.**

Look to God with joy and radiant expectation.
Delight in songs of praise and exaltation.
> **God hears our cries and saves us from troubles.**
> **God delivers us from all our fears.**

Taste and know the Creator's goodness.
Take refuge in the One who supplies all you need.
> **God is present with us here and everywhere we go.**
> **May our worship here inspire continuing praise.**

INVOCATION

As we gather in this place, we join with all your saints in every time and place, O God, to celebrate salvation. You heal the brokenness within and among us. You rescue us from the cruelty we impose on one another amid our doubts and fears and frantic scrambling for attention. Help us in these moments to know your Spirit surrounding us, to sense your love embracing us, to realize your goodness, empowering us for joyous service. Blessing and glory, wisdom and thanksgiving, honor, power, and might be to you, O God, forever and ever. Amen.

CALL TO CONFESSION

To be called saints evokes in us knowledge of the many ways we fall short of that title. Today we are summoned to the throne of God to give account to the One who knows us better than we know ourselves. We come to be purified and made whole.

PRAYER OF CONFESSION

Saving God, save us from ourselves. Rescue us from the fears that keep us from following where Jesus leads or trusting in your guidance. We have not hungered and thirsted for righteousness. We have not been pure in heart or humble-minded. We do not risk an unpopular witness or step bravely into the role of peacemaker. Our words and deeds do not praise you. Our worship lacks passion and conviction. We seek you now, O God. Redeem your children and fill us with the radiance of your self-giving love. Amen.

Assurance of Forgiveness

The realm of God is among us, and we are welcomed to experience its rewards here and now. Our Creator guides us to springs of living water, inviting us to quench our thirst. God feeds our hungers and wipes the tears from our eyes. O magnify God with me and let us exalt God's name forever. God redeems the lives of all who serve. Those who find refuge in God are purified and made whole. Sing praise to the Spirit in whom we live and move and have our being.

Collect

God of the prophets and the saints, whose presence comforts and challenges and empowers, bless us here with a thirst for your truth, an openness to your leading, and true compassion for all your people, that with radiant faces we may carry the good news of salvation among all your people, leading a chorus of praise and thanksgiving that honors you moment by moment, day by day. Amen.

Offertory Invitation

Our finest offering is our attention, moment by moment and day by day, to God's purposes for our world. We join our constant efforts to be faithful with these weekly moments of giving that celebrate the love with which God surrounds us. We are God's children, committed to caring for all of God's creation.

Offertory Prayer

We worship you night and day, gracious God, in the temple of your universe. So vast is your reality that our minds cannot comprehend, yet your presence is so real that we cannot help but rejoice. You are our refuge and deliverer and our hope for all eternity. May our offerings welcome many to the abundance of your love and move them to join with us in proclaiming, "Blessing and glory and wisdom and thanksgiving and honor and power and might be to our God forever and ever! Amen."

Commission and Blessing

Rejoice in the Sovereign and magnify God's name.
Let your worship continue night and day.
We will bless God at all times.
Praise will fill our mouths continually.
We are joined by people of every nation and tongue.
Let us celebrate the diversity of our gifts.
We rejoice in our kinship with all God's children.
Each of us has a contribution to make.
See what love God is pouring out on all of us!
We are being purified in the image of Christ.
We are blessed as saints of God.
We are learning daily to claim our identity.
Amen. **Amen.**

(See hymn 96.)

All Saints' Day   165

THANKSGIVING DAY

Fourth Thursday in November—U.S.

Second Monday in October—Canada

Deuteronomy 8:7–18   2 Corinthians 9:6–15
Psalm 34:1–10, 22   Luke 17:11–19

CALL TO WORSHIP

Bless God for the good land we have been given.
Praise God, who crowns the year with abundance.
> *We are thankful for the bounty we have enjoyed.*
> *God has been good to us through another year.*

God chooses to love us and draw us near.
God invites us to enjoy the good all around us.
> *We are grateful for food, shelter, and family.*
> *God enriches our lives with many opportunities.*

Let us renew our vows to God in this hour.
May thanksgiving overflow in acts of kindness.
> *We are here to remember and find renewal.*
> *We have come to listen to God's word.*

INVOCATION

Generous God, you are present in all times and places; capture our attention in this time and place. Open our eyes to see the wonders you provide. Open our ears to hear your commandments, your ordinances, and your statutes. Open our hearts to care deeply about people in need, whatever that need might be. Awaken our generosity and sense of justice, that we may be inspired to helpful action. Open our mouths to shout and sing together for joy, sharing the good news of salvation. Amen.

CALL TO CONFESSION

Amid the blessings God has provided, we are tempted to exalt ourselves rather than thank the Creator. We begin to think that we alone are responsible for our good fortune. In prosperous times, we are less than thankful, and in adversity we feel alienated from the source of help. Let us confront our sin.

PRAYER OF CONFESSION

O God, to whom all flesh can come and find acceptance, we bring our unfaithfulness, seeking to renew our awareness of you in every moment of every day. We confess our deeds of iniquity: our forgetfulness of your love, our unkindness to your children, our misuse of the bodies and minds you entrust to us. Despite your generosity, we have sowed sparingly for the sake of others. O God, we need your forgiveness. Awaken our thankfulness as we learn to fully appreciate all you have provided. Amen.

Assurance of Forgiveness

God offers deliverance from the bondage of our transgressions. When we are open to the Eternal One, we realize that God goes with us through the wastelands of life's calamities. God leads us out of the wilderness to find hope and profound joy. Accept the gifts God is giving you.

Collect

Healing God, whose mercy in Jesus Christ is still available to us today, may our lives aspire to the wholeness you offer, daily giving thanks in word and deed for the opportunities you afford us and for the generosity of your abundant grace, that our witness may be a force for good among your people, as we join together in praising you. Amen.

Offertory Invitation

Our generous offerings are a fitting response to a generous God, who has provided to us, in abundance, so many blessings. We are reminded that those who sow sparingly will also reap sparingly, and those who sow bountifully will also reap bountifully. Let us be joyous givers.

Offertory Prayer

For food and water, for all the blessings of the land you have given us, for family and friends who enrich our lives, our hearts overflow with thanksgiving to you, O God. We have been sheltered and educated and empowered by your generosity. In Jesus Christ, we have been shown a way to the wholeness you intend for us. Receive these offerings as a joyous expression of our gratitude. Amen.

Commission and Blessing

Go on your way, traveling by God's way.
Your trust in God is making you whole.
> *We have been cleansed and healed by God's mercy.*
> *In Christ, our broken lives are restored to wholeness.*
Be as generous with others as God is generous with you.
Share your abundant blessings with all in need.
> *Giving for others is a profound joy and privilege.*
> *We will seek ways to honor those whom we help.*
Share the gospel through your ministry of thanksgiving.
Sustain your fellow saints with gifts and prayers.
> *We live in covenant with God and one another.*
> *May God be praised in our work and in our prayers.*
Amen. **Amen.**

(See hymns 97, 98.)

Thanksgiving Day   167

Related Hymns

THE ADVENT SEASON

1

We Are Glad

First Sunday of Advent
Lavon Bayler

8.7.8.7.7.7.8.8.
(Psalm 42)

We are glad to stand before you,
Giving thanks this holy day.
You have called us all together,
Gracious God, to teach your way.
We shall turn our swords to plows,
For our God no spear allows.
Nations shall not fight each other,
Greeting all as sister, brother.

Peace shall be the mood within us,
Peace uniting all with each,
As we follow paths of justice,
People's common good to reach.
Lead us by your light, we pray,
That we may your Word obey.
May salvation draw us nearer;
Christ will come to make life clearer.

No one knows when Christ's appearing
Will be realized again.
Yet, Christ calls us to awaken,
Ready for that promised reign.
Quarrels shall be put away
As we honor Christ each day.
Linked in ways no thief can sever,
We will live in love, together.

(Psalm 122, Isaiah 2:1–5, Matthew 24:36–44, Romans 13:11–14)

(See *Fresh Winds of the Spirit*, p. 136, and *Fresh Winds, Book 2*, p. 160.)

2

Sing Your Praise

Second Sunday of Advent
Lavon Bayler

7.6.7.6. Refrain
(Royal Oak)

Refrain:
Sing your praise to God today,
Whose glory fills the earth.
Celebrate God's righteous way,
That brings new life to birth.

From Jesse's root emerges
One who in God delights.
The light of love converges
On all whom God invites.
Refrain

The poor are judged with kindness;
The meek are lifted high.
God's justice routs the blindness
That we still justify.
Refrain

The wolf and lamb together,
The leopard and the kid,
Released from hatred's tether,
Find peace none can forbid.
Refrain

Come, wondrous God, among us,
Deliverance to proclaim.
Then, faithful and courageous,
May we make love our aim.
Refrain

(Psalm 72:1–7, 18–19, Isaiah 11:1–10)

(See *Fresh Winds of the Spirit*, pp. 136–37, and *Fresh Winds, Book 2*, pp. 160–61.)

3

Remember Former Days

Second Sunday of Advent
Lavon Bayler

6.6.8.6. (S.M. Refrain)
(Marion)

Remember former days
When God was glorified,
When we were called to harmony
In Christ, the crucified.
    Know joy and peace
    And hope that God supplies.

God's promises are sure,
And meant for all to hear.
The Spirit comes to all who seek
To know that God is near.
    Know joy and peace
    And hope that God supplies.

Repent, God's realm is here.
A voice prepares the way.
Extend God's hospitality,
And bear good fruit today.
    Know joy and peace
    And hope that God supplies.

The servant Christ inspires
Our service in Christ's name.
Praise God, who grants us power to serve
And sets our hearts aflame.
    Know joy and peace
    And hope that God supplies.

(Matthew 3:1–12, Romans 15:4–13)

4

Good News Has Come

Third Sunday of Advent
Lavon Bayler

11.10.11.9.
(Russian Hymn)

Good news has come to us; good news is coming:
One who brings healing, with gladness and joy,
Sight to the blind, and for many new hearing.
God's work of justice may none destroy.

Trust in the One who bears food for the hungry,
Freedom for prisoners and hope for the poor.
God lifts the fallen, those worried and trembling,
Easing their fears, that they might endure.

God changes everything: waters the deserts,
Transforms our values, invites us to live.
No more shall riches entice or enslave us;
Mercy and kindness we seek to give.

Grant us, Almighty One, quiet endurance,
Patience to deal with the troubles we face.
Strengthen weak hands and enliven our spirits,
That we your realm may at last embrace. Amen.

(Psalm 146:5–10, Isaiah 35:1–10, Matthew 11:2–11, Luke 1:47–55,
James 5:7–10)

(See *Fresh Winds of the Spirit,* p. 137, and *Fresh Winds, Book 2,* pp. 161–62.)

5

Restore Us, God

Fourth Sunday of Advent
Lavon Bayler

8.8.8.8. (L.M.)
(Canonbury)

Restore us, God; let your face shine
On people long weighed down with fears.
Show us a sign of your intent;
Awaken hope and dry our tears.

Give ear, O Shepherd, to your flock;
Stir up your might, and come to save.
We need your healing presence here,
With love that triumphs o'er the grave.

God, hear the prayers we offer now
Amid the evil of our day.
The promise of Emmanuel
Emboldens us to choose your way.

The mystery of your Word made flesh,
In humble birth through common folks,
Arouses wonder once again,
And awe, before new life, evokes.

Restore us, God; let your face shine
Upon your people gathered here.
May we reclaim the simple joy
That comes with knowing you are near. Amen.

(Psalm 80:1–7, 17–19, Isaiah 7:10–16)

(See *Fresh Winds of the Spirit*, pp. 137–38, *Fresh Winds, Book 2*, p. 163, and *Led by Love*, p. 179.)

6

We're Called to Faith

Fourth Sunday of Advent   8.6.8.6. (C.M.D.)
Lavon Bayler   (Ellacombe)

We're called to faith that dreams and dares
Believe God's promises,
That welcomes God's surprising grace,
That stops and notices.
O save us, God, from judging those
We do not understand.
May we respond with love and care
That helps another stand.

We're called as servants and as saints,
Apostles of the Lord,
Whose birth in us is immanent
If we believe the Word.
O help us, God, to overcome
The fears that hold us back,
Our selfishness and cowardice.
Grant courage that we lack.

We're called to listen and obey,
To live with faithfulness,
Empowered by resurrection hope
To grow in holiness.
O God, assist us to belong
To Jesus Christ today,
To join the company of saints
Who live your peaceful way. Amen.

(Matthew 1:18–25, Romans 1:1–7)

(See *Fresh Winds of the Spirit*, pp. 137–38, *Fresh Winds, Book 2*, p. 163, and *Led by Love*, p. 179.)

THE CHRISTMAS SEASON

7

Sing a New Song

Christmas Day (Proper I)—A, B, C
Lavon Bayler

6.6.4.6.6.6.4.
(Italian Hymn)

Sing a new song to God,
Blessing God's holy name.
Sing all the earth.
Honor and majesty,
Strength, beauty, honesty:
These in your love we see,
Singing your worth.

You give us light and joy,
As justice comes to reign.
Hail, mighty God,
Wonderful counselor,
Peace-bringing chancellor,
Help us as we explore
Ways Jesus trod.

You judge with equity;
Your righteousness is sure.
No idol stands.
Trembling, we face our sin,
Claiming our origin.
Let life in Christ begin
As love expands. Amen.

(Psalm 96, Isaiah 9:2–7)

(See *Fresh Winds of the Spirit*, p. 139; *Fresh Winds, Book 2*, pp. 164–65; *Led by Love*, p. 178; and *Gathered by Love*, pp. 180–81.)

8

Lying in a Manger

Christmas (Propers I, II)—A, B, C
Lavon Bayler

7.7.7.7.7.7.
(Toplady)

Lying in a manger low,
Child of God, we sense love's glow.
Flowing from your humble birth,
Bringing hope and joy to earth.
May the fruit of Mary's womb
Find within our hearts a room.

Shepherds watching flocks by night,
Looking up, behold a light.
Terrified and filled with awe,
They do not, in fear, withdraw.
As they hear the angels praise,
They respond without delays.

Go to Bethlehem with haste;
See how God this world has graced.
Let amazement conquer doubt
As you live by faith devout.
Ponder in your mind and heart
Treasures God will yet impart.

Like the shepherds, we have heard
Angel songs and prophet's word.
We believe salvation's song,
Bringing hope and crushing wrong.
Christ has come amid our needs,
Calling us to godly deeds.

(Luke 2:1–20, Titus 2:11–14)

(See *Refreshing Rains of the Living Word,* p. 164; *Whispers of God,* pp. 162–63; and "Glory to God," *Gathered by Love,* p. 182.)

9

Let All Earth Rejoice

Christmas (Proper II)—A, B, C
Lavon Bayler

8.7.8.7.D.
(Austrian Hymn)

Let all earth rejoice together;
Righteousness and justice reign,
Not on thrones of garish splendor
But amid our human pain.
Listen to the angels singing,
Glory to our God on high,
Glory to the God among us,
Born that we may live, not die.

Through this baby comes salvation
Love to make us whole and free,
Fire to light the way of justice,
Goodness and integrity.
Shepherds in the fields abiding
Heard the news and rushed to see
In a stable, 'mid discomfort,
God enshrined in infancy.

All are welcome at the manger,
Called to holiness and peace.
Leave behind all worthless idols;
Let your selfish striving cease.
Know again God's loving-kindness,
Bringing lives to grand rebirth.
Let the Spirit bless you richly.
Let your praise fill all the earth.

(Psalm 97, Isaiah 62:6–12, Luke 2:1–20, Titus 3:4–7)

(See *Fresh Winds of the Spirit*, p. 140; *Fresh Winds, Book 2*, p. 165; *Whispers of God*, pp. 163–64; *Refreshing Rains of the Living Word*, p. 165; *Led by Love*, p. 180; and *Gathered by Love*, pp. 183–84.)

10

In the Beginning

Christmas (Proper III)—A, B, C
    Lavon Bayler

10.4.10.4.10.10.
(Sanden)

In the beginning was the Word of God,
The Word of life.
That word was in the paths that Jesus trod,
Confronting strife.
All things received their being and delight
Through Jesus Christ, who overcame the night.

When Jesus came to share our common lot,
There was no room.
People in power offered Christ no spot
Except a tomb.
Yet, some who listened understood God's grace
Within the truth that angel songs embrace.

Wickedness falls before God's glorious throne,
Throughout each year.
In Jesus Christ, God's being will be known
To all who hear.
Sing a new song to hail God's victory
And righteous judgments made with equity.

With joyful noise, we sing salvation's song,
And join in praise,
Sensing the power that overcomes the wrong
That marks our days.
Hills sing together; waters clap their hands
Before the light in which our Savior stands.

(Psalm 98, Isaiah 52:7–10, John 1:1–14, Hebrews 1:1–12)

(See *Fresh Winds of the Spirit*, pp. 140–41; *Fresh Winds, Book 2*, p. 166; *Whispers of God*, p. 164; *Refreshing Rains of the Spirit*, p. 166; *Gathered by Love*, pp. 185–86; and *Led by Love*, p. 181.)

11

So Soon after Christmas

First Sunday after Christmas
Lavon Bayler

11.11.11.11.
(Muller)

So soon after Christmas the terror begins
As joy turns to sorrow before Herod's sins.
Afraid of a rival to threaten his throne,
He strikes out at infants, as strangers, unknown.

When Joseph encounters a dream in the night,
The family responds and to Egypt takes flight.
God's saving grace calls for an exodus new
That ends human bondage with love strong and true.

We weep for the children whom Herod destroyed
And robbed of a life because he was annoyed.
We weep for the homeless with no place to stay,
Who wander the streets of our cities today.

"God-with-us" in Jesus, let violence end;
Bring justice to earth as you visit again.
Let meaningless suffering be with us no more;
May innocent children be spared, we implore.

Praise God, all the earth, for the hope that Christ brings
As still, through our darkness, an angel voice sings:
Fear not! and be faithful though dangers abound,
For peace and fulfillment in Christ will be found.

(Psalm 148, Matthew 2:13–23)

(See *Fresh Winds, Book 2*, pp. 164, 167, 168.)

12

We Linger at the Manger

Holy Name (January 1)—A, B, C
Lavon Bayler

8.6.8.6. (C.M.)
(Amazing Grace)

We linger at the manger bed,
Still wondering at the sight
Of strangers worshiping a child
With such amazed delight.

God sent to earth this child of love.
That we might love receive.
No longer slaves, but heirs through hope,
We, in Christ's name, believe.

How shall we glorify and praise
The God who sent this light,
Whose vast creation testifies
To wondrous power and might?

So full of majesty and grace
Is God's name on the earth!
We celebrate God's glory here
And marvel at our worth.

God names us stewards over all
The works that Love has made,
The vast resources of the earth
Before our eyes displayed.

We bow in awe that God would bless
And keep us every day.
With graciousness and confidence
And peace along our way.

(Numbers 6:22–27, Psalm 8, Luke 2:15–21, Galatians 4:4–7)

(See *Fresh Winds of the Spirit,* p. 145; *Fresh Winds, Book 2,* p. 171; *Whispers of God,* p. 167; *Refreshing Rains of the Spirit,* pp. 168–70; *Gathered by Love,* p. 192; and *Led by Love,* p. 183.)

13

O God of Strength

New Year's Day (January 1)—A, B, C
Lavon Bayler

7.6.7.6.D.
(Angel's Story)

O God of strength and mercy,
O sovereign majesty,
We look upon the heavens,
Your glory there to see.
The moon and stars proclaim you,
And distant galaxies
Announce your vast dominion
And fire our fantasies.

What worth are human beings
Amid this vast display?
Why make your home among us
When we deny your way?
Yet earth and all within it
Are placed within the hands
Of people you have trusted
As stewards of your lands.

May we, in every season
Take pleasure in our toil,
Enjoying tasks God gives us
Each day without recoil.
We feed and clothe the needy,
Their welfare to pursue,
And strangers are as family
When God makes all things new.

(Psalm 8, Ecclesiastes 3:1–13, Matthew 25:31–36, Revelation 21:1–6a)

(See *Gathered by Love*, pp. 189–91, and *Led by Love*, p. 184.)

14

God, Save Your People

Second Sunday after Christmas—A, B, C
Lavon Bayler

10.10.10.10.
(Ellers)

God, save your people, scattered through the earth.
Help us to know that you proclaim our worth.
In Jesus Christ, you sent your Word of life,
Lighting our pathway through this world of strife.

We have not seen you, yet our hearts believe,
Opening now your blessing to receive.
Make us your children, sharing in the grace,
Shown to humanity in Jesus' face.

Jesus proclaimed your truth in Word-made-flesh;
Let now that Word enlighten and refresh
Your gathered people, raising songs of praise.
Hear our rejoicing as we learn your ways.

Grant us your peace, O Shepherd of the flock.
You are our joy, our fortress and our rock.
We gain from you the strength we need each day,
As in the name of Christ we humbly pray.

Filled by the Spirit, called to holiness,
We are commissioned, to your will express.
Grant us such insight to your mystery
That we may celebrate your sovereignty. Amen.

(Psalm 147:12–20, Jeremiah 31:7–14, John 1:1–18, Ephesians 1:3–14)

(See *Fresh Winds, Book 2*, pp. 172–73; *Whispers of God*, p. 167; *Refreshing Rains of the Living Word*, p. 170; *Gathered by Love*, p. 193; and *Led by Love*, p. 185.)

Epiphany and the Season Following

15

God's Grace Is Given

Epiphany—A, B, C
Lavon Bayler

8.6.8.6.D. (C.M.D.)
(Carol)

God's grace is given for you and me
That we might understand
The mystery of Jesus Christ
And have the faith to stand
Against oppression, violence,
And all that robs the poor
Of help they need to overcome
Injustice they endure.

In faithfulness, like seers of old,
We, by a star, are led
To worship at the manger crude
That served as Jesus' bed.
As sharers in the promises
Of Jesus' power to save,
We first accept the grace, and then
Give thanks for all Christ gave.

We're called as saints to share the news
With all of humankind,
To trust the dream that sends us out
To live as God designed.
Search for the wisdom that endures
With bold new confidence
That truth and justice will prevail
And all of life make sense.

(Psalm 72:1–7, 10–14, Isaiah 60:1–6, Matthew 2:1–12, Ephesians 3:1–12)

(See appendixes of previous books of lectionary resources for other Epiphany hymns.)

Related Hymns

16

Baptized and Accepted

First Sunday after Epiphany (Baptism of Jesus)
Lavon Bayler

12.11.12.11.
(Kremser)

"Baptized and accepted," our God sends this message:
Beloved, receive now the gift of new life.
My love will come with you through each dangerous passage,
To keep you from fainting, protect you in strife.

You will not be broken, though bruised and afflicted.
You will not be harmed as for justice you seek.
I called you to righteousness; be not restricted
In offering my love as you reach out and speak.

You must understand, God is truly impartial.
No one is excluded by age, race, or creed.
So carry God's light with all strength you can marshal
To brighten the pathway for others in need.

As covenant people we're given a mission:
To open closed eyes that God's children may see,
To offer release to those held in submission
To devil's and idols' false sovereignty.

Fulfill now the righteousness God has intended
For all who are chosen to bear Jesus' name.
Let all who in Christ have been saved and befriended,
Find ways to bear witness, enjoying Love's claim.

(Psalm 29, Isaiah 42:1–9, Matthew 3:13–17, Acts 10:34–43)

(See *Fresh Winds of the Spirit*, pp. 146–47.)

17

Children, Gather

First Sunday after Epiphany (Baptism of Jesus)   8.7.8.7.
                    Lavon Bayler   (Galilee)

Children, gather at the Jordan
Where God's healing waters flow.
From all nations, come together,
That forgiveness you may know.

Come in awe that we're accepted,
When in Jesus' name we meet.
Hear the message of salvation
That your peace may be complete.

Know the Holy Spirit's power,
Here descending like a dove
On the newly baptized Christian,
Object of the Savior's love.

We remember we were baptized
In the holy triune name:
Parent, Child, and Holy Spirit,
God on us has made love's claim.

We are known, beloved, commissioned
For our service day by day.
We are called to witness boldly
By our lives, in every way.

(Matthew 3:13–17, Acts 10:34–43)

(See *Fresh Winds, Book 2,* p. 174.)

18

Called as the Church

Second Sunday after Epiphany
Lavon Bayler

6.4.6.4.D.
(Bread of Life)

Called as the church to be
Servants and saints,
May we respond, O God,
Without restraints,
As the Anointed One,
Whose name we raise,
Leads us each day and sets
Our hearts ablaze.

Spirit, descend again,
That we may feel
Your presence changing us
As you reveal
Where your Anointed One
Still can be found,
Among disciples who
With joy abound.

Thank you for grace and peace,
Gifts from your hand,
That give us strength to serve
And faith to stand.
We are enriched in love,
Knowledge and speech,
That we, in deed and word,
Your way may teach. Amen.

(John 1:29–42, 1 Corinthians 1:1–9)

(See *Fresh Winds of the Spirit,* p. 147, and *Fresh Winds, Book 2,* p. 175.)

19

God, You Have Given

Third Sunday after Epiphany
Lavon Bayler

6.6.8.6.D. (S.M.D.)
(Diademata)

God, you have given light
To guide us on our way.
Salvation is your gift of grace
For which we daily pray.
How can we be afraid,
Relying on your strength?
Whom shall we fear when you are near,
Throughout life's breadth and length?

You, God, have given joy
To those who seek your face.
Your beauty moves our hearts to praise
In this, your dwelling place.
In temples we have built,
In temples deep within,
We worship you whose love has freed
Our hearts and minds from sin.

One thing we ask of you,
And this we gladly seek:
To live within your realm each day,
To serve you week by week.
God, teach us how to live,
Rejoicing every hour,
That we may show to all the world
Your deep transforming power. Amen.

(Psalm 27:1, 4–9, Isaiah 9:1–4)

(See *Fresh Winds of the Spirit*, p. 148, and *Fresh Winds, Book 2*, p. 176.)

20

Welcome the Savior

Third Sunday after Epiphany
Lavon Bayler

5.5.6.5.6.5.6.5. Ref.
(Judas Maccabeus)

Welcome the Savior;
Gather in Christ's name.
Turn from deepest darkness;
Shout your glad acclaim.
Know God's realm is coming;
Christ has brought us near.
Pour out your repentance;
There is naught to fear.

Refrain:
Follow the Savior;
Go to share good news.
Let Christ's healing presence
All your life infuse.

Baptized and summoned,
We declare to all,
What the world calls foolish,
Faith declared by Paul:
Jesus' cross holds power
That transforms and saves
We are called as servants,
Freed from what enslaves.
Refrain

Jesus brings healing
For the sick and lost,
Pouring out his life blood,
Counting not the cost.
Listen to the message:
Christ has made us one.
Overcome divisions;
Live as Christ has done.
Refrain

(Matthew 4:12–23, 1 Corinthians 1:10–18)

21

Rejoice, O Hills

Fourth Sunday after Epiphany
Lavon Bayler

9.8.9.8.
(St. Clement)

Rejoice, O hills, that God has blessed us.
Give thanks, O mountains lifted high.
God's foolishness is meant to test us.
God's wisdom calls for our reply.

We dare to take the cross as banner,
Though stumbling block to some it be.
We turn away from evil slander
To know again Love's purity.

We bring to God our zeal for justice,
And offer our humility.
May we be kind to all who trust us,
That they Christ's sacrifice may see.

May all who mourn be given comfort,
And all who hunger be fulfilled.
Let righteousness and humble effort
Build lasting peace that you have willed.

Rejoicing, we are filled with gladness,
As Christ's disciples, called and blessed.
God's comfort wipes away our sadness
And offers us a blessed rest.

(Psalm 15, Micah 6:1–8, Matthew 5:1–12, I Corinthians 1:18–31)

(See *Fresh Winds of the Spirit,* pp. 148–49, and *Fresh Winds, Book 2,* pp. 177–78.)

22

We Humble Ourselves

Fifth Sunday after Epiphany
Lavon Bayler

10.10.11.11.
(Hanover)

We humble ourselves; we fast and we pray.
Where are you, O God? We need you today.
Our voices implore you to show us your way.
We ask you to notice the faith we display.

We seek to be salt that brings out the taste
Of life at its best, discerned and embraced.
We long for the light that permits us to be
A beacon of hope, that your servants may see.

Oh help us obey commandments you give
That guide and empower and teach us to live,
No longer for self, but that nations may find
True justice and freedom for all humankind.

You visit us when we share broken bread
In ritual feast or from tables spread
To welcome the homeless, oppressed, and denied.
Our bones are made strong and our needs satisfied.

Your wisdom, O God, inspires us to see
Around us each day profound mystery.
In Christ crucified our salvation is sealed;
In gifts of the Spirit, your love is revealed. Amen.

(Psalm 112:1–10, Isaiah 58:1–12, Matthew 5:13–20,
1 Corinthians 2:11–16)

(See *Fresh Winds of the Spirit*, p. 149, and *Fresh Winds, Book 2*, pp. 179–80.)

Hymns for Epiphany and the Season Following

23

God of Judgment

Sixth Sunday after Epiphany
Lavon Bayler

7.7.7.7.
(Mercy)

God of judgment, truth, and grace,
Here we long to see your face.
Teach us what we need to know;
Send us forth your love to show.

You have taught us we must choose
Life or death, to love or lose.
Life is found when we obey;
Let not hearts be turned away.

Hate and falsehood you deplore.
Jealousy shall be no more.
Help us, God, to overcome
Ways that we are quarrelsome.

Not just acts but our intent.
Give us reason to repent.
Hear our prayers, O God of life.
Calm our fears and heal our strife.

When we're tempted, God, to stray,
Keep us in your wholesome way.
Fix our eyes on your commands.
To your work we set our hands.

We are ready, God, to grow.
Set our hearts and lives aglow.
May we reconcilers be,
Tuned to your eternity. Amen.

(Deuteronomy 30:15–20, Psalm 119:1–8, Matthew 5:21–37,
I Corinthians 3:1–9)

(See *Fresh Winds of the Spirit,* p. 150, and *Fresh Winds, Book 2,* pp. 181–82.)

Related Hymns

24

God of Holiness

Seventh Sunday after Epiphany
Lavon Bayler

6.5.6.5.6.6.6.5.
(St. Dunstan's)

God of all holiness,
Teach us, your servants,
How to be holy, too,
In love's observance.
Give understanding and
Help us to keep your law
That we may worship you
With life and death awe.

Confirm your promises
To those who fear you.
Keep us from vanities
That we may hear you:
Rain falls and sun will shine
On good and bad, all mine,
And you shall hate no one;
See in them my sign.

According to your grace,
We lay foundations
On which your church may build
Great expectations
For true community
That all your love may see
And honesty may mark
This place of safety. Amen.

(Leviticus 19:1–2, 9–18, Psalm 119:33–40, Matthew 5:38–48,
1 Corinthians 3:10–11, 16–23)

(See *Fresh Winds of the Spirit*, p. 151, and *Fresh Winds, Book 2*, pp. 183–84.)

25

You Are the One

Eighth Sunday after Epiphany
Lavon Bayler

8.8.8.8. (L.M.)
(Duke Street)

You are the One we seek to serve,
God, whose compassion none deserve.
Daily you answer when we call,
Comforting, judging great and small.

You feed the hungry, quench their thirst,
Though you have seen us at our worst.
No one escapes your watchful eye,
As you our deepest needs supply.

Barriers are overcome in you,
As, in your light, we see anew
Ways out of prisons we create,
To follow Christ in paths made straight.

We lift our hearts in songs of praise,
Pond'ring the myst'ry of your ways.
We are to be your covenant
To every humble supplicant.

Stewards of all that we possess,
We seek to use our wealth to bless
All those with whom this day we share,
Eager to show how much you care. Amen.

(Psalm 131, Isaiah 49:8–16a, Matthew 6:24–34, I Corinthians 4:1–5)

(See *Fresh Winds of the Spirit*, p. 152, and *Fresh Winds, Book 2*, p. 185.)

Related Hymns

26

Blest Be Our God

Ninth Sunday after Epiphany
Lavon Bayler

8.6.8.6.D. (C.M.D.)
(Forest Green)

Blest be our God, whose wondrous love
Sustains 'mid life's alarms,
Whose help is ever near at hand
To shelter us from harm.
In you we find a refuge strong,
O God of righteousness.
Our hearts take courage as you lead
Through all life's storms and stress.

Redeemed by you, O faithful God,
We join the saints in praise,
Rejoicing as we wait to hear
Your message for these days.
We will not turn from your commands,
Intending to obey.
The Word you lay upon our hearts
We will, in trust, display.

We'll write that Word on minds and souls;
We'll teach it to the young,
Until your will is recognized
By every heart and tongue.
As love awakens us each morn,
We'll thank you for the day,
And through its hours 'til we retire,
Remembering, we'll pray. Amen.

(Deuteronomy 11:18–21, 26–28, Psalm 31:1–5, 19–24)

(See *Fresh Winds, Book 2,* pp. 212–13.)

Hymns for Epiphany and the Season Following

27

Help Us Build

Ninth Sunday after Epiphany
Lavon Bayler

7.7.7.7.7.7.
(Dix)

Help us build upon the rock,
Not upon the shifting sands,
As the winds and rains of life
Draw us from your law's demands.
God, we put our faith in you,
Knowing you will see us through.

In the gospel we delight,
Thanking you for news that saves,
Sensing in love's healing power
Wholeness that each person craves.
We will never be ashamed,
Knowing we, by Christ, are named.

Justified by faith, not works,
We are given gifts of grace.
You, O God, forgive the sins
We are seeking to replace
With the righteousness you give,
That empowers us to live.

As we build communities
That embrace the love you teach
Grant, by Christ's authority,
That our work may ever reach
Helping hands to aid and bless
All your children in distress. Amen.

(Matthew 7:21–29, Romans 1:16–17, 3:22b–28 (29–31))

28

Let Your Day Dawn

Last Sunday after Epiphany (Transfiguration)
Lavon Bayler

8.7.8.7.D.
(Beach Spring)

Let your day dawn, gracious Savior,
On your people gathered here.
We would heed the prophet's message
As your morning stars appear.
Your commandments will instruct us,
And your word set hearts aflame.
May your glory reign among us
As we magnify your name.

To your holy mountain lead us
That your vision we may see.
Grant that we, as your disciples
May perceive your majesty.
Let us hear again the summons:
"This is my beloved one;
Listen now with all your senses.
Let my will in you be done."

Through the clouds and shadows, reach us
With your touch that calms our fear,
As your saints from other ages
Tell us you are ever near.
May our faces show the radiance
That we see, O Christ, in you.
We would share the joy that fills us
When our hearts to you are true. Amen.

(Exodus 24:12–18, Psalm 2, Matthew 17:1–9, 2 Peter 1:16–21)

THE LENTEN SEASON

29

God of Mercy

Ash Wednesday (A, B, C)
Lavon Bayler

7.8.7.8.7.7.
(Grosser Gott, Wir Loben Dich)

God of mercy, hear our cry.
Wash us; blot out our transgressions.
Cleanse from sin and purify
All who make sincere confession.
We return to you this day,
Weeping, fasting, as we pray.

You are gracious to forgive
Those who bow with contrite spirit.
By your wisdom, may we live,
Recognizing, as we hear it,
Truth and purpose you impart
Into each receptive heart.

Reconcile us through your grace
On this day of our salvation.
May we find, through your embrace,
Meaning in our tribulation.
In your service, we belong;
Bless our work, and keep us strong.

Teach us how to give our best,
Not for praise or recognition,
But because our lives are blessed
And we have but one ambition:
Finding our true home in you,
Trusting Love makes all things new. Amen.

(Psalm 51:1–17, Joel 2:1–2, 12–17, Matthew 6:1–6, 16–21,
2 Corinthians 5:20b–6:10)

(See *Fresh Winds of the Spirit*, p. 154; *Fresh Winds, Book 2*, p. 187; *Whispers of God*, p. 177; *Refreshing Rains of the Living Word*, p. 186; *Led by Love*, p. 202; and *Gathered by Love*, pp. 222–24.)

30

Our Hiding Place

First Sunday in Lent
Lavon Bayler

6.6.8.6. (S.M.)
(Lake Enon)

You are a hiding place
In trouble and distress.
Your love, O God, surrounds us here,
To comfort and to bless.

O help us, God, to face
Our dodging and deceit,
The ways we cloak iniquity
In self-disguised conceit.

We offer prayers to you,
Confessing sin and guilt.
You know evasions we have tried,
Excuses we have built.

We turn, in trust, to you,
Believing we can change
Our self-defeating tendencies
Through counsel you arrange.

We open hearts to you,
As you instruct and teach.
We ask you, God, to guide our thoughts,
Our actions and our speech.

We find true happiness
In knowing you forgive.
In true community with you,
We're learning how to live. Amen.

(Psalm 32)

(See *Fresh Winds of the Spirit*, p. 155, *Fresh Winds, Book 2*, p. 188, and *Refreshing Rains of the Living Word*, p. 187.)

31

We Lift Our Eyes

Second Sunday in Lent
Lavon Bayler

11.10.11.10.
(Ancient of Days)

We lift our eyes to hills in all their splendor,
Asking from where our help will come today.
Then we remember: God is our defender,
Ever creating, wonders to display.

God does not sleep, but watches as we slumber,
Keeping us strong through all our waking hours.
We need not fear the terrors that we number;
Nothing in life or death can match God's powers.

God of the ages, you have called your people,
Leading us forward, blessing us each day,
Shielding our lives and keeping us from evil
As we respond, your purpose to obey.

May we, like Abraham, believe your promise,
Daring to follow you in paths unknown.
We seek your help; be ever our accomplice
In kindly actions by which love is shown.

Not by our works, but by your grace supported,
We seek this day to grow in faith and trust.
You call us forth from death, and ways distorted,
Giving directions that are true and just. Amen.

(Genesis 12:1–4a, Psalm 121, Romans 4:1–5, 13–17)

(See *Fresh Winds of the Spirit*, p. 156, and *Fresh Winds, Book 2*, p. 189.)

32

We Seek Your Presence

Second Sunday in Lent
Lavon Bayler

6.6.8.6.D. (S.M.D.)
(Terra Beata)

We seek your presence, God,
While lifting up our eyes
Beyond our self-absorbed routines,
Above earth's merchandise.
We long to see the face
Of Jesus Christ today,
To hear again the messages
That point us to Love's way.

We worship you in awe
Before the One you sent,
To open eyes and challenge us
To ponder and repent.
May we be born anew,
To dwell within the light
That shines from Christ to give us life,
That will our souls ignite.

So send your wind, O God,
To blow among us here,
To whisper of your steadfast love
That wipes away our fear.
And free us to believe
The One who saves and heals.
That we in Jesus Christ may live
By all that Love reveals. Amen.

(Psalm 121, Matthew 17:1–9, John 3:1–17)

(If the transfiguration story in Matthew is being used today, see hymn 28.)

33

God, Hear Your People

Third Sunday in Lent
Lavon Bayler

8.8.8.8. (L.M.)
(Hamburg)

God, hear your people, gone astray.
Thirsty and tired, we turn to pray.
Give us a drink of waters pure
That we may faithfully endure.

Turn us away from loud complaints
And from our surging doubt's restraints.
Help us to trust the offer made
Of living water Christ displayed.

Then, justified by faith, not deeds,
We'll know the peace that meets our needs.
Touched by your grace, in which we stand,
We'll feel the blessing of your hand.

Then, though we suffer, we'll endure,
Learning to trust your promise sure.
In Jesus Christ, we're reconciled,
Loved and forgiven, not reviled.

Come, let us make a joyful noise
That all our energy employs,
Singing to God our songs of praise,
In truth and spirit all our days. Amen.

(Exodus 17:1–7, Psalm 95, John 4:5–42, Romans 5:1–11)

(See *Fresh Winds of the Spirit*, pp. 156–57, and *Fresh Winds, Book 2*, pp. 190–92.)

Related Hymns

34

Jesus, Lend Your Light

Fourth Sunday in Lent
Lavon Bayler

7.7.7.7.7.7.
(Redhead 76)

Jesus, lend the world your light.
Open our unseeing eyes.
May we know the gift of sight
That your healing touch supplies.
Then, through insights we receive,
Help us deeply to believe.

We confess our narrow view,
Swayed by prejudice and sin.
Seeing handsomeness and hue,
We can miss the heart within.
When we judge so hastily,
We may not your glory see.

Guide us in the paths you choose,
Gracious Shepherd, Leader, Friend,
When we're tempted to confuse
Our delights with tests you send.
Lead us through our doubt and fear
By your mercy, ever near.

Bring us to discipleship
That discerns your truth each day.
Then, by brave apostleship,
May we boldly serve your way,
Daring to obey your will,
Your high purpose to fulfill. Amen.

(1 Samuel 16:1–13, Psalm 23, John 9:1–41, Ephesians 5:8–14)

(See *Fresh Winds of the Spirit,* pp. 158, 169, 191–92, and *Fresh Winds, Book 2,* pp. 193, 262–63.)

35

We Cry from Valleys

Fifth Sunday in Lent
Lavon Bayler

7.6.7.6.D.
(Aurelia)

We cry from shadowed valleys,
Dried up, in deep despair.
O God, we have forgotten
Your steadfast love and care.
Our minds, so set on riches,
This mortal life can win,
Are hostile to your law, and
Forget our origin.

O God, we wait upon you,
Attentive to your voice.
Come, lift us from our graves and
Restore to us the choice
Of following the Savior
In paths of righteousness.
We feel your hand upon us,
Intent to save and bless.

Released from death's dominion,
Unbound, revived, set free,
We rise, by God's forgiveness,
From our iniquity.
Your winds, O God, blow through us,
Removing stains of sin,
And we discover life when
Your Spirit dwells within. Amen.

(Psalm 130, Ezekiel 37:1–14, John 11:1–45, Romans 8:6–11)

(See *Fresh Winds of the Spirit*, p. 159, *Fresh Winds, Book 2*, pp. 194–95, and *Whispers of God*, p. 196.)

36

Raise High Your Branches

Palm/Passion Sunday
Lavon Bayler

8.6.8.6. (C.M.)
(Azmon)

Raise high your branches; shout your praise,
Our Savior to adore.
Sing loud hosannas; fill your days
With thanks forevermore.

Our Savior comes on borrowed beast,
In true humility,
Among the greatest and the least
With love's nobility.

As gates of welcome open wide,
We come in Jesus' name.
The One whom hatred crucified
Releases us from shame.

The Stone, rejected, has become
An anchor in life's storms.
The Savior, killed as troublesome,
Redeems us and transforms.

Fulfill in us, each day we live,
Your gracious promises,
Poured out, O God, that we might give
Through loving practices. Amen.

(Psalm 118:1–2, 19–29, Matthew 21:1–11)

(See *Fresh Winds of the Spirit*, p. 159, and *Fresh Winds, Book 2*, p. 197.)

37

God, Be Gracious

Passion/Palm Sunday
Lavon Bayler

7.7.7.7.7.7.
(Dix)

God, be gracious; hear us now,
In our great distress and grief.
In humility, we bow,
Sorrowing in disbelief.
How could we betray a friend?
This is not what we intend.

As disciples long ago
Vowed to follow, even die,
When they heard the rooster crow,
Knew they had no alibi,
We, like them, the Christ deny,
And our Savior crucify.

We, who share the cup and bread,
Still forget to watch and pray.
Taught and baptized, blessed and fed,
We have turned from Jesus' way.
God, we trust your saving power.
Come, transform us in this hour.

Lead us from the tombs of death,
Where our good intentions lie.
Raise us up and give new breath,
That our lives may testify
To your steadfast love and grace,
Reaching out through time and space. Amen.

(Psalm 31:9–16, Isaiah 50:4–9a, Matthew 26:14–27:66,
Philippians 2:5–11)

(See *Fresh Winds of the Spirit*, p. 160, and *Fresh Winds, Book 2*, pp. 196–97.)

38

Christ Leads Us Forward

Monday of Holy Week (A, B, C)
Lavon Bayler

10.10.10.10.
(Eventide)

Christ leads us forward through this holy week,
Bearing God's love and justice toward the cross,
Revealing light from God to all who seek
Truth and salvation in the midst of loss.

Christ comes as servant to our troubled earth,
Teaching the ways that God would have us live,
Calling for righteousness to match the worth
God has proclaimed in us and vows to give.

Christ mediates the covenant made new,
Off'ring redemption that forgives and frees,
Opening eyes to see the larger view
That looks beyond another's frailties.

Christ helps us honor one another's gifts,
Keeping us safe and granting confidence
To share a faith that quietly uplifts,
Drawing from all their highest excellence.

Christ bids us join the feast that God provides,
As we prepare to journey toward the light
Of Easter morning, where our hope abides.
May we in faithful, joyous praise unite.

(Psalm 36:5–11, Isaiah 42:1–9, John 12:1–11, Hebrews 9:11–15)

(See *Whispers of God*, p. 183; *Refreshing Rains of the Living Word*, p. 194; *Gathered by Love*, p. 239; and *Led by Love*, p. 212.)

39

O God, Our Hope

Tuesday of Holy Week (A, B, C)
Lavon Bayler

8.8.8.8.6.
(St. Margaret)

O God, our hope, receive our praise.
We put our faith and trust in you.
Walk with us through these evil days.
That we, with Christ, may keep our gaze
On what is right and true.

Our souls are troubled as we flee
The cross of suffering and shame.
Your love, rejected on the tree,
Gives strength the foolish cannot see,
That we, in Christ, may claim.

We thank you, God, that though we're weak,
You choose to call us to the light.
You are the source of life we seek.
You give us courage as we speak,
And set our hearts aright.

We want to follow and to serve,
To bear good fruit in Jesus' name,
To spend our strength without reserve,
That scoffing doubters may observe
Love's power that we proclaim. Amen.

(Psalm 71:1–14, Isaiah 49:1–7, John 12:20–36, 1 Corinthians 1:18–31)

(See *Whispers of God*, p. 184; *Refreshing Rains of the Living Word*, p. 194; *Gathered by Love*, pp. 240–41; and *Led by Love*, p. 213.)

40

Witnesses Surround Us

Wednesday of Holy Week (A, B, C)
Lavon Bayler

6.5.6.5.D
(King's Weston)

Witnesses surround us
In this holy week,
As we, sins confessing,
Hope and courage seek.
Shadows of betrayal
Haunt us on our way.
Keep us from dishonor,
Jesus Christ, we pray.

With your perseverance,
May we run the race
That is yet before us,
As you set the pace.
Pioneering Jesus,
Faith's perfecter strong,
May we never weary
Though the way is long.

Every day, awaken
Eyes and ears and mind,
That we may be faithful,
Sensitive and kind.
Christ, by your example,
May we share and teach.
Help us in our serving
Many lives to reach. Amen.

(Psalm 70, Isaiah 50:4–9a, John 13:21–32, Hebrews 12:1–5)

(See *Whispers of God*, p. 184; *Refreshing Rains of the Living Word*, p. 195; *Gathered by Love*, p. 242; and *Led by Love*, p. 214.)

41

So Precious in God's Sight

Holy Thursday (A, B, C)
Lavon Bayler

6.7.6.7.6.6.6.6.
(Darmstadt)

So precious in God's sight
Is Jesus Christ, our Savior.
In life and death, our Lord
Most surely knew God's favor.
Yet still he faced a cross,
Betrayal by a friend,
Denial, scorn, and loss,
With no one to defend.

We, by God's bounty blessed,
Awakened, taught, and grateful,
Are called to follow Christ
And challenged to be faithful.
We, too, may need to face
Resistance to Love's way,
As we Christ's steps retrace
And his command obey.

Disciples live by love
For God and one another.
We share the bread and cup
With every sister, brother.
As servants, we prepare
To go where we are sent,
Salvation to declare,
Christ's caring to present.

(Exodus 12:1–14, Psalm 116:1, 2, 12–19, John 13:1–17, 31b–35,
I Corinthians 11:23–26)

(See *Gathered by Love*, p. 243, *Led by Love*, p. 215, and *Fresh Winds, Book 2*, pp. 199, 201.)

42

From Garden to the Cross

Good Friday (A, B, C)
Lavon Bayler

6.6.8.6.D. (S.M.D.)
(Terra Beata)

From garden to the cross,
Our Savior treads once more,
Betrayed, arrested, and denied
In ways that we ignore.
God, hear our earnest prayer,
Why does it come to this?
Must Jesus die from our neglect
And fearful cowardice?

We find it hard to speak
A word on Christ's behalf.
We fear the ridicule of friends,
And foes' disdaining laugh.
God, save your straying flock,
Intent on our own way.
Forsake us not; we need you here,
Amid our shocked dismay.

The covenant God writes,
Through Christ, upon our hearts,
Inspires an answering faith and love,
And confidence imparts.
God, help us stand with Christ,
To risk and serve, with care
For all your children, near and far,
And for your reign prepare. Amen.

(Psalm 22, Isaiah 52:13–53:12, John 18:1–19:42, Hebrews 10:16–25)

(See *Fresh Winds of the Spirit*, p. 164; *Fresh Winds, Book 2*, pp. 200–202; *Whispers of God*, p. 186; *Refreshing Rains of the Living Word*, pp. 197–98; *Gathered by Love*, pp. 244–46; and *Led by Love*, p. 216.)

43

Look, the Tomb Is Sealed

Holy Saturday (A, B, C)
Lavon Bayler

8.7.8.7.
(Rathbun)

Look, the tomb is sealed securely.
Death has won a victory.
Killed by ways we live impurely,
Christ within the grave must be.

Idols claim our fond attention;
Things we have and things we crave
Vie against our good intentions
To distract us and deprave.

All our days are full of trouble,
Faithlessness and dull routine.
Serving God becomes a struggle,
And we know ourselves unclean.

Rescue us, O God, our refuge,
From our lawlessness and sin.
Save us from the fire and deluge;
Let new life in us begin.

Teach us how to serve each other
As we seek to do your will.
May we yet Christ's joy discover
And his disciplines fulfill.

Let Christ rise again among us,
Saving us from living death.
Come, renew our sense of purpose.
Breathe through us Love's vital breath. Amen.

(Psalm 31:1–4, 15–16, Job 14:1–14, Matthew 27:57–66, 1 Peter 4:1–8)

(See *Gathered by Love*, p. 248, and *Led by Love*, p. 217.)

THE EASTER SEASON

44

Jesus Has Risen

Easter Sunday
Lavon Bayler

14.14.4.7.8.
(Lobe den Herren)

Jesus has risen; why come you with sorrow and weeping?
This is the time to rejoice, to awake from your sleeping.
Recount the deeds
Of One who meets human needs,
Giving yourself to Christ's keeping.

Rise and give thanks for the marvelous gift of salvation.
Join with disciples in seeking Christ's manifestation.
See and believe;
Christ touches us as we grieve,
Turning despair to elation.

Christ calls our names and appears to us while we are praying,
Healing, forgiving, and lifting up all who were straying.
Go forth to tell
Good news of One who makes well
Those who God's way are obeying.

Glad songs of victory echo through all of creation.
We are to carry their message to every nation.
Christ is alive,
Seeking our souls to revive
With ever-new revelation.

(Psalm 118:1–2, 14–24, John 20:1–18, Acts 10:34–43, Colossians 3:1–4)

(See *Fresh Winds of the Spirit*, p. 166; *Fresh Winds, Book 2*, pp. 203–4; *Whispers of God*, p. 187; *Refreshing Rains of the Living Word*, p. 200; *Gathered by Love*, p. 251; *Led by Love*, p. 221.)

45

At the Day's Dawning

Easter Sunday (alt.)
Lavon Bayler

5.6.8.5.5.8.
(Schönster Herr Jesu)

At the day's dawning.
Lead us to view the tomb.
Lightning and earthquake greet us there.
Fear not, a voice cries,
Hear how Christ denies
The cruel claims of death's despair.

You look for Jesus.
You will not find him here.
Come, see the place where Jesus lay.
Crucified, buried,
Your sins he carried
Through death to life in God's new day.

Jesus has risen!
Now quickly go and tell
All the disciples; they will see
Jesus among them,
Never to condemn,
But bearing love that sets us free.

Jesus says: Greetings!
Know now the peace God gives.
God chooses you to spread good news.
By deeds testify
That God will reply
To fervent prayers, and sin excuse.

(Matthew 28:1–10, Acts 10:34–43)

(See *Fresh Winds, Book 2,* p. 203.)

46

At End of Day

Easter Evening (A, B, C)
Lavon Bayler

10.10.10.10.
(Sine Nomine)

At end of day, we walk along life's road,
Talking about the Easter episode.
Confusion mixes with the tears that flowed.
Where is salvation? Where is God's presence?

We cannot recognize a presence here
When hearts are filled with doubts and numbed by fear.
How can we know that Christ is drawing near?
Where is salvation? Where is God's presence?

We will not trust a vision that pretends
Death is erased by life that never ends.
Yet God, in Christ, our questioning transcends.
Here is salvation, God's presence with us.

How slow we are the prophets to believe!
Yet, as the Scriptures open, we receive
A firm assurance that does not deceive.
Here is salvation, God's presence, with us.

As bread is broken, eyes are opened wide.
Hearts burn within as we with Christ abide.
Love has reclaimed the One we crucified.
God's love still heals us, and peace is given.

Proclaim good news in this and ev'ry land.
Christ walks among us, leading by the hand
Disciples who still witness as God planned.
God's love still heals us, and peace is given

(Luke 24:13–49)

(See *Fresh Winds, Book 2*, pp. 206–7; *Whispers of God*, p. 189; *Refreshing Rains of the Living Word*,
p. 201; *Gathered by Love*, pp. 252–53; and *Led by Love*, p. 222.)

47

Blest God Who Gives Birth

Second Sunday of Easter
Lavon Bayler

8.8.8.8.8.8.
(Melita)

Blest be our God who gives new birth,
Whose gift in Christ proclaims our worth.
Receive our thanks and highest praise,
As, in your presence all our days,
We seek to follow where Christ leads
And honor you in all our deeds.

Our hearts are glad, our tongues rejoice,
As soul and flesh to hope give voice.
Your presence shows the path of life
Through times of doubt, distress, and strife.
Come, bless us now as we confess
True sorrow at our faithlessness.

The lesser gods that we create,
And things that we accumulate,
Cannot our needs accommodate
Or lift from us our sins' cruel weight.
But you, O God, have raised us up
To share with Christ the bread and cup.

Believing though we have not seen,
May no encounter seem routine.
Let Jesus in our midst appear,
That we the word of peace may hear.
Then send us out as Christ was sent
To live our lives as sacrament. Amen.

(Psalm 16, John 20:19–31, Acts 2:14a, 22–32, I Peter 1:3–9)

(See *Fresh Winds of the Spirit,* p. 167, *Fresh Winds, Book 2,* pp. 208–9, and *Gathered by Love,* p. 285.)

48

Invoke the Name

Third Sunday of Easter
Lavon Bayler

8.6.8.6.D. (C.M.D.)
(All Saints New)

Invoke the name of God today:
Impartial Judge, our hope.
God sees our actions, hears us pray,
And gives us strength to cope
With fears and dangers that beset
Our journey on life's road.
May we invest, without regret,
The trust that Jesus showed.

In Jesus Christ, we're born anew
And saved from futile ways.
To solemn vows, may we be true
Throughout our earthly days.
Baptized, forgiven, gifted by
The Holy Spirit's power,
We sing, with voices lifted high,
Of faith God brings to flower.

At table with the risen Christ,
We do not recognize
The One who, for us, sacrificed,
Now living in disguise
In friends and neighbors, far and near,
Who share this planet earth.
Hearts burn once more as you appear,
Proclaiming each one's worth.

(Psalm 116:1–4, 12–19, Luke 24:13–35, Acts 2:36–41, I Peter 1:17–23)

(See *Fresh Winds of the Spirit,* p. 168, and *Fresh Winds, Book 2,* pp. 207, 210–11.)

49

Wonders and Signs

Fourth Sunday of Easter
Lavon Bayler

8.8.8.8. (L.M.)
(Angelus)

Wonders and signs were all around
When the apostles prayed and served.
All who believed let love abound,
Meeting the needs that they observed.

With glad and generous hearts they shared
Goods held in common, God to praise.
Daily they showed the world they cared,
Seeking to follow Jesus' ways.

We have been called to follow, too,
Striving to do what's good and right.
As Christ was ever faithful, true,
We, in Christ's service, now unite.

We know the voice of One who calls,
Jesus, our Shepherd, strong and brave,
And so we vow, whate'er befalls,
We want to give as Jesus gave.

Help us to live abundantly,
In glad response to saving grace.
May we endure triumphantly,
Amid the insults we may face.

You are the shepherd who restores
Life in its fullness when we fail.
Merciful goodness underscores
Your loving care that will prevail. Amen.

(Psalm 23, John 10:1–10, Acts 2:42–47, 1 Peter 2:19–25)

(See *Fresh Winds of the Spirit*, p. 169; *Whispers of God*, pp. 191–92; *Refreshing Rains of the Living Word*, pp. 204–5; *Fresh Winds, Book 2*, p. 212; *Led by Love*, p. 225; *Gathered by Love*, p. 258; and "God Is My Shepherd," in *The New Century Hymnal*.)

50

Let Your Face Shine

Fifth Sunday of Easter
Lavon Bayler

6.4.6.4.6.6.6.4.
(St. Edmund)

Let your face shine on us,
Jesus, today,
That we may clearly see
Your holy way.
Blessed by your presence here,
Taking away our fear,
May we your love display
In all we say.

Help us to grow in faith,
Trusting in you.
Lead us and guide our thoughts;
Help us be true.
Rescue us when we fall,
Let us your way recall.
May every prayer renew
Life's larger view.

As you have chosen us,
May we proclaim
Your mighty acts in deeds
Done in your name.
As greater works we do,
Your love will see us through
All our distress and pain.
Come, God, to reign. Amen.

(Psalm 31:1–5, 15–16, John 14:1–14, Acts 7:55–60, 1 Peter 2:2–10)

(Dedicated to the 1996 confirmation class of the Congregational UCC of Geneva, Illinois. See *Fresh Winds of the Spirit,* p. 170, and *Fresh Winds, Book 2,* pp. 212–13.)

51

Unknown God, We Search

Sixth Sunday of Easter
Lavon Bayler

7.6.7.6.D.
(Boundless Mercy)

Unknown God, we search for you
In our human ignorance.
All you've chosen to reveal
Challenges our pretense.
Not in shrines of human hands
But in lives committed
You, O God, still choose to dwell
Where we act as kindred.

Bless, O God, your people here
As we sing your praises.
You have tested, saved, and led
As your love amazes.
Hear our prayers as we deplore
All the ways we fail you.
Raise us from our sinful ways
To the life you value.

In your love we live and move
And discover meaning,
Not in silver, gold, or stone
But in faithful being.
May we meet your test each day,
Tried and true and honest,
Giving you our very best,
Living all we've promised. Amen.

(Psalm 66:8–20, Acts 17:22–31)

(See *Fresh Winds of the Spirit,* pp. 170–71.)

52

Send Your Advocate

Sixth Sunday of Easter
Lavon Bayler

8.7.8.7.D.
(Beecher)

Send your Advocate among us,
God, whose love has blessed us here.
May your Spirit dwell within us,
Cleansing us from doubt and fear.
Let your truth surround and hallow
All we seek to do or say.
Eagerly we vow to follow
As Christ Jesus leads the way.

If we suffer on life's journey,
May it be for doing good.
We will trust your love and mercy,
Knowing we are understood.
You, O God, with patient kindness
Watch us when we disobey,
Sending messengers to find us
When our lives have gone astray.

You remind us, we are baptized,
Cleansed by water and by grace,
Never orphaned, though we're chastised,
Offered, in your realm, a place.
Thus we live with hope abounding,
Praying for a conscience clear,
As your reign of love, astounding,
Brings our resurrection near. Amen.

(John 14:15–21, 1 Peter 3:13–22)

(See *Fresh Winds, Book 2*, p. 214.)

53

We Seek Your Wisdom

Ascension Day (or Seventh Sunday of Easter)   11.10.11.10.
          Lavon Bayler   (Bonhoeffer)

We seek your wisdom, God of all the ages,
As you reveal the greatness of your power.
We want to follow Christ with lives enlightened
By hope to which you call us in this hour.

We give you thanks for all who lived before us,
Whose faith in you and love for all the saints
Inspire our prayers of penitence and sorrow
For wrong we've done and self-absorbed complaints.

As we have been baptized with living water,
Let now your Holy Spirit come and stay.
Grant strength to all who join in joyous witness,
With shouts of praise to honor you this day.

Continue every day your revelation
That opens minds and hearts to understand.
May your forgiveness change our ways of doing,
As we extend to all a helping hand.

As you have lifted Christ from death's dominion,
Raise us, we pray, to claim our heritage.
Grant us the faith and love of early Christians
As we, your church, in caring acts engage. Amen.

(Psalm 47, Luke 24:44–53, Acts 1:1–11, Ephesians 1:15–23)

(See *Led by Love*, p. 228; *Gathered by Love*, p. 262; *Refreshing Rains of the Living Word*, pp. 207–8; *Whispers of God*, p. 194; and *Fresh Winds, Book 2*, pp. 215–16.)

54

The Hour Has Come

Seventh Sunday of Easter
Lavon Bayler

6.6.6.6.8.8.8.
(Rhosymedre)

The hour has come, O God,
To glorify your name,
So we may know your love,
Eternally a flame,
That sends us out to share your word
With all who have not seen or heard
The wonders that your truth conferred.

Oh, make us one in Christ,
Whose blessed name we bear,
That, humbly following,
Our lives may show your care.
Anxieties we cast aside,
And discipline ourselves inside
To calmly, in full trust, abide.

Your Spirit we await,
Continuing in prayer,
Anticipating power
This planet to repair.
Let enemies and hatred flee
Before the joyous company
That hails your awesome majesty. Amen.

(Psalm 68:1–10, 32–35, John 17:1–11, Acts 1:6–14,
I Peter 4:12–14, 5:6–11)

(See *Fresh Winds of the Spirit,* p. 172, and *Fresh Winds, Book 2,* pp. 217–18.)

PENTECOST AND THE SEASON
FOLLOWING

55

How Manifold the Gifts

Pentecost (A, B, C)
Lavon Bayler

8.6.8.6.D. (C.M.D.)
(Materna)

How manifold the gifts of God,
In rich variety.
One Spirit activates them all:
Faith, wisdom, prophecy.
Discernment, healing, miracles,
And knowledge all supply
The church, as Christ's community,
With works to magnify.

The Holy Spirit comes again,
With wind and tongues of fire,
Empowering speech that all may hear,
Devotion to inspire.
The world will ever stand amazed
When faithful ones respond
To power that God supplies to those
Whose vision sees beyond.

Christ gives us peace and sends us forth
To witness and forgive,
To share the good that God supplies
So humankind might live
As one in Christ, both Jew and Greek,
United, slave and free.
May all the earth praise God today
In joyous harmony.

(Psalm 104:24–34, 35b, John 20:19–23, Acts 2:1–21,
1 Corinthians 12:3b–13)

(See *Fresh Winds of the Spirit*, p. 173; *Fresh Winds, Book 2*, pp. 219–21; *Refreshing Rains of the Living Word*, p. 209; *Gathered by Love*, p. 266; and *Led by Love*, p. 232.)

56

God, We Are Thirsty

Pentecost (Alt.)
Lavon Bayler

5.6.8.5.5.8.
(Schönster Herr Jesu)

God, we are thirsty,
Longing for pure water,
Where shall we find the help we need?
Pour out your truth here
In principles clear,
That all the world may hear and heed.

We would believe you,
Trust you and obey you.
Let now your Spirit flow today
Like living water,
Ever to foster
Our cleansing, and your power convey.

We are astonished
By wind and tongues of fire,
Spreading with rich diversity
Through varied people,
Serving as channels
For unexpected unity.

May we, like prophets,
Carry your truth abroad,
Sharing good news that changes lives.
Give us the vision
To make decisions
With insight that your love supplies. Amen.

(Numbers 11:24–30, John 7:37–39, Acts 2:1–21)

57

Creation Continues

Trinity Sunday
Lavon Bayler

11.10.11.10.11.10.
(Finlandia)

In the beginning, you, O God, created
The vast expanse of matter, time, and space.
We gaze into the heav'ns in all their grandeur,
And wonder why you've given us a place,
So crowned with glory, honor, and dominion,
On this good earth, where we can know your grace.

We marvel at the passing of the seasons,
The changes that proclaim creation still
Continues day and night around and in us.
We see your works on ev'ry vale and hill,
As seeds are sown and crops are brought to harvest,
And life goes on according to your will.

You grant us light to guide our onward journey,
And guide our feet in ways that we should go.
All humankind bears your eternal image,
And benefits from gifts that you bestow.
We give you thanks for all that you have given
To fill our days with joy, and help us grow.

Send us your wind, the Spirit blowing through us,
To energize and recreate each day
Communities of trust and loving service,
Whose words and deeds proclaim your holy way.
Then, mindful of our need for rest and worship,
We honor you, while gathering to pray. Amen.

(Genesis 1:1–2:4a, Psalm 8)

(See *Fresh Winds of the Spirit*, p. 174, *Fresh Winds, Book 2*, p. 223, and *Gathered by Love*, p. 268.)

58

We Are Descendants

Proper 4 (May 29–June 4)
Lavon Bayler

10.10.10.10.
(National Hymn)

We are descendants of your righteous ones,
Those who obeyed, your daughters and your sons,
Greeting your covenant with joyous praise
Through fearful nights and problem-laden days.

You were their refuge through all times of change,
When your commands, O God, seemed harsh and strange.
Saved from the floods to populate the earth,
They were amazed as you proclaimed life's worth.

God, give us strength to face the violence
That we, with hate, so callously dispense,
Or, yet, ignore in others if we see
No harm for us in their iniquity.

Forgive us, God, for breaking covenant
In all the subtle ways that we invent.
Help us, we pray, your image to receive
Into our lives, with courage to believe.

We have been blessed with gifts so manifold!
Heaven and earth, and wonders yet untold,
Proclaim your majesty, O God of Light.
May we, your people, worship you aright. Amen.

(Genesis 6:9–22, 7:24; 18:14–19, Psalm 8)

(See *Fresh Winds, Book 2,* pp. 212–13, 226. See also hymn 27 in this book.)

59

Praise God for Memories

Proper 5 (June 5–11)
Lavon Bayler

7.6.7.6.D.
(Lancashire)

Praise God for sacred mem'ries
That bring us here today.
Let happiness surround us
As we rejoice and pray
That God will always bless us
Wherever we may go,
As in the past God guided
Our way and helped us grow.

We stand in awe before you,
God, for you have led
Our ancestors before us
When to this land they fled.
You helped them build a nation,
Inspiring them to form
Communities of faith where
True caring was the norm.

You challenged them to follow
The Christ, whose healing touch
Restored the lost and broken
While loving them so much
That prejudice was challenged
And hope was offered all.
God, renew our vision
That we may heed your call. Amen.

(Genesis 12:1–9, Psalm 33:1–12, Matthew 9:9–13, 18–26)

(This hymn was first sung during high school reunion weekend in Newton, Iowa, when persons who had been members of St. John United Church of Christ renewed their ties with one another during worship at First Congregational UCC. The building housing St. John UCC, rural Newton, had burned when struck by lightning twenty-five years before, and the congregation disbanded. See *Fresh Winds, Book 2,* p. 224.)

60

God Appears

Proper 6 (June 2–18)   7.7.7.7.D.
Lavon Bayler   (Martyn)

God appears in stranger's garb,
With surprises we resist,
Bringing news we disregard,
Challenges too soon dismissed.
Laughing at God's promises,
We, like Sarah, need to know,
God, whose love astonishes,
Wills that we should learn and grow.

Nothing is too wonderful
For the God in whom we trust.
Prayers, sincere and purposeful,
Reach our God, whose care is just.
When we do not understand
Suff'ring, loss, and endless pain,
God in Christ is near at hand
Helping us to live again.

Justified by faith alone,
We receive the gift of peace,
Selfishness is overthrown,
Anxious thoughts and deeds decrease.
We endure, with hope and joy,
Through the grace in which we stand,
As we all our gifts employ,
May our faith and love expand.

(Genesis 18:1–15, 21:1–7; Psalm 116:1–2, 12–19; Romans 5:1–8)

(See *Fresh Winds, Book 2*, pp. 192, 210.)

61

Our Savior Traveled

Proper 6 (June 12–18)
Lavon Bayler

8.8.8.8. (L.M.)
(Herr Jesu Christ, Dich Zu
Uns Wend)

Our Savior traveled through the land,
That common folks might understand
Good news that Love had come to reign,
To heal their ills and ease their pain.

Without a shepherd, they appeared
Harassed and helpless, not revered.
Christ had compassion on the lost
And cared for them despite the cost.

He called disciples, sent them out
To deal with fear and sin and doubt.
A harvest plentiful awaits
The lab'rers Jesus consecrates.

And still today, authority
Is giv'n to use Love's energy
To serve and heal in Jesus' name,
The lost and helpless to reclaim.

We're called to use our gifts of grace,
God's suff'ring people to embrace.
All we receive, we pass along,
Inviting all to sing Love's song.

(Matthew 9:35–10:8)

(See *Fresh Winds, Book 2,* p. 227.)

62

God, Preserve Your Servants

Proper 7 (June 19–25)
Lavon Bayler

8.7.8.7.8.7.
(Lauda Anima)

God, preserve your faithful servants,
Cast aside by human pride,
Jealousy, and alienation.
Be to them a friend and guide.
Help them in their days of trouble;
Be forever by their side.

We have known your goodness, ever
Saving and protecting all
Who cry out with supplications
When they stumble, fail, or fall.
Hear our cries of desperation
As your promise we recall.

You are gracious and forgiving.
Come to heal our spirits now.
We have been the ones unmindful
Of the hurts that we allow.
We have turned away the troubled,
We have broken many a vow.

May all nations come before you,
Bowing down to glorify
You, O God, whose great compassion
Saves us, though we crucify.
For the waters of salvation,
We will lift our praises high. Amen.

(Genesis 21:8–21; Psalm 86:1–10, 16–17)

❀

Hymns for Pentecost and the Season Following

63

How Shall We Live?

Proper 7 (June 19–25)
Lavon Bayler

6.6.8.6. (S.M.)
(Dennis)

How shall we live in grace?
How shall we die to sin?
Baptized into the death of Christ,
We rise, reborn within.

God's glory grants anew
The union that we seek
With Christ, our teacher, leader, friend,
In whom we serve and speak.

Disciples, we are called
To represent Christ here,
God's truth to tell, God's love to show
In ways that conquer fear.

God values ev'ry one.
Each creature God has made
Is counted, treasured, reconciled,
Though they rebelled and strayed.

Our loyalty to Christ
Surpasses human ties.
The cross commands our faithfulness,
As we evangelize.

We give our lives away,
That all the world may know
The God we worship and adore
Assists us as we grow.

(Romans 6:16–11, Matthew 10:24–39)

(See *Fresh Winds, Book 2,* p. 230.)

64

Abraham Rose

Proper 8 (June 26–July 2)
Lavon Bayler

8.6.8.6. (C.M.)
(Beatitudo)

Abraham rose in early morn,
Taking his only son,
Ready to sacrifice and mourn
This long-awaited one.

Terror and sorrow mingled there,
High on the mountainside.
A father hastened to prepare
To have his dreams denied.

"If this is what God wants of me,
I will obey and trust.
Here is my best, spent willingly,
For you, O God, are just."

But the father heard his name:
"Please do not harm the lad.
You have responded to my claim,
Your faith has made me glad.

"Here is the fitting sacrifice
I have provided you.
You would have paid the highest price
In worship brave and true."

Now let us trust God's steadfast love,
Making God's will our choice,
Seeking salvation from above,
As faithful hearts rejoice.

(Genesis 22:1–14, Psalm 13)

(See *Fresh Winds, Book 2*, p. 225.)

65

God, We Present Ourselves

Proper 8 (June 26–July 2)
Lavon Bayler

6.4.6.4.6.6.4.4.
(More Love to You)

God, we present ourselves
This day to you.
Take all our sins away;
Help us be true.
As you bring life anew,
Grant grace to see us through.
Each passing hour,
Grant us your power.

We are not under law,
But under grace.
Yet, we would be your slaves,
In Love's embrace,
Daily obeying you,
Your purpose to pursue,
Sharing your word
'Til all have heard.

We welcome those you send,
Prophet and friend.
Pray, help us minister,
Not just pretend.
May we put others first,
Seeking to quench their thirst
With water pure,
Life to ensure. Amen.

(Matthew 10:40–42, Romans 6:12–23)

66

You Have Blessed Us

Proper 9 (July 3–9)
Lavon Bayler

10.7.10.7. Ref.
(I Am Yours)

You have blessed us, God, on life's journey long,
Giving guidance on our way.
We would worship you with our loyalty,
Joyous gladness to display.

Refrain:
We will praise you in our words and deeds,
Giving thanks that you reveal
To the least of us the love you have for all,
And the calming words that heal.

We confess that we are at war within
As we try to do what's right.
Come and rescue us from our wretchedness,
In your law to find delight.
Refrain

Come to me, Christ said, all you weary ones,
Come, and be my honored guest.
Lay your burdens down, and refreshment find,
For I want to give you rest.
Refrain

Take my yoke, Christ said, and learn from me,
Find my yoke and burden light,
And, with gentleness and humility,
In God's gracious will unite.
Refrain
Amen.

(Genesis 24:42–49, Psalm 45:10–17, Matthew 11:25–30,
Romans 7:15–25a)

(See *Fresh Winds, Book 2*, p. 232.)

67

Send Your Word

Proper 10 (July 10–16)
Lavon Bayler

8.7.8.7.D.
(Bradbury)

Send your word to light our pathway,
Our awareness to increase.
You have granted, as a birthright,
Minds embracing life and peace.
God, we praise you, praise and thank you,
For the gifts that you bestow.
As your Spirit dwells within us,
You incline our hearts to grow.

When we struggle, you are with us.
When we from your precepts stray,
You incline our hearts to trust you
And return to Jesus' way.
God, we praise you, praise and thank you,
For the guidance you provide.
You revive us when we flounder
And restore us to your side.

In your law is perfect freedom
From the bondage of our sin.
As we let your Spirit lead us,
We discover strength within.
God, we praise you, praise and thank you,
For the joy that we have known.
We will go where you may send us;
We would make your ways our own. Amen.

(Genesis 25:19–34, Psalm 119:105–112, Romans 8:1–11)

68

The Crowds Gathered

Proper 10 (July 10–16)
Lavon Bayler

7.6.7.6.D.
(Es Flog Ein Kleins Waldvogelein)

The crowds 'round Jesus gathered
To listen as he taught
Of seeds a sower scattered
And yields beyond their thought.
For God will bring the harvest
Of fruits a hundredfold
Despite resistant hardness
And all that we withhold.

God's word is for our hearing,
As seeds are for the soil,
But much is interfering,
God's harvest to despoil.
Like thorns, the world's distractions
Choke out the truth we seek,
For wealth has its attractions
And cares can leave us weak.

O God, grant understanding
And willingness to learn,
So soil where seeds are landing
May yield a high return.
May depth and strong endurance
Accompany our joy,
And Love give reassurance
No evil can destroy. Amen.

(Matthew 13:1–9, 18–23)

(See *Fresh Winds, Book 2*, p. 233.)

69

You, God, Have Searched Me

Proper 11 (July 17–23)
Lavon Bayler

10.10.10.10.
(Toulon)

You, God, have searched me, you know all my ways;
You are aware of all my yesterdays.
You know my thoughts before they reach my tongue;
You understand the songs that I have sung.

When I lie down in utter weariness,
You come in dreams to fill my emptiness
With hope and promises to challenge fear,
Gently assuring me that you are near.

There is no place that I can flee from you;
No other one can pardon and renew.
If I ascend to heaven, you are there;
Plunged to the depths, I'm still within your care.

Your presence guides and takes me by the hand,
Showing me greater things than I had planned.
You fill my heart with reverence and awe;
Help me, O God, to trust and keep your law.

May I each day discern your truth and light,
Testing my thoughts and seeking to unite
My ways with yours for all eternity.
Help me this day your perfect will to see. Amen.

(Genesis 28:10–19a, Psalm 139:1–12, 23–24)

70

Creation Waits

Proper 11 (July 17–23)
Lavon Bayler

8.6.8.6.D. (C.M.D.)
(St. Matthew)

Creation waits with eagerness
For fruits of righteousness
Among God's children, chosen heirs,
Whom Christ has come to bless.
Our slav'ry we would leave behind;
Adopted, glorified,
To shine as brightly as the sun
As we in Christ abide.

We are not debtors to the flesh,
Mere creatures of the dust.
Teach us to follow and obey,
In faithfulness and trust.
O Holy Spirit, lead us now
Away from death to life,
So we may know a patient hope
That overcomes all strife.

May we be children of your realm,
Strong plants from fertile seed.
Keep us away from choking weeds
Of fear, decay, and greed.
May we be gathered by your grace,
To yield abundantly
At harvest time when Christ returns
In glorious sov'reignty. Amen.

(Matthew 13:24–30, 36–43, Romans 8:12–25)

(See *Fresh Winds, Book 2*, pp. 234–35.)

71

Worship God

Proper 12 (July 24–30)
Lavon Bayler

8.7.8.7.7.7.
(Unser Herrscher)

Worship God, whose loving presence
Welcomes us in covenant.
Sing your praise with growing rev'rence,
Giving thanks as celebrant
Of the good that God supplies,
Miracles before our eyes.

Worship God, who judges fairly
All the people of the earth.
We are beneficiary
Of the love that gives us worth.
Let us praise our God each day,
Finding strength as we obey.

Worship God and tell the story
Of the promises God keeps.
As our forebears knew God's glory,
Let our hearts explore the deeps
Of our valued chosenness,
Knowing God will save and bless.

Worship God, whose works continue
Through the Word alive in us
That announces, "God is with you!"
To a struggling populace,
Past the limits we now see,
God helps build community.

(Psalm 105:1–11, 45b)

(See *Fresh Winds, Book 2*, p. 235.)

72

Come, Spirit of God

Proper 12 (July 24–30)
Lavon Bayler

11.11.11.11.
(St. Denio)

Come, Spirit of God, to examine our hearts,
And teach us to value the truth Christ imparts,
For we, in our weakness, know not how to pray,
Yet you intercede for us, showing Love's way.

Though often your people have misunderstood,
We sense that all things work together for good,
For those who, in love, are committed each day
Your way to pursue and your will to obey.

You call us to live by your glorious will,
As saints and disciples, Christ's work to fulfill.
We know you are for us though some may oppress,
When others condemn, you are with us to bless.

No hardship, distress, persecution, or sword
Can separate us from Christ Jesus our Lord,
For we have been loved in high moments and low
By One who is with us wherever we go.

May we grow each day in the image of Christ,
Who, for our salvation from sin, sacrificed,
In life and in death, what the world has esteemed
That we might be healed, justified, and redeemed. Amen.

(Romans 8:26–39)

(See *Fresh Winds of the Spirit*, p. 81, and *Fresh Winds, Book 2*, pp. 236–37.)

73

O God, Attend Our Cries

Proper 13 (July 31–August 6)
Lavon Bayler

6.6.8.6. (C.M.)
(Festal Song)

O God, attend our cries;
Give ear to all our prayers.
From you, let vindication come.
Be present through our cares.

We wrestle through the night,
And struggle day by day
To find the paths that you intend
And follow in your way.

You try our hearts and test
For ways that we transgress.
We pray that you will find in us
No sham or wickedness.

We seek your name, O God,
And ask you to address
Our questions and petitions now,
To answer and to bless.

Your steadfast love provides
A refuge from distress,
From adversaries threatening
To harm us and oppress.

O God, we seek your face,
In dreams and when we wake.
May all we say and do reflect
Your love, for others' sake. Amen.

(Genesis 32:22–31, Psalm 17:1–7,15)

(See *Fresh Winds*, Book 2, p. 230.)

74

We Have Heard

Proper 13 (July 31–August 6)
Lavon Bayler

Irregular
(Battle Hymn of the Republic)

We have heard the voice of Jesus
Calling all of us to feed
All the hungry, thirsting multitudes
Who live in fear and need.
We can feed them with the joyous news
That they are loved and freed
As children of God's love.

Refrain:
Join in songs of adoration,
Filling this and ev'ry nation,
Living out our true vocation,
As children of God's love.

May God's faithful ones inherit
What the patriarchs received:
All the promises in covenant
God gave when they believed.
May forgiveness come to all who have
The Holy Spirit grieved.
Restore us in God's love.
Refrain

God, equip us for your service
In the work we do each day.
Be our constant inspiration
In our struggles and our play.
May the food that you supply be blessed
Among us as we pray
For strength to share your love.
Refrain

(Matthew 14:13–21, Romans 9:1–5)

(Prepared for and first sung at worship at St. Michael United Church of Christ, West Chicago, Illinois. See *Fresh Winds, Book 2,* p. 239.)

75

We Thank You, God

Proper 14 (August 7–13)
Lavon Bayler

8.6.8.8.6.
(Rest)

We thank you, God, and sing your praise,
And marvel at your deeds.
Your miracles surround our days;
Your care is known through all the ways
You meet our many needs.

When we, like Joseph, seem to be
Most favored on the earth,
Grant us profound humility
That we, with you, may rightly see
Each other person's worth.

So long ago your guiding hand
Kept Joseph from despair.
When nothing went as he had planned
And brothers sent him from their land,
He still was in your care.

Your love brought good where evil reigned,
For Joseph, and for us,
For you kept faith when we complained,
Supporting us when courage waned
And times were perilous.

O God, forgive the treachery
We kindle or allow.
Save us from subtle bigotry
That we may build community
And hatred disavow.

(Genesis 37:1–4, 12–28, Psalm 105:1–6, 16–22)

(See *Fresh Winds, Book 2*, p. 235.)

Related Hymns

76

We Rejoice

Proper 14 (August 7–13)
Lavon Bayler

7.8.7.8.8.8.
(Liebster Jesu)

We rejoice; your Word is near,
On our lips and in our hearing,
Teaching us to dare, not fear,
As we wait for Christ's appearing.
Fill our hearts with joyous praises
As your presence now amazes.

You have bid us come to you
When the storms of life are raging.
We would here our faith renew,
In your service re-engaging.
As you now uplift our thinking,
Keep our fragile hopes from sinking.

We confess what we believe:
You have sent to us a Savior.
Daily we your gifts receive;
Daily we enjoy your favor.
May we now take heart, reclaiming,
All your church has been proclaiming.

We rejoice that we are sent
As disciples with a mission,
Carrying your high intent
That we find our common vision
In communities of caring
In which all are gladly sharing. Amen.

(Matthew 14:22–33, Romans 10:5–15)

(See *Fresh Winds, Book 2*, p. 239.)

77

How Pleasant When Kindred

Proper 15 (August 14–20)
Lavon Bayler

6.6.11.6.6.11.D.
(The Ash Grove)

How pleasant when kindred,
Received and uplifted,
By pardon and grace, live in God's unity.
Sent forth by commission,
To live out Christ's mission,
We welcome the stranger to community.
How pleasant when giving
Springs forth from thanks living
To offer a helpfulness meeting true need.
We ask God who made us
To strengthen and aid us
In list'ning to others and living our creed.

May none be rejected
But rather respected
As precious and cherished, as soulmates and kin.
Remove hateful anger
Betrayal and rancor
From all of our hearts, and divert us from sin.
May all now find pleasure
In giving full measure
Of self and of substance to ease others' pain.
Unite us in caring,
Inspiring our sharing,
That we, from this day, may embody God's reign. Amen.

(Genesis 45:1–15, Psalm 133, Matthew 15:21–28,
Romans 11:1–2a, 29–32)

78

Gifted by Grace

Proper 16 (August 21–27)
Lavon Bayler

10.6.10.6.8.8.8.6.
(All Is Well)

Gifted by grace, we serve in many ways,
Giving God thanks and praise.
Differing strengths empower all we do,
As God's love sees us through.
'Mid troubling times, when hopes are dim,
We find the strength to sing this hymn:
Blest be the God of all the earth
Who proclaims each one's worth.

We are assured that God is on our side;
Help is never denied.
When raging waters threaten to destroy,
God can turn fear to joy.
When enemies invade our thought,
When we forget what Christ has taught,
God's mercy helps us interweave
Hope with all we receive.

We build the church whose mission cannot fail;
Jesus Christ will prevail.
Let us embrace God's good and perfect will,
Christ's intent to fulfill.
No longer to this world conformed,
May we, in spirit, be transformed
To claim and use our gifts each day
As we work, as we pray.

(Exodus 1:8–2:10, Psalm 124, Matthew 16:13–20, Romans 12:1–8)

(See *Fresh Winds, Book 2*, p. 243.)

79

When Moses Saw

Proper 17 (August 28–September 3)
Lavon Bayler

8.6.8.6.8.6.
(Coronation)

When Moses saw the burning bush
And turned aside to see,
He sensed that this was holy ground
And asked what this might be.
He heard God's call to leave his flock
And set the captives free.

When people live in misery,
God knows their suffering.
Our words and work are needed now,
A better day to bring.
We seek for all the strength God gives,
That all might praises sing.

Glory to God; let hearts rejoice
And marvel at the deeds
And miracles that come to pass
When selfless love proceeds
To work for justice, truth, and right
While meeting people's needs.

The God we know sends each of us
On missions we can do.
We have the keys to God's own realm,
And visions to pursue.
God blesses us each day we live,
And Love will see us through.

(Exodus 3:1–15, Psalm 105:1–6, 13–26, 45b (Matthew 16:19))

80

We Stand Before God

Proper 17 (August 28–September 3)
Lavon Bayler

8.6.8.6.D. (C.M.D.)
(Ellacombe)

We stand before the burning bush
And wonder at the news
That we are called by you, O God,
The way of Christ to choose.
We want to be true followers,
But it is hard to know
How we can serve most faithfully
And help your church to grow.

You promise to be with us here
When we take up the cross,
But we are frightened when we think
Of likely pain and loss.
We grieve that our companionship
Through years of fruitful toil
Will end as we depart or stay,
But serve on different soil.

You ask us to rejoice in hope,
To never lag in zeal.
You urge, as we rejoice and weep,
Come, feel what others feel.
You bid us live in harmony,
To find your way of peace,
And so we ask, for days ahead:
May mutual care increase. Amen.

(Exodus 3:1–15, Matthew 16:21–28, Romans 12:9–21)

(Sung on September 1, 1996, at a service of celebration and farewell at First Congregational United
Church of Christ, Naperville, marking the beginning of Hope United Church of Christ, a mission
fellowship seeking to minister to the city's newest residents.)

81

When We Are Gathered

Proper 18 (September 4–10)
Lavon Bayler

10.10.10.10.
(Slane)

When we are gathered, by twos or by threes,
God is among us and hears all our pleas.
If we agree, God has promised to do
All that we ask, as Christ's way we pursue.

Love one another, fulfilling God's law,
Keeping commandments and living with awe,
Praising our Maker with dancing and song;
Showing that we to our Savior belong.

Welcome salvation that surely is near;
Night is far gone and the light chases fear.
Live now with honor, not quarreling or greed,
Following Jesus, in word and in deed.

If we have grievances, we will confront
One who offends us, and tell what we want,
Seeking to reconcile, and to forgive,
That we in unity henceforth may live.

Grant new beginnings to all who believe
As we give thanks for the gifts we receive.
We are awakened, O God, by your light;
Help us to love and to do what is right. Amen.

(Psalm 149, Matthew 18:15–20, Romans 13:8–14)

(See *Fresh Winds, Book 2*, p. 244.)

82

We Marvel at God's Leading

Proper 19 (September 11–17)   7.6.7.6.D.
Lavon Bayler   (Munich)

We marvel at God's leading,
And bow in reverent awe,
While trembling in the presence
Of One whose word is law.
We know ourselves as debtors,
Forgiven and set free,
Yet failing to have patience
To hear our neighbor's plea.

The heritage of Israel
Is one in which we share.
As people fled from Egypt,
They knew that God was there,
For cloud and light protected
When Pharaoh's hordes pursued,
And people of the promise
Were strengthened and renewed.

God's saving hand provided
Escape from fearsome foes,
And still God's hand is guiding
Through all our joys and woes.
We live by love, not judgment,
For we belong to Christ,
Whose mercy conquered hatred,
Who, for us, sacrificed.

(Exodus 14:19–31, Psalm 114, Matthew 18:21–35, Romans 14:1–12)

(See *Fresh Winds, Book 2,* p. 246.)

83

Hear Our Complaints

Proper 20 (September 18–24)
Lavon Bayler

8.8.8.8. (L.M.)
(Hesperus (Quebec))

Hear our complaints, O God Most High.
Hear all your people as they cry,
Longing for bread and water pure,
Seeking survival, to endure.

You heard your children long ago,
Facing oppression, harm, and woe.
You led them through the wilderness,
Granting relief from their distress.

You promised them both bread and meat,
Giving them just enough to eat.
Yet there are many more today,
Starving and grieving while we play.

We hear your call to give them bread,
Even as we are overfed.
This is much more than we can do.
Will manna come to see them through?

Grant us the courage so to give,
That all of us may simply live,
Giving you thanks in word and deed,
Seeking your strength for all we need. Amen.

(Exodus 16:2–15, Psalm 105:1–6, 27–45)

84

Following Christ

Proper 20 (September 18–24)
Lavon Bayler

8.6.8.6. (C.M.)
(St. Agnes)

Following Christ is life to me;
Dying is also gain.
Living for Christ, I long to see
Vistas where God will reign.

Laboring here for others' good,
Seeking their faith and joy,
My boast in Christ is understood:
Trust no one can destroy.

Keep me from harmful jealousy
When you forgive the lost,
Giving them all you give to me,
Gen'rous, beyond all cost.

May we live out the gospel news
In actions day by day
That will reflect our Savior's views
And help our neighbors pray.

May all now share abundantly
In our Redeemer's grace,
Knowing that Love has set us free,
All of our sins to face.

So, as we struggle day by day
To live more faithfully,
May all we suffer pave the way
For Love's eternity. Amen.

(Matthew 20:1–6, Philippians 1:21–30)

(See *Fresh Winds, Book 2,* p. 247.)

85

Why Test Our God?

Proper 21 (September 25–October 1)
Lavon Bayler

6.6.8.4.D.
(Leoni)

Why did we test our God,
Insisting on our due,
While God supplied abundantly
More than we knew?
Like Israelites of old,
Who thirsted and complained,
We question, Is God with us here?
Is Love restrained?

Incline your ears and hear
The psalmist speak again
Of glorious deeds and wondrous acts:
God's great amen.
Pure water streamed from rocks
To quench the wanderer's thirst.
Led by their God, with cloud and fire,
They seas traversed.

Then Jesus came to teach,
That we might look beyond
Our own ambitions and conceits
And then respond
With minds attuned to Christ
Who, in humility,
Became obedient, to death,
And set us free.

(Exodus 17:1–7, Psalm 78:1–4, 12–16, Philippians 2:1–13)

86

Who Will Inherit?

Proper 21 (September 25–October 1)   10.10.10.10.
 Lavon Bayler   (Morecambe)

Who will inherit places in God's realm?
Who will believe the way that Christ has taught?
Our good intentions hardly overwhelm,
Nor have our ways reflected righteous thought.

Those whose acknowledged sin leads to belief
May be included earlier than we
Who take for granted pardon and relief
And, feigning goodness, fail our wrongs to see.

Christ gives encouragement to all who seek
On bended knee, with trembling and with fear,
To put aside ambition and conceit,
Off'ring compassion and a list'ning ear.

Sharing the Spirit, finding unity
In humble love that seeks each other's good,
Our joy is made complete in harmony
When we the mind of Christ have understood.

Let us exult in Christ and raise the name
Of One whose sacrifice transforms and saves.
We would obey the Word that we proclaim,
Working to please our God, whose love forgave.

(Matthew 21:23–32, Philippians 2:1–13)

(See *Fresh Winds, Book 2,* p. 249, and *Fresh Winds of the Spirit,* p. 187.)

87

The Earth Is Yours

Proper 22 (October 2–8)
Lavon Bayler

6.6.8.6. (S.M.)
(St. Thomas)

The earth is yours, O God,
And we are tenants here.
May we be ready every day,
With joy, when you appear.

You judge our stewardship,
Our losses and our gains.
You know when we are filled with zeal
And when our passion wanes.

Increase our faith in Christ,
That resurrection power
May waken us from selfish pride,
Transforming us this hour.

We seek to be the church,
Christ's body on this earth,
Continuing the work of One
Whose love proclaims our worth.

Come, reign among us here,
Equipping us to serve,
That we may bear the fruit of love
And give without reserve. Amen.

(Matthew 21:33–46, Philippians 3:4b–14)

(See *Fresh Winds, Book 2*, p. 245.)

88

Praise to Our God

Proper 23 (October 9–15)
Lavon Bayler

11.10.11.10.
(Morning Star)

Praise to our God who is near and forgiving.
Praise for the promises we have received.
Love that is steadfast surrounds all our living.
Granting more wonders than we have believed.

God has delivered a people from bondage,
Guiding their footsteps through pathways unknown.
Yet they create other objects for homage,
Worshiping idols no god would condone.

God is the host who invites to a banquet
All of earth's children, life's riches to share.
Yet there are many without robe or basket,
Empty and hopeless with no one to care.

We are the ones who forget our Creator,
We are the people who revel in sin,
Living as if we were merely spectator
Rather than servant, new ways to begin.

Therefore, beloved, my sisters and brothers,
Be of one mind in the gospel each day.
Put aside worry while praying for others,
Letting God's peace guard your hearts in Christ's way.

Choose what is pleasing to God who will teach us;
Do what is true, just, and worthy of praise.
Let no impurity stain or impeach us
As we stand firm in the love Christ conveys.

(Exodus 32:1–14, Psalm 106:1–6, 9–23, Matthew 22:1–14,
Philippians 4:1–9)

(See *Fresh Winds, Book 2*, pp. 247, 252.)

89

What Shall We Give?

Proper 24 (October 16–22)
Lavon Bayler

6.6.8.6. (S.M.)
(Trentham)

What shall we give to God?
How shall we meet love's test?
All that we have is not our own,
For God our lives has blessed.

May there be prayers of thanks,
Offered for all to hear,
That, in our joyous gratitude,
The world may know God near.

May there be caring acts,
Offered in Jesus' name,
That faith and hope and steadfast love
May God's good news proclaim.

May there be mercy shown
To all who live in dread,
That, by the Holy Spirit's power,
The joy we know may spread.

Let us, then, dedicate
All that we give and keep,
That what we sow may offer growth
For other hands to reap.

(Exodus 33:12–23, Psalm 99, Matthew 22:15–22, 1 Thessalonians 1:1–10)

(See *Fresh Winds, Book 2*, p. 255.)

90

God Is Our Dwelling

Proper 25 (October 23–29)   7.6.7.6.D.
     Lavon Bayler   (Nyland)

In God we have our dwelling,
As does the universe.
Surrounding all creation,
Its light years to traverse,
The Spirit here enfolds us
With steadfast love and power.
Come, celebrate God's presence
In this and every hour.

A thousand years are nothing
Amid infinity,
Yet every moment matters
Within God's sovereignty.
Here everyone is valued;
To all our God lays claim,
Inviting our allegiance,
And calling us by name.

God promises a homeland,
A place where we belong.
God calls us to be holy,
And turn from doing wrong.
We shall not act unjustly,
Deferring to the great,
But, loving every neighbor,
Refuse to judge or hate.

(Repeat verse one.)

(Leviticus 19:1–2, 15–18, Deuteronomy 34:1–12, Psalm 90:1–6, 13–17)

91

God of Steadfast Love

Proper 25 (October 23–29)
Lavon Bayler

8.7.8.7.D.
(Hyfrydol)

God of steadfast love and mercy,
Look upon your servants here,
As we seek your love and favor,
Pardon and release from fear.
Meet us in our pain and sorrow;
Take away deceit and wrongs.
Prosper all our words and labor;
Make us glad to sing your songs.

We have heard the great commandments
Jesus chose and taught his friends:
With our hearts and souls to love you
With a zeal that never ends.
Using minds and strength to honor
You and every neighbor, too,
May we give ourselves with gladness,
Confident your word is true.

Grant us courage in our witness
To the gospel, day by day.
Help us live its caring message
As we follow Jesus' way.
May we gently nurse your children
Toward the health that you intend,
Showing kindness and compassion,
Your dominion to extend. Amen.

(Psalm 90:1–6, 13–17, Matthew 22:34–46, I Thessalonians 2:1–8)

(See *Fresh Winds, Book 2*, p. 257.)

92

Teach Us, O Savior

Proper 26 (October 30–November 5)
Lavon Bayler

10.10.10.10.
(Sursum Corda)

Teach us, O Savior, ways that we might live,
True to your covenant, our best to give.
May your commandments guide us on our way,
Prompting our finest efforts day by day.

May we be drawn to worship and to pray
By the example all your deeds display.
Help us become disciples, pure and true,
Finding identity through serving you.

When we betray you, when our words offend,
Help us your high intent to comprehend,
That we may change the ways that we relate,
Learning to listen carefully and wait.

Grant us to see the needs that others hide,
That we may empathize, with you as guide,
Walking beside them, helping bear the load,
Sharing the love that you so often showed.

Unite your people in one family,
Sisters and brothers, living faithfully.
Lead us to find fulfillment as we grow,
Thanking our God, through every joy and woe.

(Joshua 3:7–17, Psalm 107:1–07, 33–37, Matthew 23:1–12,
I Thessalonians 2:9–13)

(See *Fresh Winds, Book 2,* pp. 258–59.)

93

God, We Praise You

Proper 27 (November 6–12)
Lavon Bayler

8.7.8.7.8.7.7.
(Cwm Rhondda)

God, we praise you through our serving.
Let no lesser gods distract
Our attention and our yearning
From your Word that bids us act,
Planning wisely, with alertness,
Though by enemies attacked,
Though by enemies attacked.

We have chosen, most sincerely,
Faith in your abiding word.
And we long to know more clearly
Truths through which our hopes are stirred.
We'll encourage one another,
That your message may be heard,
That your message may be heard.

Keep us faithful in our teaching
Generations yet to come.
We, your pardon now beseeching,
Want to be more venturesome,
Reaching children with the gospel,
As disciples they become,
As disciples they become. Amen.

(Joshua 24:1–3a, 14–25, Psalm 78:1–7, Matthew 25:1–13,
I Thessalonians 4:13–18)

(See *Fresh Winds, Book 2*, p. 260.)

Related Hymns

94

Lift Up Your Eyes

Proper 28 (November 13–19)
Lavon Bayler

7.6.8.6.8.6.8.6.
(St. Christopher)

Lift up your eyes, O people,
As servants of life's best,
And recognize the talents God
Invites us to invest
In building up each other, and
Encouraging each one
To realize the realm of God
Among us here begun.

The talents God has given
Are destined for the light,
To spend in ways that offer hope
To those now lost in night.
We pray that we may faithfully
Fulfill our destiny
As stewards of the grace of God,
Engaged in ministry.

Have mercy on us, Savior,
When we betray your trust.
Restore us in your steadfast love
When we have been unjust.
If we are hurt or wronged, may we
Have courage to forgive.
Restore our faith in humankind
And teach us how to live. Amen.

(Psalm 123, Matthew 25:14–30, I Thessalonians 5:1–11)

(See *Fresh Winds, Book 2*, p. 262.)

95

Make a Joyful Noise

Proper 29 (Reign of Christ)
Lavon Bayler

7.7.7.7.D.
(Spanish Hymn)

Make a joyful noise and sing
Hymns that make the heavens ring.
God, our Shepherd, summons all
From the places where we fall,
Scattered and undisciplined,
Blown by every passing wind,
Now to worship and explore
Ways our spirits yet may soar.

Praising God, we enter in,
Here to face unwitting sin.
Do we welcome strangers here?
To the prisoner offer cheer?
Do the weary find a friend,
Working hard for hunger's end?
Sick and naked, thirsty, too,
Do they get some help from you?

Answering the Savior's call,
We our sad neglect recall.
Yet, we are by love embraced,
Welcomed here, and not disgraced.
God forgives the penitent,
Honoring our new intent,
Faithfully to serve each day,
Recommitted to Christ's way.

(Psalm 100, Ezekiel 34:11–16, 20–24, Matthew 25:31–46)

(See *Fresh Winds, Book 2,* p. 263.)

SPECIAL DAYS

96

Rejoicing with the Saints

All Saints' Day (November 1)
Lavon Bayler

6.6.6.6.6.6.
(Laudes Domini)

Rejoicing with the saints,
Resisting all complaints,
We worship and adore
With shout of joyous praise
The One who fills our days
With vistas to explore.

Our souls make humble boast
In God who is our host
Along this pilgrim way.
Oh, magnify with me
God's glorious sovereignty
On this and every day.

We listen for the word
Crowds on the mountain heard
When Jesus called them blessed.
Those hungry, poor, and weak,
The merciful and meek,
Were given Jesus' best.

May we be pure in heart
And seek to do our part
To live as God intends.
We turn from wickedness,
Thirsting for righteousness,
And peace that never ends.

(Psalm 34:1–10, 22, Matthew 5:1–12, 1 John 3:1–3, Revelation 7:9–17)

(See *Fresh Winds, Book 2,* pp. 265–66.)

97

Praise to You, O God

Thanksgiving Day
Lavon Bayler

8.7.8.7.8.7.
(Regent Square)

Praise to you, O God, in Zion,
You who answer heartfelt prayer.
We repeat our vows before you,
Our commitment to repair.
You have promised to forgive us
As we now our sins declare.

You have fed us with abundance
Meant for all of us to share.
You have multiplied our riches,
Kept us in your love and care.
Yet we hoard what you have given,
Thinking we have naught to spare.

Help us now to be more thankful
For your gracious providence,
Gladly sharing all you give us,
Sowing with new confidence,
Cheerfully to share the harvest
In renewed obedience.

We are happy to be near you,
Serving in your courts today,
Joining in a great thanksgiving,
Humbly gathering to pray.
By your mercy, heal and save us.
May we follow Jesus' way. Amen.

(Deuteronomy 8:7–18, Psalm 65, Luke 17:11–19, 2 Corinthians 9:6–15)

(See *Fresh Winds, Book 2*, pp. 267–69.)

98

Thank You, Creator

Thanksgiving Day
Lavon Bayler

8.8.8.8.8.8. (L.M. Ref.)
(St. Catherine)

Thank you, Creator, mighty God;
Thank you for life and health and food.
We have received abundantly
Gifts of your grace, each day renewed.
We thank you, God; we praise your name.
Each day we will your love proclaim.

All that we have belongs to you;
Our wealth is not by our own hand.
May our good works reflect our vow
To live each day by your command.
We thank you, God; we praise your name.
Each day we will your love proclaim.

Thank you for mercy, freely given.
Thank you for faith that conquers fear.
You give us confidence to live
With hope and joy and love sincere.
We thank you, God; we praise your name.
Each day we will your love proclaim.

Renew in us your covenant,
As we fulfill our ministry,
With saints and sinners every day,
Sharing your generosity.
We thank you, God; we praise your name.
Each day we will your love proclaim. Amen.

(Deuteronomy 8:7–18, Psalm 65, Luke 17:11–19, 2 Corinthians 9:6–15)

99

God Who Has Led Us

Church Anniversary
Lavon Bayler

8.8.4.4.D. with Alleluias
(Lasst uns erfreuen)

God, who has led us through the years,
Loving, supporting, calming fears,
Hear our praises: Alleluia!
You have been faithful every day
Though we have wandered from your way.
We would thank you! Alleluia!
Alleluia, alleluia, alleluia!

Out of our varied history,
You have developed Unity.
Hear our praises. Alleluia!
As, in your church, we celebrate
All you have helped us to create,
We would thank you! Alleluia!
Alleluia, alleluia, alleluia!

Looking ahead, we seek to know
Where you, O God, would have us go
As we praise you. Alleluia!
Shape and expand our ministry,
That we may build community,
As we thank you. Alleluia!
Alleluia, alleluia, alleluia!

Grant us the vision to embrace
People of every land and race
As we praise you. Alleluia!
May we, your children, sense our worth,
Sharing your love through all the earth
As we thank you. Alleluia!
Alleluia, Alleluia, Alleluia!

(Commissioned for the Tenth Anniversary of Unity United Church of Christ, Trumbull, Connecticut.)

100

Amazing God, Whose Mercy

Installation
Lavon Bayler

10.10.10.8.
(Sine Nomine)

Amazing God, whose mercy overflows
In acts of ministry your grace bestows,
Upbuild us here, your purpose to disclose,
In living wholeness, in loving wholeness.

Save us from idols of prosperity:
Spending our days for things that we can see.
Transform our arrogant hypocrisy
In living wholeness, in loving wholeness.

Thank you for gifts that we can use for you,
Varying gifts equipping us anew.
To work for justice, healing to pursue,
In living wholeness, in loving wholeness.

Challenge us now in our conformity
To ways that contradict community,
That we may celebrate diversity
In living service, in loving service.

Renew our minds that we may know you still,
Leading us on, your purpose to fulfill
In servanthood, responsive to your will,
In living service, in loving service.

Bless now the leader(s) we install today.
May (his/her/their) discipleship your word convey
As, full of hope, (he/she/they) follow(s) Jesus' way
In living service, in loving service. Amen.

(Written for and sung at the 36th Annual Meeting of the Illinois Conference, United Church of Christ, June 1996.)

Indexes

ALPHABETICAL INDEX OF HYMNS

(by hymn number)

TOPICAL INDEX OF HYMNS

(by hymn number)

Called as the Church 18
Christ Leads Us Forward 38
Come, Spirit of God 72
Following Christ 84
Gifted by Grace 78
God, We Praise You 93
How Shall We Live? 63
Jesus Has Risen 44
Jesus, Lend Your Light 34
Let Your Day Dawn 28
Our Savior Traveled 61
Rejoice, O Hills 21
Send Your Advocate 52
So Precious in God's Sight 41
The Crowds Gathered 68
We Rejoice 76
We Seek Your Wisdom 53
You Are the One 25

Doubt
At End of Day 46
God, Hear Your People 33
Jesus, Lend Your Light 34
Lying in a Manger 8
Our Savior Traveled 61
Send Your Advocate 52

Easter Season
At End of Day 46
At the Day's Dawning 45
Blest God Who Gives Birth 47
Invoke the Name 48
Jesus Has Risen 44
Let Your Face Shine 50
Send Your Advocate 52
The Hour Has Come 54
Unknown God, We Search 51
We Seek Your Wisdom 53
Wonders and Signs 49

Education (see Teaching)

Epiphany and Season Following
Baptized and Accepted 16
Blest Be Our God 26

Called as the Church 18
Children, Gather 17
God of Holiness 24
God of Judgment 23
God, You Have Given 19
God's Grace Is Given 15
Help Us Build 27
Let Your Day Dawn 28
Rejoice, O Hills 21
We Humble Ourselves 22
Welcome the Savior 20
You Are the One 25

Eternal Life
At End of Day 46
Following Christ 84
God of Judgment 23
Send Your Advocate 52
We Seek Your Presence 32
We're Called to Faith 6

Faith
Blest Be Our God 26
Called as the Church 18
Christ Leads Us Forward 38
From Garden to the Cross 42
God Appears 60
God, Hear Your People 33
God, We Praise You 93
God's Grace Is Given 15
Help Us Build 27
How Manifold the Gifts 55
Invoke the Name 48
Jesus, Lend Your Light 34
Let Your Face Shine 50
Lift Up Your Eyes 94
Lying in a Manger 8
O God, Our Hope 39
Our Hiding Place 30
Praise God for Memories 59
Thank You, Creator 98
The Earth Is Yours 87
We Are Descendants 58
We Humble Ourselves 22

Ordination, Installation, Commissioning

Pain and Suffering

Peace

Penitence (see Confession, Repentance)

Pentecost and Season Following

Prayer

Repentance (see also Confession)

Resurrection

INDEX OF SCRIPTURE READINGS

(The italicized scriptures indicate the alternate series of readings
for the Sundays following Pentecost)

Ascension Day
Pentecost Alt.
Proper 7

Alone
After Christmas 1
Lent 2, 6
Easter Season 6

Amazement
Christmas, Proper II
January 1—Holy Name
After Epiphany 1, 5, 8, Last
Lent 3
Holy Week—M, Sat
Easter Day 1, Evening
Pentecost 1, Alt.
Trinity Sunday
Proper 7, 8, 10, 14, 18, 20, 22, 23,
24

Ancestors
Lent 3
Proper 11, 17, 18, 19, 20, 23, 25,
26, 27

Anger
Advent 4
Epiphany
After Epiphany 6
Holy Week—Sat
Proper 15, 17

Anguish
After Epiphany 3
Holy Week—F
Proper 13

Anticipation
Advent 1, 4
Ash Wednesday
Pentecost Alt.
Proper 5, 9, 18

Anxiety (see Fear)

Apathy
Proper 25

Apostles (see also Disciples)
Proper 25

Appearances
Advent 1
Lent 4
Proper 6

Appreciation
Proper 10
Thanksgiving Day

Arrogance
Holy Week—M

Ascension
Ascension Day

Assurance
Lent 2, 3, 5
Easter Evening
Easter Season 4
Proper 5, 11, 12, 14, 18, 20, 21,
24, 28

**Astonishment (see also
Amazement)**
Lent 2
Easter Evening
Pentecost 1, Alt.

Attention
Lent 3
Easter Season 6
Proper 13

Attitudes
Advent 3
Holy Week—F
Proper 10

Authority
Christmas, Proper I
January 1—Holy Name
Proper 4

Awaken(ing)
Advent 1, 4
Christmas, Proper I
After Epiphany Last
Lent 4
Holy Week—W, F
Easter Day 1
Proper 18

Awareness
January 1—New Year
After Epiphany 5
Easter Season 6
Proper 7, 22, 28
Thanksgiving Day

Awe and Wonder
Advent 1, 2
Christmas, Propers I and II
After Christmas 1
January 1—Holy Name, New
    Year
After Epiphany 5, Last
Lent 3
Holy Week—Th, F
Easter Day Alt., Evening
Easter Season 4, 5, 7
Ascension Day
Trinity Sunday
Proper 5, 7, 10, 11, 13, 14, 22 23,
    24, 25

Baptism
Advent 2
After Epiphany 1, 2
Lent 2
Easter 3, 6
Ascension Day
Trinity Sunday
Proper 7

Beatitudes
After Epiphany 4
All Saints' Day

Beauty
Christmas, Proper III
January 1—Holy Name
After Epiphany 3
Easter Season 3
Proper 8, 12

Belief(s), Believers
Advent 4
After Christmas 2
After Epiphany 1, 7, Last
Lent 2, 4, 5
Holy Week—Tu
Easter Day 1
Easter Season 5
Pentecost 1, Alt.
Proper 8, 14, 15, 18

**Beloved (see also God's
Love)**
After Epiphany 1, 6, Last

Best
Advent 1
January 1—New Year
After Epiphany 4, 5, 7, 9, Last
Lent 2
Holy Week—M, Th, Sat
Easter Season 6, 7
Trinity Sunday
Proper 12, 23

Betrayal
Lent 6
Holy Week—W, Th, F
Easter Day 1
Proper 15

Better Way
Pentecost Alt.
Proper 19

Bewilderment
Holy Week—Sat

Birth
Advent 1
Christmas, Proper II
Easter Season 2, 3

Bitterness
Advent 4

Blessing(s)
Advent 1
Christmas, Propers I and II
January 1—Holy Name
After Epiphany 3, 4, 6, 8, 9
Lent 1, 4, 6
Holy Week—M
Easter Evening
Easter Season 2, 6, 7
Pentecost Alt.
Trinity Sunday
Proper 4, 5, 8, 9, 13, 15, 19, 21,
    24, 25, 26, 28, 29
All Saints' Day
Thanksgiving Day

Blindness
Advent 3
Christmas, Proper III
After Christmas 2
Proper 15, 29

Boasting
After Epiphany 7, 9

Body of Christ
Holy Week—W, Sat
Easter Season 3, 5, 7
Ascension Day
Pentecost
Proper 14, 16, 22, 28, 29

Bondage
After Epiphany 5

Proper 6, 11, 18, 27
Thanksgiving Day

Born Anew
Lent 2
Easter Season 3

Bounty
Advent 1
After Christmas 2
After Epiphany 7
Holy Week—Th
Trinity Sunday
Proper 6, 8, 13, 15, 23
Thanksgiving Day

Bow Down
Lent 3
Easter Season 7
Proper 7, 9, 17, 19

Bread
Lent 1
Holy Week—W, Th
Easter Evening
Easter Season 4
Proper 5, 20

Breath(e)
Holy Week—Sat
Easter Season 2, 6
Pentecost

Brightness
Christmas, Proper III
Epiphany
After Epiphany Last
Lent 4
Easter Day 1

Brokenness
After Epiphany 6
Ash Wednesday
Easter Day 1
Proper 7, 13, 15, 18
All Saints' Day

Brothers and Sisters
After Christmas 1
January 1—Holy Name
Lent 3
Holy Week—Th
Easter Day 1
Easter Season 5, 6
Ascension Day
Trinity Sunday
Proper 17, 19, 25

Brutality
Holy Week—W

Build(ing)
After Epiphany 3, 5
Easter Season 5
Pentecost
Proper 7, 16, 28

Burdens
After Epiphany 8
Proper 6, 9, 26

Burning Bush
Proper 17

Burnt Offerings
After Epiphany 4

Busyness
Advent 3
After Christmas 1, 2
After Epiphany 1, 9
Holy Week—Tu
Easter Day Alt.
Easter Season 2, 3
Proper 9, 17

Call(ed)
Christmas, Proper II
Epiphany
After Epiphany 1, 4, 5, 6, 7

Ash Wednesday
Lent 4, 5
Holy Week—Tu
Easter Day 1
Easter Season 3, 6
Ascension Day
Proper 5, 7, 11, 18, 20, 22, 27, 29
All Saints' Day

Calm
After Epiphany 8

Care, Caring
January 1—Holy Name, New
     Year
After Epiphany 7, 9
Lent 6
Holy Week—M, Th, Sat
Easter Season 2, 4, 5, 6, 7
Pentecost 1, Alt.
Trinity Sunday
Proper 4, 5, 6, 7, 9, 10, 13, 14, 15,
     16, 18, 19, 21, 25, 26, 29
Thanksgiving Day

Celebration
After Christmas 2
After Epiphany 8
Lent 6
Holy Week—Th
Easter 1, Alt., Evening
Easter Season 2, 4, 7
Ascension Day
Trinity Sunday
Proper 4, 7, 8, 9, 10, 13, 18, 27
All Saints' Day

Challenge(s)
After Epiphany 2, 6
Ash Wednesday
Lent 2, 3, 4, 6
Holy Week—Th, F
Easter Day, Alt., Evening
Easter Season 7

Proper 4, 5, 6, 12, 14, 17, 21, 27
All Saints' Day

Change

January 1—New Year
After Epiphany 1, 3, 5, 6, 9, Last
Lent 4
Easter Day 1, Evening
Ascension Day
Pentecost Alt.
Proper 4, 6, 12, 17, 20, 21, 26, 29

Children of God

Advent 4
Christmas, Propers I and III
After Christmas 1, 2
January 1—Holy Name
After Epiphany 3, 4, 8, 9, Last
Lent 4
Holy Week—M, Tu
Easter Day Alt.
Easter Season 3, 7
Ascension Day
Pentecost
Proper 4, 6, 8, 10, 11, 15, 16, 19,
        20, 24, 27, 28
All Saints' Day

Choice(s)

Advent 4
After Epiphany 6
Lent 1
Holy Week—M
Proper 18, 20, 23, 27

Chosen

After Christmas 2
Holy Week—M, Tu
Easter Season 5
Proper 5, 20, 24

Christ's Coming (Appearance)

Christmas, Proper I
Easter Sunday 1, Evening

Christ's Example

After Epiphany 3
Holy Week—Tu, Th, F
Easter Season 4, 5
Proper 12

Christ's Leading

Christmas, Proper I
After Epiphany 2, 3
Lent 3, 6
Holy Week—Tu, Th
Easter Day Alt.
Easter Season 4, 5
Proper 11, 12, 14

Christ's Name

After Epiphany 1
Easter Season 2, 3, 4, 5
Ascension Day
Pentecost
Proper 5, 8, 10, 13, 17, 21

Christ's Presence

Lent 5
Holy Week—Tu
Easter Day Alt., Evening
Easter Season 2, 3, 5, 6
Proper 20, 21

Christ's Promises

Trinity Sunday

Christ's Teachings

After Epiphany 3, 4
Holy Week—Th, F
Easter Season 6
Ascension Day
Proper 7, 12, 23, 26

Church

After Epiphany 1, 2, 3, 6, 7, 9,
        Last
Ash Wednesday
Lent 1, 2, 6

Holy Week—W, F, Sat
Easter Season 5, 7
Ascension Day
Pentecost
Proper 4, 5, 9, 10, 14, 16, 18, 20,
    21, 22, 23, 24, 27, 28, 29

Cleansing
Advent 3
After Epiphany 2
Ash Wednesday
Lent 3
Holy Week—F
Easter Evening
Proper 10, 15
Thanksgiving Day

Clouds
After Epiphany Last
Ash Wednesday
Holy Week—Tu, W
Pentecost, Alt.
Proper 19

Comfort
After Christmas 2
After Epiphany 4, 8
Easter Season 4
Proper 6, 7, 9
All Saints' Day

Commandments
After Christmas 2
After Epiphany 4, 7, 9
Easter Season 6
Proper 4, 6, 13, 18, 22, 25, 27, 28
Thanksgiving Day

Commendation
After Epiphany 8

Commission(ed)
Christmas, Proper III
After Epiphany 2
Proper 6

Commitment
Christmas, Propers II and III
January 1—Holy Name
Epiphany
After Epiphany 1, 2, 3, 4, 9, Last
Ash Wednesday
Lent 6
Holy Week—Th, F, Sat
Easter Day Alt.
Easter Season 2, 3, 5, 6
Pentecost
Proper 6, 8, 10, 14, 26
All Saints' Day

Communion
January 1—Holy Name
Ash Wednesday
Lent 3, 5
Holy Week—Th, F
Trinity Sunday
Proper 25

Community
Christmas, Proper III
After Christmas 1, 3
After Epiphany 6, 9, Last
Ash Wednesday
Lent 1, 4
Easter Day Alt.
Easter Season 2, 4, 5, 6
Ascension Day
Proper 6, 7, 9, 12, 13, 15, 16, 17,
    18, 19, 20, 21, 22, 24, 25, 26,
    28
All Saints' Day

Compassion
Advent 3
Christmas, Proper III
After Epiphany 8
Lent 4, 5
Holy Week—M, Sat
Easter Day Alt.

Proper 6, 8, 9, 13, 16, 20, 21, 25,
    29
All Saints' Day

Complacency
After Epiphany 5, Last
Easter Season 6

Complain(er)(ts)
Lent 3
Proper 9, 13, 17, 20

Concern
Lent 3
Pentecost Alt.
Proper 4, 9, 10, 12, 13, 21, 24

Condemn(ation)
Proper 10, 18

Confess(ion)
After Christmas 1
January 1—New Year
After Epiphany 1, 2, 6
Ash Wednesday
Lent 5
Easter Evening
Proper 4, 5, 6, 10, 13, 15, 24, 27
Thanksgiving Day

Confidence
Advent 4
Epiphany
Lent 2
Holy Week—W, Th
Easter Day Alt.
Easter Season 7
Pentecost 1
Trinity Sunday
Proper 7, 9, 12, 14, 16, 23, 26, 28

Conformity
Proper 16

Confront(ation)
Christmas, Proper III
After Epiphany 6

Confusion
Holy Week—W
Proper 25

Conscience
Holy Week—F

Consciousness
Pentecost Alt.

Consumers
Pentecost Alt.

Control
Pentecost 1

Convictions
Proper 24

Cornerstone
Easter Day Alt.
After Easter 5
Proper 22

Cost
Lent 6
Holy Week—Th
Proper 7, 21

Counsel(or)
Advent 2
Proper 26

Courage
Christmas, Proper II
After Epiphany 6, 9, Last
Lent 1, 2, 5, 6
Easter Day 1, Evening
Easter Season 2
Trinity Sunday

Proper 4, 5, 12, 15, 17, 20, 25, 26,
27

Covenant
Christmas, Proper III
After Epiphany 1, 8
Lent 6
Holy Week—M, Th
Proper 4, 6, 8, 12, 13, 27
Thanksgiving Day

Cowardice
Lent 6

Creation, Creator
Christmas, Proper III
After Christmas 1
January 1—Holy Name, New
Year
After Epiphany 8
Lent 1, 2
Easter Day Alt.
Easter Season 5, 6, 7
Pentecost 1
Trinity Sunday
Proper 5, 6, 7, 8, 12, 13, 15, 16,
17, 24, 25, 26, 27
All Saints' Day
Thanksgiving Day

Creativity
After Epiphany 9

Cries
January 1—New Year
After Epiphany 2
Lent 1, 5
Holy Week—F, Sat
Proper 7, 13, 26
All Saints' Day

Cross
After Epiphany 3, 4
Ash Wednesday

Lent 2, 6
Holy Week—Tu, W, Th, F, Sat
Easter Day 1
Proper 7, 17

Crown of Thorns
Holy Week—F

Crucifixion
Lent 6
Easter Day Alt.
Easter Season 2

Cruelty
Holy Week—Tu

Cup
Lent 6
Holy Week—Th
Easter Evening
Easter Season 3, 4
Proper 6, 8

Cynicism
Holy Week—F

Damage
Holy Week—Sat

Daring (see also Risk)
Advent 4
After Epiphany 9
Holy Week—Sat
Pentecost 1, Alt.
Proper 5, 28

Darkness
After Epiphany 3
Easter Season 5
Proper 11, 18

Dawn
After Epiphany Last
Easter Day 1

Dead, Death
Advent 3
After Christmas 1
After Epiphany 6
Lent 2, 3, 5
Holy Week—Tu, Th, F, Sat
Easter Day 1, Alt., Evening
Easter Season 2, 6
Trinity Sunday
Proper 5, 6, 7, 10, 11, 12, 19, 21

Dead Works
Holy Week—M

Deceit, Deception
Lent 6
Holy Week—M, F, Sat
Proper 12, 13, 14, 15

Decisions
After Epiphany 6
Proper 24, 27

Dedication
After Epiphany 9
Ash Wednesday
Holy Week—M, Tu
Easter Day 1
Easter Season 3, 4, 5
Trinity Sunday
Proper 8, 12, 15, 19
Thanksgiving Day

Deeds
January 1—New Year
After Epiphany 4
Holy Week—F
Easter Season 3
Proper 8, 12, 15, 19
Thanksgiving Day

Delight
Advent 2
After Epiphany 5, 7

Lent 1
Holy Week—M
Easter Day Alt.
Proper 6, 8, 9
All Saints' Day

Deliverance
Holy Week—W, Th, F
Easter Season 5
Proper 23
All Saints' Day

Denial
Christmas, Proper II
After Epiphany 6
Lent 6
Holy Week—F
Easter Day 1
Easter Season 6
Ascension Day
Pentecost 1
Proper 9, 17

Depth
Holy Week—M
Easter Season 3
Pentecost Alt.
Proper 10

Desert (see Wilderness)
Lent 1
Proper 26

Desires
After Epiphany 6

Desolation
Easter Season 7

Despair
After Epiphany 2, 3
Holy Week—Tu, F, Sat
Easter Day 1
Easter Season 2

Pentecost 1
Proper 10

Destiny
After Epiphany Last

Devotion
After Epiphany 4
Pentecost Alt.
Proper 27

Differences
Holy Week—F
Easter Season 3, 5
Proper 14, 18

Difficulties
Lent 1, 2
Holy Week—Th

Dimness
After Epiphany 1

Direction
Lent 6
Pentecost 1, Alt.
Proper 6, 26

Discipleship
After Epiphany 2, 8, 9
Ash Wednesday
Lent 3, 4, 6
Holy Week—M, W, Th, F
Easter Day 1, Alt., Evening
Easter Season 2, 3, 7
Pentecost 1, Alt.
Trinity Sunday
Proper 4, 6, 7, 8, 10, 29

Discipline(s)
After Epiphany 6
Holy Week—Th
Easter Season 6, 7
Proper 29

Dishonesty
After Epiphany 6

Distractions
After Epiphany 9
Lent 1
Easter Day Alt.
Easter Season 6
Proper 23, 27

Distress
After Christmas 1
January 1—New Year
Lent 5
Proper 7, 9, 12, 13, 15, 23

Diversity
Advent 1
After Christmas 2
After Epiphany 3, 7
Lent 4
Proper 10
All Saints' Day

Divisions
After Epiphany 3
Proper 7, 16

Doom
Lent 6

Doubt(s)
After Christmas 2
After Epiphany 4
Lent 2, 3, 6
Easter Day Alt., Evening
Easter Season 2, 5, 7
Pentecost Alt.
Trinity Sunday
Proper 6, 12, 14, 21, 29
All Saints' Day

Dove
After Epiphany 1

Drama
Holy Week—W, Th
Pentecost Alt.

Dreams, Dreamers
Epiphany
After Epiphany 9
Holy Week—Sat
Pentecost 1, Alt.
Proper 11, 14, 25

Drink
Holy Week—M
Pentecost Alt.
Proper 20

Dry Bones
Lent 5

Ears
Advent 3
After Epiphany 5
Lent 1
Holy Week—W
Easter Season 3, 5
Proper 9, 13, 21
Thanksgiving Day

Emmanuel
Advent 4

Empowerment
After Epiphany 5, 6, 8, 9, Last
Ash Wednesday
Lent 5
Easter Day Alt.
Easter Season 2, 6, 7
Ascension Day
Pentecost 1, Alt.
Trinity Sunday
Proper 6, 8, 16, 18, 19, 20, 24, 29
All Saints' Day

Emptiness
Advent 3, 4

After Christmas 1
Easter Day 1
Proper 5, 9, 27

Encouragement
After Epiphany 6
Lent 3, 5
Holy Week—F
Proper 21, 27, 28

Endurance
Ash Wednesday
Lent 3
Holy Week—Tu, W
Easter Season 3

Enemies
Advent 4
After Epiphany 3, 4, 7
Easter Day 1
Easter Season 5
Proper 14, 16, 18

Energy
Advent 4
January 1—New Year
After Epiphany 9
Lent 3, 4, 5
Easter Season 3
Proper 10, 14, 16, 17, 18, 22, 26

Enlighten(ment)
After Christmas 2
Ascension Day
Proper 22, 29

Enrichment
Proper 5
Thanksgiving Day

Estrangement
After Epiphany 6

Eternal (Life), Eternity
Christmas, Proper II

January 1—New Year
Lent 2, 3
Easter Season 2, 7
Pentecost Alt.
Trinity Sunday
Proper 8, 9, 11, 15, 24, 25, 27, 29
All Saints' Day

Evil
Advent 2, 4
Christmas, Proper III
After Epiphany 4, 5
Lent 2, 4, 6
Holy Week—F
Easter Evening
Easter Season 7
Proper 15, 17, 19
Thanksgiving Day

Excellence
Proper 23

Excitement
Ash Wednesday
Pentecost Alt.

Excuse(s)
Lent 4
Easter Season 5

Existence
Lent 2, 4

Expectations
January 1—New Year
After Epiphany 6, 7, 9
Lent 5
Holy Week—Th
Easter Day Alt.
Pentecost 1
Proper 4, 8, 15, 17, 19, 29
All Saints' Day

Exultation
Proper 8
All Saints' Day

Eyes
Advent 3
After Epiphany 1, 5, 6, Last
Lent 1, 2, 3, 4
Holy Week—M, W
Easter Season 3, 5
Ascension Day
Proper 8, 12, 28, 29
All Saints' Day
Thanksgiving Day

Failure
After Epiphany 2
Lent 2, 6
Holy Week—Tu
Proper 4

Faith
Advent 4
After Christmas 2
Epiphany
After Epiphany 3, 5, 7, 9
Lent 1, 2, 5
Holy Week—M, W, Th, F
Ester Day Alt., Evening
Easter Season 2, 3,4, 6, 7
Ascension Day
Pentecost Alt.
Proper 4, 7, 10, 11, 12, 13, 14, 16,
    17, 20, 21, 23, 25, 27, 28, 29

Faithfulness
Advent 3
Christmas, Propers II and III
After Christmas 1
January 1—Holy Name
Epiphany
After Epiphany 2, 9, Last
Ash Wednesday

Lent 1, 2, 3, 6
Holy Week—M, Tu, W, Th, F
Easter Evening
Easter Season 5, 6, 7
Trinity Sunday
Proper 4, 5, 7, 8, 13, 14, 15, 18,
    21, 22, 25, 27, 28, 29
All Saints' Day

Falseness

January 1—Holy Name
After Epiphany 2, 4, 7, 8, 9
After Pentecost 4, 5, 13, 23, 24, 27, 28

Family (of God, of Faith)

Christmas, Proper III
January 1—New Year
After Epiphany 1, 6, 9
Easter Season 3
Proper 10, 14, 22, 23
Thanksgiving Day

Fanatical

Pentecost 1

Fasting

Ash Wednesday

Father/Mother

Lent 5

Fear(s)

Advent 3, 4
After Christmas 1
After Epiphany 2, 3, 9, Last
Lent 2, 6
Holy Week—Tu, Th, F
Easter Day 1, Alt., Evening
Easter Season 2, 4, 6, 7
Pentecost
Proper 6, 7, 11, 13, 14, 16, 19, 22,
    23, 28
All Saints' Day

Feast, Festival

Holy Week—M
Easter Evening
Proper 18, 23, 27

Feeding, Fed, Food

January 1—New Year
After Epiphany 5, 8
Proper 10, 13, 20
All Saints' Day
Thanksgiving Day

Feet

Proper 10

Fire, Flames

Advent 2
After Epiphany Last
Holy Week—F
Easter Season 2
Pentecost 1, Alt.
Proper 17, 18, 19

First Things First

After Epiphany 8

Flesh

After Christmas 1, 2
January 1—Holy Name
After Epiphany 6
Lent 5, 6
Pentecost Alt.
Proper 20
Thanksgiving Day

Follow(ers)

After Epiphany 3, 9, Last
Lent 2, 4, 5, 6
Holy Week—Tu, W, Th
Easter Day Alt.
Easter Season 4, 5, 6
Pentecost Alt.

Proper 4, 5, 11, 14, 16, 17, 18, 20,
  21, 26, 29
All Saints' Day

Food (see Fed)
Advent 3
January 1—New Year
After Epiphany 6, 8
Easter Day 1
Proper 20

Foolishness
After Epiphany 3, 4, 7
Holy Week—Tu

Foot Washing
Holy Week—Th

Forbidden Fruits
Lent 1

Forget(fulness), Forgotten
Christmas, Propers II and III
After Epiphany 8
Easter Season 2, 7
Proper 8, 27
Thanksgiving Day

Forgiveness
Christmas, Propers II and III
After Christmas 1, 2
January 1—Holy Name, New
  Year
After Epiphany 1, 3, 4, 6, 8, 9
Ash Wednesday
Lent 1, 5
Holy Week—M, W, Th, Sat
Easter Day 1
Easter Season 3, 5, 6
Ascension Day
Proper 5, 6, 7, 8, 9, 10, 11, 12, 14,
  15, 16, 17, 18, 19, 24, 25, 27
Thanksgiving Day

Forsaken (not)
Christmas, Proper II
After Epiphany 3, 6
Lent 6
Holy Week—F

Fortress
After Epiphany 9
Holy Week—Tu, Sat
Easter Season 5

Foundation
After Epiphany 5, 7, 9
Proper 4

Freedom, Freeing
After Christmas 1
After Epiphany 1, 5, 7, 8
Lent 1, 5
Holy Week—M
Pentecost Alt.
Proper 4, 6, 7, 8, 10, 11, 13, 15,
  16, 17, 18, 22, 26, 27

Friends
Advent 1
January 1—New Year
After Epiphany 4, 7, Last
Lent 3
Holy Week—M, Th
Easter Season 4
Ascension Day
Proper 8, 10, 14, 23
Thanksgiving Day

Fruit(s)
Advent 2
Lent 1
Holy Week—Tu, Th
Easter Season 6
Proper 10, 11, 12, 17, 20, 26

Fulfillment, Full Life
Advent 4

After Christmas 1, 2
After Epiphany 4, 7, Last
Lent 6
Holy Week—M
Easter Evening
Easter Season 2, 5
Trinity Sunday
Proper 5, 7, 12, 18, 23

Futility
Easter Season 3

Future
January 1—New Year

Gathering
Epiphany
Holy Week—M, Sat
Easter Season 4
Pentecost 1, Alt.
Proper 4, 7, 8, 13, 15, 16
All Saints' Day

Generosity
After Christmas 1
Epiphany
After Epiphany 2, 5, 7, 8
Ash Wednesday
Lent 1, 4, 6
Holy Week—Sat
Easter Season 4
Ascension Day
Proper 4, 8, 12, 13, 14, 16, 19, 20,
    23, 29
Thanksgiving Day

Gentleness
Easter Season 4, 6
Proper 9, 25

Gifts, Giving
Epiphany
After Epiphany 3, 4, 5, 8, Last
Ash Wednesday

Lent 2, 4, 6
Holy Week—M, Tu, W, Th, F
Easter Day 1, Evening
Easter Season 3, 4, 5, 6, 7
Pentecost 1, Alt.
Proper 5, 7, 9, 12, 15
All Saints' Day
Thanksgiving Day

Gladness
Advent 3
After Christmas 1, 2
After Epiphany 2
Holy Week—Th
Easter Day 1, Alt.
Easter Season 2, 4, 7
Proper 6, 9, 29

Gloom
Holy Week—F

Goals
Easter Season 7
Proper 22

God's Benefits
Easter Season 6

God's Call (see Call)
Epiphany
After Epiphany 1, 4, 5, 6, 7
Ash Wednesday
Lent 2, 5
Holy Week—Tu
Easter Evening
Easter Season 3
Pentecost
Proper 5, 9, 15, 17

God's Care
Christmas, Proper II
After Christmas 1
January 1—Holy Name
After Epiphany 5, 8, 9

Lent 2, 3, 5
Holy Week—F
Easter Season 4, 7
Trinity Sunday
Proper 7, 10, 12, 19

God's Counsel
After Epiphany 6
Lent 1
Easter Season 2
Proper 5

God's Earth
January 1, New Year

God's Family
Easter Day Alt.

God's Faithfulness
Christmas, Proper III
After Epiphany 2, 9
Proper 16, 18, 29

God's Favor
Easter Season 6
Proper 24, 25

God's Gift(s)
Advent 4
Christmas, Propers I, II, and III
January 1—Holy Name, New
    Year
Epiphany
After Epiphany 2, 5, 7
Ash Wednesday
Lent 1, 2, 4
Holy Week—W
Easter Evening
Easter Season 3, 4, 6, 7
Ascension Day
Pentecost 1, Alt.
Proper 6, 8, 10, 11,12, 13, 15, 16,
    19, 20, 21, 22, 26, 29
Thanksgiving Day

God's Glory
Advent 2
Christmas, Propers I, II, and III
After Christmas 1, 2
January 1—Holy Name
Epiphany
After Epiphany 1, 5, 9, Last
Lent 5
Holy Week—Tu, W, Th
Easter Day 1
Easter Season 5
Pentecost 1, Alt.
Trinity Sunday
Proper 4, 6, 7, 12, 13, 16, 18, 20,
    22, 26

God's Goodness
Advent 4
Christmas, Proper II
After Christmas 1, 2
Epiphany
After Epiphany 1, 9
Lent 4
Easter Day 1
Easter Season 4, 5, 6
Trinity Sunday
Proper 13
All Saints' Day

God's Greatness
Christmas, Proper I
Holy Week—W
Proper 29

God's Guidance
After Epiphany 1, 5, 6
Ash Wednesday
Lent 6
Holy Week—M, Sat
Easter Season 7
Pentecost
Proper 7, 9, 10, 11,18, 19, 20, 22,
    23, 29
All Saints' Day

God's Holiness
Christmas, Proper I
Proper 9, 20

God's Inclusiveness
Holy Week—W, Th, F
Easter Day 2

God's Invitation
Ash Wednesday
Holy Week—M, Th

God's Kindness
Christmas, Proper II and III
Easter Day Alt.

God's Law
After Epiphany 2, 6, 7, 9
Lent 5
Holy Week—F
Proper 4, 6, 9, 10, 13, 16, 18, 20,
    22, 27

God's Leading
After Christmas 1
After Epiphany 1
Lent 1, 5
Holy Week—Sat
Easter Season 4
Proper 7, 11, 15, 18, 19
All Saints' Day
Thanksgiving Day

God's Love
Advent 2, 3, 4
Christmas, Propers I, II, and III
After Christmas 1, 2
After Epiphany 1, 2, 7, 8, 9, Last
Ash Wednesday
Lent 2, 3, 5, 6
Holy Week—Tu, W, Th, F, Sat
Easter Day 1, Alt., Evening
Easter Season 3, 4, 5, 6, 7
Ascension Day

Trinity Sunday
Proper 6, 7, 8, 10, 11,12,
    13,14,16, 18, 19, 20,
    21,22,23, 25, 26, 27, 28, 29
All Saints' Day
Thanksgiving Day

God's Majesty
January 1—Holy Name, New
    Year
After Epiphany 1, Last
Easter Season 7
Trinity Sunday
Proper 19
All Saints' Day

God's Patience
Easter Day Alt.

God's Peace
Advent 3
Christmas, Propers I and III
Lent 3
Easter Day Alt.
Pentecost
Proper 10

God's Power
Advent 4
Christmas, Propers II and III
After Epiphany 1, 3, 6
Easter Day, Alt., Evening
Easter Season 7
Pentecost 1
Proper 10
All Saints' Day

God's Presence
Advent 3, 4
Christmas, Propers II and III
After Christmas 1
January 1—New Year
Epiphany
After Epiphany 5, 6, 8, 9, Last

Ash Wednesday
Lent 1, 3, 6
Holy Week—Tu, F, Sat
Easter Day 1
Easter Season 2, 3, 6, 7
Ascension Day
Pentecost, Alt.
Trinity Sunday
Proper 4, 5, 6, 11, 12, 13, 14, 17,
    18, 19, 20, 21, 22, 24, 25, 26,
    27, 28
All Saints' Day

God's Promises
Advent 3, 4
Christmas, Proper I
After Epiphany 4, 5
Ash Wednesday
Easter Season 3
Ascension Day
Pentecost 1, Alt.
Proper 4, 5, 6, 11, 17, 18, 19, 20,
    25, 27

God's Protection
Proper 13, 14, 16, 27

God's Purposes
Advent 4
After Christmas 1
Epiphany
After Epiphany Last
Easter Day Alt.
Proper 5, 21, 25
All Saints' Day

God's Realm/Reign/Rule
Advent 2, 3
Christmas, Proper II
January 1—Holy Name, New
    Year
After Christmas 2
Epiphany
After Epiphany 3, 4, 5, 8, 9, Last

Lent 2, 3
Holy Week—Tu, F
Easter Day 1
Easter Season 6, 7
Ascension Day
Trinity Sunday
Proper 4, 6, 9, 10, 11, 12,15, 16,
    17, 20, 24, 26, 27
All Saints' Day

God's Saving Acts
Easter Season 5
Proper 27

God's Silence
Holy Week—F

God's Voice (see also Voices)
Ester Season 3, 4, 7
Proper 12, 17

God's Way(s)
Advent 2
Christmas, Proper I
Epiphany
After Epiphany 1, 6, 7, 9
Ash Wednesday
Lent 1, 4
Holy Week—W, Th
Easter Evening
Pentecost 1
Proper 4, 5, 11, 20, 25
Thanksgiving Day

God's Will
Advent 1
After Christmas 1, 2
January 1—Holy Name
Epiphany
After Epiphany 2, 4, 5, 6, 7, 9
Lent 4
Holy Week—F, Sat
Easter Day, Alt.
Trinity Sunday

Proper 4, 8, 9, 11, 12, 13, 15, 16,
24, 25, 27
Thanksgiving Day

God's Word
Advent 2
Christmas, Proper III
After Christmas 2
Epiphany
After Epiphany 9
Lent 1, 5
Holy Week—M
Easter Season 3, 5
Proper 5, 8, 10, 13, 14, 15, 16, 17,
20, 25, 26, 27
Thanksgiving Day

God's Works
After Christmas 1
After Epiphany 5
Lent 4
Holy Week—Tu
Pentecost 1, Alt.
Trinity Sunday
Proper 9, 12, 13, 14, 19, 20, 21,
23, 25

God's Wrath
Proper 23, 28

Good
Advent 4
Lent 4
Holy Week—Th
Easter Day, Alt.
Easter Season 6
Pentecost 1, Alt.
Trinity Sunday
Proper 9, 10, 11, 12, 14, 15, 16,
17, 19, 20, 21, 24, 29
Thanksgiving Day

Good Deeds
Christmas, Proper I

After Epiphany 5, 9
Holy Week—F
Easter Day Alt.
Proper 23

Good News
Advent 3
Christmas Propers I, II, and III
January 1—Holy Name
Epiphany
After Epiphany 2, 3, 8, Last
Lent 5, 6
Holy Week—M, Tu, W, Sat
Ester Day 1, Alt., Evening
Ascension Day
Pentecost 1, Alt.
Proper 4, 6, 7, 8, 11, 12, 14, 18,
25, 29
All Saints' Day
Thanksgiving Day

Goodness
Holy Week—Sat
Easter Season 2, 4
Proper 9, 29

Gospel
Epiphany
After Epiphany 2, 3,9
Holy Week—Sat
Proper 4, 8, 20, 24, 25
Thanksgiving Day

Grace, Gracious
Advent 4
Christmas, Propers I and II
After Christmas 1, 2
Epiphany
After Epiphany 2, 6, 7, 9
Ash Wednesday
Lent 1, 2, 3, 4, 5
Holy Week—Sat
Easter Season 7
Trinity Sunday

Proper 4, 5, 6, 7, 8, 9, 14, 16, 24,
27
Thanksgiving Day

Gratitude
Advent 4
Christmas, Proper III
January 1—Holy Name
Epiphany
After Epiphany 6
Lent 3
Holy Week—W
Proper 6, 7, 8, 9, 10, 19
Thanksgiving Day

Great and Glorious Day
Pentecost, Alt.

Greed
Lent 1
Proper 11, 25

Grief (see also Sorrow)
Lent 6
Holy Week—F, Sat
Easter Day, Alt.

Growth
After Epiphany 5, 8
Lent 6
Easter Day, Alt.
Easter Season 5
Ascension Day
Pentecost 1
Proper 8, 10, 12,15, 20, 22, 27
All Saints' Day

Grumble
Advent 3

Guests
Easter Evening

Guidance
January 1—Holy Name

After Epiphany 1, 5, 6
Ash Wednesday
Holy Week—M
Pentecost
Proper 18

Guilt
Holy Week—W
Easter Season 6
Proper 29

Hands
After Epiphany 8
Ash Wednesday
Lent 2, 3
Holy Week—M, Th
Easter Season 6
Pentecost Alt.
Proper 5, 11, 13,14, 21, 24

Happy
Christmas, Proper III
After Epiphany 6, Last
Proper 5

Harmony
Advent 2
Epiphany
Proper 17, 27

Harp, Lyre, etc.
Christmas, Proper III

Harvest
Lent 3
Proper 6, 10, 11, 26

Hate
Easter Evening

Health, Healing
Advent 3, 4
Christmas, Propers II and III
After Epiphany 1, 3, 5, 8, 9
Ash Wednesday

Lent 1, 4
Holy Week—Tu
Easter Day 1, Alt., Evening
Easter Season 3, 4, 5
Proper 6, 7, 8, 10, 13, 15, 16, 18,
    20, 29
All Saints' Day
Thanksgiving Day

Hearing
Advent 3
Christmas, Proper III
After Epiphany 4, 6
Ash Wednesday
Lent 3, 5
Holy Week—M
Easter Season 3, 5, 6
Pentecost Alt.
Proper 5, 6, 7, 10, 11, 13, 20, 21,
    26
Thanksgiving Day

Hearts
Advent 3, 4
Christmas, Propers II and III
After Epiphany 4, 5, 6, 9, Last
Ash Wednesday
Lent 1, 2, 3, 4
Holy Week—W, Th, F, Sat
Easter Evening
Easter Season 2, 3, 5
Ascension Day
Proper 4, 6, 9, 10, 11, 12, 14, 15,
    20, 25, 26, 27
Thanksgiving Day

Heirs
Christmas, Proper II
January 1—Holy Name

Helper, Helping
Advent 4
After Christmas 1
After Epiphany 2, 6, 7, 8
Lent 1, 2

Holy Week—Tu, W, Th, F, Sat
Easter Season 5, 6
Pentecost, Alt.
Proper 5, 7, 9, 13, 14, 16, 19, 24,
    26
Thanksgiving Day

Hidden
Proper 8, 10

Holiness
After Epiphany 7
Ash Wednesday
Proper 25

Holy Ground (Places)
After Epiphany 7
Proper 17

Holy Name
Christmas, Proper II
January 1—Holy Name

Holy People
Christmas, Proper II
After Epiphany 7

Holy Spirit
Advent 2
After Christmas 2
After Epiphany 1, 2, 7, Last
Ash Wednesday
Lent 1
Easter Season 2, 3, 7
Ascension Day
Pentecost 1, Alt.
Trinity Sunday
Proper 6, 10, 12, 15, 16, 20, 24
All Saints' Day

Holy Way
Advent 3

Home(s)
After Epiphany 9

Easter Season 7
Proper 15

Honesty
Christmas, Proper III
After Epiphany 7, 9
Holy Week—M
Proper 12, 21, 23, 26

Honor(able)
Advent 2
After Christmas 1, 2
January 1—Holy Name
After Epiphany 4, 5
Easter Season 6
Proper 8, 9, 18, 23, 26
Thanksgiving Day

Hope
Advent 2, 3
Christmas, Propers I, II, and III
After Epiphany 1, 9, Last
Ash Wednesday
Lent 3, 5
Holy Week—Tu, F, Sat
Easter Day 1, Evening
Easter Season 2, 3, 6, 7
Ascension Day
Pentecost 1
Trinity Sunday
Proper 5, 6, 10, 11, 13, 15, 16, 17,
    22, 24, 26, 27, 29
All Saints' Day
Thanksgiving Day

Hosanna
Lent 6
Easter Sunday 1

Hospitality
Proper 6, 17

Humility
Christmas, Proper II

January 1—Holy Name, New
    Year
After Epiphany 4, 5
Ash Wednesday
Lent 2, 6
Easter Season 5
Proper 7, 9, 16, 18, 21, 24, 25, 26
All Saints' Day

Hunger
Advent 1, 3
January 1—New Year
After Epiphany 4, 5, 8
Proper 13, 15, 26, 29
All Saints' Day

Hurts
Holy Week—M
Proper 15

Identity
Advent 1
January 1—Holy Name
Proper 11, 14, 18
All Saints' Day

Idols
After Epiphany 2
Lent 1
Holy Week—M, Sat
Proper 22, 23, 24, 27

Image
After Christmas 1
Trinity Sunday
Proper 6, 11, 27
All Saints' Day

Imagination
Pentecost
Proper 5

Impatience
Advent 3

Impulses
Lent 1

Inequality
Proper 29

Inheritance
January 1—Holy Name
After Christmas 2
Easter Season 2
Ascension Day
Proper 5, 12, 29

Iniquities (see Sin)

Insensitivity
Proper 16

Insight
Trinity Sunday
Proper 14, 16, 25, 29

Inspiration
After Epiphany Last
Holy Week—M, F
Easter Day 1, Evening
Easter Season 2, 5
Pentecost 1, Alt.
Proper 11, 23, 26
Thanksgiving

Instruction
Advent 1
Lent 1
Ascension Day
Proper 10, 16

Integrity
Lent 4

Intentions
After Epiphany 1, 4
Holy Week—M, Th, F
Proper 8, 27, 28

Intervention
Proper 8

Invest
After Epiphany 8
Lent 5
Pentecost
Proper 8, 27, 28

Invitation
After Christmas 1
After Epiphany 3, 4
Lent 4
Holy Week—M
Proper 9, 12, 14, 23
Thanksgiving Day

Isolation
Easter Season 5
Proper 9

Issues
Proper 13

Jealousy
Advent 1
After Epiphany 6
Proper 14, 15, 18, 20

Jesus Christ
Advent 2
Christmas, Propers II and III
After Christmas 1, 2
January 1—Holy Name
After Epiphany 2, 4, 5, 8, 9, Last
Ash Wednesday
Lent 1, 2, 3, 5, 6
Holy Week—M, Tu, W, Th, F, S
Easter Day 1, Alt.
Easter Season 2, 3, 4, 5, 6, 7
Ascension Day
Pentecost 1, Alt.
Trinity Sunday
Proper 4, 5, 6, 7, 8, 9, 10, 12, 13,

14, 15, 16, 18, 19, 21, 24, 25,
27, 28, 29
All Saints' Day
Thanksgiving Day

Journey
After Epiphany Last
Ash Wednesday
Lent 2
Easter Season 3, 6
Proper 5, 9, 20

Joy
Advent 2, 3
Christmas, Propers I and III
After Christmas 1, 2
January 1—Holy Name, New
Year
Epiphany
After Epiphany 1, 2, 3, 5, 7, 8
Ash Wednesday
Lent 1, 2, 3, 4, 5, 6
Holy Week—M, W
Easter Day 1, Alt.
Easter Season 2, 4, 7
Ascension Day
Pentecost 1, Alt.
Proper 6, 8, 9, 10, 11, 14, 16, 18,
20, 23, 24, 25, 26, 27, 28, 29
All Saints' Day
Thanksgiving Day

Joyful Noise
Lent 3
Proper 29

Judgment(al)
Advent 3, 4
January 1—New Year
Epiphany
After Epiphany 5, 8
Lent 4
Holy Week—M, Th, Sat

Easter Season 3, 5
Proper 5, 12, 16, 19, 27, 28, 29

Just, Justice
Advent 2
Christmas, Propers I and III
Epiphany
After Epiphany 1, 4, 5, 7
Lent 4
Holy Week—M, Tu
Easter Season 7
Proper 4, 5, 13, 23, 24, 28, 29
Thanksgiving

Justification
Proper 4

Keys
Proper 16

Kindness
January 1—New Year
After Epiphany 4
Ash Wednesday
Proper 13, 19
Thanksgiving Day

Kneel
Christmas, Proper II
Lent 3

Knowledge
After Christmas 2
After Epiphany 2, 4, Last
Ash Wednesday
Easter Season 3, 6
Ascension Day
Pentecost 1
Proper 8, 11, 12, 19, 24

Labor(ers)
Easter Season 5, 6
Proper 6, 20

Lamp(s)
After Epiphany Last
Proper 10, 27

Last Supper
Holy Week—Th

Law
Proper 4, 8, 9

Laughter
Advent 4

Lead(er, ship, ing)
After Epiphany Last
Lent 6
Easter Season 4
Pentecost 1, Alt.
Proper 5, 15, 16

Learn(ers, ing)
After Epiphany 2, 5
Ash Wednesday
Holy Week—Th
Easter Day Alt.
Easter Season 2
Pentecost Alt.
Proper 7, 9, 15, 27
All Saints' Day

Leaven
Easter Evening

Life
Advent 4
Christmas, Proper III
After Christmas 1
After Epiphany 1, 3, 6, 7, Last
Lent 5, 6
Holy Week—M, Sat
Easter Evening
Easter Season 2, 3, 6
Pentecost 1, Alt.

Trinity Sunday
Proper 4, 5, 6, 7, 9, 10, 11, 12, 14,
        15, 16, 19, 23, 24,25, 26, 27

Lifted Up
After Christmas 1
After Epiphany 4
Lent 5
Easter Season 5
Ascension Day
Proper 5, 9, 14, 28

Light
Advent 1, 4
Christmas, Propers I, II, and III
After Christmas 2
Epiphany
After Epiphany 1, 3, 5, Last
Lent 4, 5, 6
Holy Week—M, Tu, F, Sat
Easter Season 5
Proper 7, 8, 10, 11,18, 20, 26, 27,
        28

Limitations
Lent 1, 4
Easter Season 4
Trinity Sunday

Lips
Ash Wednesday
Proper 13, 14

Listen(ing)
Advent 4
After Epiphany 1, 2, 5, 9
Lent 1, 3, 4, 5
Holy Week—Sat
Easter Season 3, 6
Pentecost 1
Proper 4, 6, 7, 11, 15, 18, 21, 25,
        27
Thanksgiving

Living Bread
After Epiphany 8
Easter Evening

Living Hope
Easter Day 1
Easter Season 2

Living Water
After Epiphany 5, 8
Lent 3, 4
Pentecost 1, Alt.
All Saints' Day

Living Way
Holy Week—F

Loneliness
January 1—New Year

Longing
Advent 4

Look (Up)
Christmas, Proper I
Easter Day 1
Proper 11

Loss(es), Lost
After Christmas 1, 2
January 1—New Year
After Epiphany 3
Lent 5
Holy Week—Tu, Th, F
Easter Season 4
Proper 12, 14, 21, 26

Loving God, Neighbor
After Christmas 1
January 1—New Year
After Epiphany 5, 6, 7, Last
Ash Wednesday
Lent 3, 6
Holy Week—Tu, Th, Sat

Easter Day 1, Alt., Evening
Easter Season 3, 6,7
Pentecost
Proper 4, 6, 7, 8, 11, 14, 17, 18, 21, 25, 27, 28, 29

Loyalty
Christmas, Proper I
After Epiphany 6
Lent 6
Easter Day 1, Evening
Easter Season 7
Proper 8, 22, 27

Manger
Christmas, Propers I and II
January 1—Holy Name

Meaning
After Christmas 1
After Epiphany Last
Lent 2, 4
Holy Week—Tu
Easter Day 2
Easter Season 3
Proper 20, 25, 28, 29

Meditation
Pentecost Alt.
Proper 9, 23, 24, 27

Meekness
Advent 2
After Epiphany 4

Members of One Body
Pentecost 1

Memory
Proper 4

Mercy, Merciful
Advent 3
Christmas, Proper II

After Christmas 1
All Epiphany 2, 4
Ash Wednesday
Lent 4, 6
Holy Week—Th
Easter Season 4, 5
Proper 5, 9, 13, 15, 19, 24, 28
Thanksgiving

Message, Messengers
Christmas, Proper III
January 1—Holy Name
After Epiphany 1, 3
Lent 2, 3
Holy Week—W
Easter Day 1
Easter Season 3, 4
Pentecost, Alt.
Proper 6, 21, 24

Messiah
After Epiphany 2
Proper 26

Minds
After Epiphany 5, 9
Ash Wednesday
Lent 6
Holy Week—W, F
Easter Day 1
Pentecost 1
Proper 10, 14, 16, 17, 21, 23, 25
All Saints' Day
Thanksgiving Day

Ministry, Mission
Advent 4
Christmas, Proper II
Epiphany
After Epiphany 1, Last
Lent 1, 2, 5, 6
Holy Week—W, Sat
Easter Season 3, 4
Pentecost 1, Alt.

Proper 4, 6, 8, 9, 10, 11, 14, 15,
   16, 18, 27, 29
Thanksgiving Day

Miracles
Christmas, Proper III
Proper 14, 17, 20

Motives
Holy Week—M
Proper 19, 24

Mountain(s, tops)
Advent 1, 2
After Epiphany 4, Last
Lent 3
Holy Week—M
Easter Evening
Proper 8

Mourning
January 1—New Year
After Christmas 2
After Epiphany 4
Ash Wednesday
Lent 6
Holy Week—F, Sat

Mystery
Christmas, Proper III
January 1—Holy Name
After Christmas 2
Epiphany
After Epiphany 5, 8, Last
Lent 2
Holy Week—W
Ascension Day
Trinity Sunday
Proper 23

Name(s, ed)
January 1—Holy Name
Lent 6
Holy Week—Tu

Easter Day 1
Easter Season 4
Trinity Sunday
Proper 14, 16, 24

Needs, Needy
Advent 2, 3
After Christmas 1
January 1—New Year
After Epiphany 5, 8
Lent 1, 5
Holy Week—W, Th, F
Easter Season 4, 5, 7
Pentecost Alt.
Proper 5,6, 7, 8, 9, 13, 27, 29
Thanksgiving Day

Neglect
Advent 4
Lent 5
Trinity Sunday
Proper 24

Neighbors
After Epiphany Last
Lent 3
Proper 4, 8, 12, 20, 25, 27

New Beginnings
Lent 6
Proper 4, 18

New Commandment
Holy Week—Th

New Day
Christmas, Proper I
After Epiphany Last

New Life
Advent 4
Christmas, Propers I and III
January 1—Holy Name

Epiphany
After Epiphany 6, 9, Last
Lent 2, 5, 6
Holy Week—M, F
Easter Day 1, Alt., Evening
Easter Season 2, 4
Ascension Day
Pentecost
Proper 5, 6, 10, 15

New Possibilities
January 1—New Year
After Epiphany 1, Last
Lent 4
Easter Season 5
Proper 4, 7

New Song
Christmas, Propers I and III
After Epiphany 2
Lent 3
Proper 18

New Thing
After Epiphany 1
Holy Week—M
Proper 25

New Ways
Advent 4
After Christmas 1
Lent 2
Holy Week—M, F
Proper 4, 16, 18

Nourishment
Proper 9, 26

Obedience
Advent 4
January 1—Holy Name
After Epiphany 6, 9
Lent 1, 4, 6

Holy Week—F
Easter Season 3, 5
Trinity Sunday
Proper 8, 15, 16, 21, 26, 27

Offering(s)
Lent 6
Holy Week—Tu, W
Easter Season 6
Pentecost Alt.
Proper 5, 7, 9, 10, 11, 14, 15, 18,
    26, 27, 28
Thanksgiving Day

Oneness
Pentecost 1
Proper 4

Openness
January 1—Holy Name, New
    Year
Ash Wednesday
Lent 1, 2, 3, 4
Easter Evening
Easter Season 2, 3
Ascension Day
Pentecost 1, Alt.
Proper 6, 9, 10, 12, 13, 15, 18, 20,
    23, 26
All Saints' Day
Thanksgiving Day

Opportunities
January 1—New Year
Epiphany
After Epiphany 8, 9, Last
Ash Wednesday
Holy Week—Tu, Th
Easter Season 2, 4, 5, 7
Proper 4, 5, 6, 10, 13, 15, 20, 21,
    27, 29
All Saints' Day
Thanksgiving Day

Opposition
Lent 6
Easter Season 6

Oppression
Advent 3
Epiphany
After Epiphany 1, 3, 5
Easter Season 5
Proper 16, 17, 19, 28, 29

Outreach
Proper 9, 24

Pain
Advent 4
January 1, New Year
Holy Week—F, Sat
Easter Season 4, 5
Proper 8, 18

Partiality
Proper 24

Partnership
Proper 24

Passion(s)
Christmas, Proper I
Holy Week—Sat
Proper 8, 12
All Saints' Day

Passover
Holy Week—Th

Path(s) of Life
Advent 1
After Epiphany 7
Ash Wednesday
Lent 4
Easter Season 2, 4, 5
Proper 10, 11

Patience
Advent 3
Ash Wednesday
Easter Day Alt.
Proper 11, 17, 19

Peace(makers)
Advent 1, 2, 4
Christmas, Propers I and III
After Christmas 2
Epiphany
After Epiphany 1, 3, 4
Lent 3, 4
Holy Week—Th
Easter Day 1, Alt., Evening
Easter Season 2
Pentecost
Proper 4, 6, 7, 8, 15, 17, 23, 28
All Saints' Day

Peculiar People
Easter Evening

Perfect(er)
After Epiphany 7
Holy Week—W, F, Sat
Proper 13

Pleasure
January 1—New Year
Lent 1
Holy Week—M
Proper 15

Poor, Poverty
Advent 2, 3
Epiphany
After Epiphany 3, 4, 5
Holy Week—W
Easter Season 5
Pentecost Alt.
Proper 7, 9, 16

Possessions, Possessiveness
After Christmas 1

After Epiphany 4, 6, 8
Lent 1
Easter Season 4
Proper 22, 27

Possibilities
January 1—New Year
After Epiphany 1, 4, Last
Lent 4, 6
Easter Season 5, 7
Trinity Sunday
Proper 5, 6, 10, 14

Power(s)
Advent 3, 4
Christmas, Proper III
Epiphany
After Epiphany 4, 9
Ash Wednesday
Lent 2
Holy Week—Tu, W, Th
Easter Day Alt.
Easter Season 7
Ascension Day
Pentecost 1, Alt.
Proper 4, 12, 16, 18, 25

Praise
Advent 2, 3
Christmas, Proper III
After Christmas 1
January 1—Holy Name, New
    Year
Epiphany
After Epiphany 4, 5, 6, 9
Ash Wednesday
Lent 1, 3, 4, 5, 6
Holy Week—Tu, F
Easter Season 3, 4, 6, 7
Ascension Day
Pentecost 1, Alt.
Trinity Sunday
Proper 5, 6, 9, 10, 12, 13,14,15,
    16, 18, 19, 20, 23, 24, 26

All Saints' Day
Thanksgiving Day

Prayer
Advent 2, 4
January 1—New Year
After Epiphany 4, 8, 9, Last
Ash Wednesday
Lent 1, 4, 6
Holy Week—F
Easter Day 1, Alt.
Easter Season 3, 4, 5, 6, 7
Ascension Day
Pentecost Alt.
Proper 4, 5, 6, 7, 11, 12, 13, 14,
    15, 16, 17, 22, 23, 24, 27
Thanksgiving Day

Precious
Holy Week—Th
Easter Season 3
Proper 12

Prejudice
After Epiphany 5
Easter Season 2
Proper 24

Pretension
Advent 3
Ash Wednesday
Lent 1
Holy Week—W
Easter Season 4
Proper 12, 14, 16, 21, 24,25,26,
    29

Pride
Advent 3
January 1—Holy Name
After Epiphany 2, 6, 9
Proper 4, 16, 24, 28

Priorities
January 1—New Year

Epiphany
After Epiphany 2, 5, 6
Holy Week—Tu
Easter Evening
Easter Season 3
Proper 9, 21

Prison(ers)
January 1—New Year
After Epiphany 1, 8
Holy Week—M
Easter Season 7

Privilege
Easter Season 7
Proper 8, 16, 21, 25, 29
Thanksgiving Day

Promises
Advent 4
Christmas, Proper I
After Epiphany 6
Lent 2, 5, 6
Easter Day 1, Alt.
Easter Season 3
Ascension Day
Proper 11, 13

Prophecy, Prophets
Advent 4
After Epiphany Last
Pentecost 1, Alt.
Proper 25
All Saints' Day

Pure, Purified, Purity
After Epiphany 4
Ash Wednesday
Holy Week—M
Easter Season 3, 5
Proper 22, 23, 26
All Saints' Day

Purpose
Advent 4

After Christmas 1, 3
After Epiphany 9
Lent 5, 6
Pentecost
Proper 9, 15, 29

Quality
Lent 3
Proper 15, 18, 22, 23,24

Quarreling
Advent 1
After Epiphany 3, 6
Lent 3
Proper 18, 19

Questions
Easter Season 2, 5
Proper 15, 21, 25, 26

Quiet
Advent 3, 4
After Epiphany 8
Ash Wednesday

Radiance
After Christmas 2
Epiphany
All Saints' Day

Rebellion
Lent 3
Holy Week—W

Rebirth
Christmas, Proper II
January 1—New Year
Lent 2

Reconciliation
After Epiphany 6
Ash Wednesday
Proper 11, 15, 17, 18

Redeemer, Redemption
Christmas, Proper II
After Christmas 1, 2
Lent 5
Holy Week—M, Tu
Easter Season 3
Proper 22, 26
All Saints' Day

Refuge
Advent 3
After Epiphany 9, Last
Holy Week—M, Tu, Sat
Easter Season 2, 5
Proper 4, 13
All Saints' Day

Rejoicing
Advent 2, 3
Christmas, Propers I, II, and III
After Epiphany 4, 5
Lent 6
Holy Week—Th
Easter Day 1, Alt., Evening
Easter Season 2, 5
Ascension Day
Proper 5, 6, 8, 9, 10, 12, 14, 20,
    23, 27
All Saints' Day

Relationships
Advent 4
After Epiphany 6
Lent 2, 3, 4, 6
Holy Week—Tu
Easter Season 3, 4, 5
Pentecost Alt.
Proper 4, 5, 13, 15, 19, 22, 23, 25,
    27, 28

Remembering
Christmas, Proper II
Lent 1, 2
Holy Week—Th, F

Easter Season 5
Proper 12, 18
Thanksgiving Day

Renewal
Christmas, Proper II
After Epiphany 2
Ash Wednesday
Holy Week—Tu
Easter Season 2, 6
Pentecost 1, Alt.
Trinity Sunday
Proper 7, 8, 9, 13, 16, 26
Thanksgiving Day

Rejection
Lent 2
Holy Week—F
Easter Season 6
Proper 7, 19

Repentance (see also Confession)
Advent 2, 4
January 1—New Year
After Christmas 2
After Epiphany 3
Lent 1
Easter Season 3, 6
Ascension Day

Rescue
After Christmas 2
Holy Week—Tu
Easter Season 5
Proper 29
All Saints' Day

Resources
Epiphany
After Epiphany 8
Lent 5
Ascension Day
Pentecost 1
Proper 4, 5, 9, 13, 17, 23

Responsibility
January 1—Holy Name, New
Year
After Epiphany 2, 4, 6
Holy Week—W
Easter Season 5
Trinity Sunday
Proper 24

Responsiveness
Christmas, Proper II
After Christmas 1, 2
January 1—Holy Name, New
Year
After Epiphany 6, 9, Last
Ash Wednesday
Lent 1, 4, 5
Holy Week—F, Sat
Easter Day 1, Evening
Easter Season 5
Pentecost Alt.
Proper 7, 9, 10, 19, 21, 22, 24, 25,
27, 28

Restoration
After Epiphany 5
Ash Wednesday
Lent 4, 6
Holy Week—M
Easter Season 4, 7
Proper 5, 12, 13

Resurrection
Lent 5, 6
Easter Day 1, Alt., Evening
Easter Season 2, 6
Trinity Sunday
Proper 7, 10, 22

Revelation
Advent 4
January 1—Holy Name
After Christmas 2
Epiphany

After Epiphany 5, Last
Lent 1, 6
Easter Day 1, Evening
Easter Season 3, 4
Ascension Day
Trinity Sunday
Proper 4, 8, 9, 10, 11, 24, 29

Reverence
Advent 2
Lent 5
Easter Season 6
Proper 15

Reward(s)
After Epiphany 7
Ash Wednesday
Proper 8

Riches (see also Wealth)
Epiphany
Lent 3
Pentecost, Alt.
Proper 9, 10, 16, 29

Ridicule
Lent 2, 6

Right
After Epiphany 4, 7, 8
Lent 4
Holy Week—Th
Easter Day Alt.
Easter Season 4
Proper 13, 24

Righteousness
Advent 2
Christmas, Proper I
After Epiphany 1, 4, 5,6, 8
Ash Wednesday
Lent 5, 6
Holy Week—M, Tu

Easter Day 1, Alt.
Easter Season 7
Proper 4, 5, 8, 11, 13, 22, 23, 24, 25
All Saints' Day

Rise, Risen
Lent 3
Holy Week—Th, Sat
Easter Day 1, Alt, Evening
Easter Season 2, 3, 5
Ascension Day
Proper 11, 14

Risk (see also Daring)
After Christmas 1
Lent 6
Holy Week—Th, Sat
Easter Day Alt.
Easter Season 4, 6
Pentecost 1, Alt.
Proper 5, 13, 26, 29
All Saints' Day

Rituals
After Epiphany 2

Rock
After Epiphany 9
Lent 3
Holy Week—Tu
Easter Season 5
Proper 22

Roots
Proper 10

Routines
After Epiphany 2
Pentecost Alt.

Ruler(s)
After Epiphany Last

Lent 3, 5
Holy Week—Tu
Proper 17

Sacrifice
Ash Wednesday
Lent 6
Holy Week—Tu, Th
Easter Season 3, 6
Proper 4, 6, 12, 16

Sadness
Holy Week—Sat

Search
Proper 11, 21

Secret
Proper 17

Security
Advent 1
Lent 2, 3
Pentecost Alt.
Proper 13, 21, 28

Seeds
Proper 10, 11, 12

Seek(ers)
January 1—New Year
Ash Wednesday
Easter Season 3
Pentecost 1
Proper 8,17, 26, 28

Seeing
Christmas, Proper III
After Epiphany Last
Easter Season 6
Pentecost 1
Proper 10, 12
Thanksgiving Day

Self-centered, Self-concerned, Self-serving
After Epiphany 6
Lent 1, 5
Holy Week—Sat
Easter Season 3
Proper 7, 21

Self-examination
Ash Wednesday
Lent 1
Easter Season 7
Proper 5, 23

Selfishness
Easter Day Alt.
Easter Season 4
Proper 5, 12, 24

Sent
Christmas, Proper III
Lent 2
Easter Season 2
Pentecost 1

Separation from God
Holy Week—Sat
Proper 12

Servants, Service
Advent 3
After Christmas 1
January 1—Holy Name
Epiphany
After Epiphany 2, 3, 5, 6, 7, 8, 9, Last
Ash Wednesday
Lent 2, 6
Holy Week—M, Tu, Th, Sat
Easter Day 1, Alt.
Easter Season 2, 5, 6, 7
Ascension Day
Pentecost 1

Trinity Sunday
Proper 4, 6, 7, 8, 9, 10, 11, 14, 15,
    16, 18, 21, 22, 24, 25,26, 27,
    28
All Saints' Day

Shadows
After Epiphany 1, 3, 5, 8, Last
Lent 3, 4
Holy Week—M
Easter Sunday 1

Shame
Lent 4
Holy Week—Tu, W
Easter Day 1
Easter Season 5
Proper 8

Sharing
January 1—New Year
Epiphany
After Epiphany 3, 5, 8, 9
Ash Wednesday
Lent 1, 2, 3, 4, 5
Holy Week—Th, Sat
Easter Season 2, 4, 6, 7
Pentecost Alt.
Proper 5, 6, 7, 10, 12, 13,14, 15,
    20, 21, 26, 29
Thanksgiving Day

Sheep/Goats
January 1—New Year
Easter Season 4

Shelter
Advent 3
After Epiphany 3
Proper 4, 15
Thanksgiving Day

Shepherd(s)
Advent 4

January 1—Holy Name
After Christmas 2
Lent 4
Easter Season 4
Proper 6, 29

Sick
January 1—New Year
Proper 29

Signs
Advent 4
After Epiphany 4
Lent 1
Holy Week—Th, F
Pentecost Alt.
Proper 24, 25

Silence, Stillness
Christmas, Proper II
After Epiphany 6
Lent 6

Silver and Gold
Easter Season 3

Sin, Sinners
After Christmas 1
After Epiphany 6, 9
Ash Wednesday
Lent 3, 4, 5
Holy Week—W, F, Sat
Easter Season 3
Proper 4, 5, 6, 7, 9, 10, 11, 13, 15,
    18, 21, 22, 23,24, 25, 27, 29
Thanksgiving Day

Sincerity
Easter Evening
Proper 6, 27

Sing(ing), Song(s)
Advent 3
Christmas, Propers I, II, and III

After Christmas 2
After Epiphany 2, 3
Lent 3
Easter Day Alt.
Easter Season 3, 7
Ascension Day
Pentecost 1, Alt.
Proper 12, 14, 16, 18, 20, 24
All Saints' Day
Thanksgiving Day

Sisters and Brothers
After Christmas 1
January 1—Holy Name
Lent 3
Holy Week—Th
Easter Day 1
Easter Season 5, 6
Ascension Day
Proper 17, 19, 25

Slander
After Epiphany 7

Slavery
Pentecost Alt.

Sleeping
Advent 1
Lent 2, 6
Proper 18

Sons and Daughters
Pentecost Alt.

Sorrow (see also Grief)
Advent 3
After Christmas 2
Holy Week—F, Sat
Proper 13

Soul
After Epiphany 9

Easter Season 2, 3, 4
Proper 9, 22, 25, 26

Sowing Bountifully or Sparingly
Thanksgiving Day

Spirit
January 1—Holy Name
After Epiphany 1, 5, 6, 7, Last
Ash Wednesday
Lent 1, 2, 3, 5
Holy Week—M, Sat
Easter Day 1, Evening
Easter Season 6
Ascension Day
Pentecost 1, Alt.
Proper 5, 7, 9, 10, 11, 12, 13, 27, 28
All Saints' Day

Spiritual Ancestors
Lent 3
Proper 8, 11, 17, 18, 19, 20 23, 25, 26, 27

Spiritual Blessings
After Christmas 2

Spiritual Gifts
After Epiphany 2, 5

Spiritual Nourishment
After Epiphany 6
Easter Season 5
Pentecost 1
Proper 16, 27

Standards
Easter Season 7

Star(s)
Epiphany
After Epiphany Last

Steadfast Love
After Christmas 1
After Epiphany 2, 9
Ash Wednesday
Lent 1, 5, 6
Holy Week—M, Sat
Easter Day 1, Alt.
Easter Season 6
Proper 7, 8, 13, 23, 25, 26, 29

Stewardship
January 1—Holy Name, New
    Year
After Epiphany 6, 8
Easter Season 4
Trinity Sunday
Proper 4, 5, 14, 17, 20, 28

Stillness
Advent 3
Holy Week—Sat
Proper 4

Still Waters
Lent 4
Easter Season 4

Stone(s)
Easter Day 1, Alt.
Easter Season 5

Storms
Proper 4, 14

Story
Lent 3
Holy Week—F
Easter Season 6

Stranger(s)
January 1—New Year
After Epiphany 7
Easter Season 4

Pentecost 1
Proper 8, 29

Strength(ened)
Advent 3, 4
After Christmas 1, 2
January 1—New Year
After Epiphany 1, 2, 3, 4, 5, 6, 9
Lent 6
Holy Week—Tu, Th, F
Easter Day 1, Alt., Evening
Easter Season 7
Proper 4, 5, 7, 12, 13, 17, 19, 20,
    23, 24

Struggle
Lent 2
Easter Season 6
Proper 21

Stumbling (Block)
Lent 5
Holy Week—Tu
Proper 13, 16, 19

Suffering
After Christmas 1
After Epiphany 8
Lent 6
Holy Week—F, Sat
Easter Day 1
Easter Season 4, 6, 7
Pentecost 1, Alt.
Proper 17, 19, 20

Surprises
Easter Day 1, Evening
Pentecost 1, Alt.
Proper 9, 12, 17, 20, 25

Swords
Holy Week—F
Proper 7

Symbol
Holy Week—W

Table
Holy Week—Th
Easter Evening
Proper 15, 23

Talents
Proper 5, 28

Teacher, Teaching
After Epiphany 1, 3, 9
Lent 1, 2, 5
Holy Week—W
Easter Season 4, 6
Proper 4, 6, 7, 8, 9, 10, 13, 16, 19,
    21, 26, 27

Tears
Advent 4
January 1—New Year
Holy Week—F, Sat
Easter Evening
All Saints' Day

Temptation
After Christmas 2
Lent 1, 2, 3
Easter Day 1
Easter Season 4
Trinity Sunday
Proper 5, 16, 18, 19, 29

Tension
Holy Week—Tu

Terror
Lent 6
Easter Day Alt., Evening

Test
After Christmas 1

Lent 3
Proper 8, 11, 22

Thanks(giving)
Christmas, Proper II
After Christmas 2
Epiphany
After Epiphany 4, 6, 9
Ash Wednesday
Lent 3, 6
Holy Week—Th, F, Sat
Easter Day 1, Alt.
Pentecost 1
Proper 5, 6, 7, 9, 12, 14, 15, 16,
    17, 20, 23, 26, 28, 29
All Saints' Day
Thanksgiving Day

Think, Thoughts
After Christmas 1
After Epiphany Last
Ash Wednesday
Lent 4, 6
Easter Season 3
Proper 5, 8, 10, 11, 15, 16, 22, 26

Thirst
January 1—New Year
After Epiphany 4, 5, 8
Lent 3
Pentecost 1, Alt.
Proper 8, 13, 26, 29
All Saints' Day

Time (and Space)
After Epiphany 6, 7, Last
Lent 3, 6
Holy Week—W, Sat
Ascension Day
Easter Season 7
Trinity Sunday
Proper 6, 9, 13, 14

Time, Talent, Treasure
After Epiphany 3, 9, Last
Lent 4, 5
Holy Week—W
Easter Day Alt.
Easter Season 7
Pentecost 1, Alt.
Trinity Sunday
Proper 14, 28

Tithes and Offerings
Lent 3, 4
Holy Week—Th
Easter Day Alt.
Easter Season 5
Proper 4, 10, 14, 16, 20, 25

Togetherness
After Epiphany 9, Last
Ash Wednesday
Holy Week—W, F
Easter Season 3, 4, 7
Ascension Day
Proper 9, 11, 13, 15, 23
All Saints' Day
Thanksgiving Day

Tongues
Holy Week—W
Pentecost 1
Proper 11, 19, 21
All Saints' Day

Touch
Ash Wednesday
Lent 4
Easter Day 1
Easter Season 2, 3
Pentecost Alt.
Proper 5, 6, 13, 23, 24

Toys
Proper 23, 27

Transformation
Christmas, Proper III
Ash Wednesday
Lent 4, 6
Holy Week—M
Easter Season 2
Ascension Day
Pentecost Alt.
Proper 10, 16, 22

Transgressions (see Sins)

Treasures
Proper 8, 12

Tremble
Christmas, Propers I and II
Epiphany
After Epiphany 9, Last
Holy Week—Th
Pentecost Alt.
Proper 17, 19, 22

Trials
Lent 1, 2
Easter Season 2, 7

Trouble(s)
After Epiphany 3
Holy Week—M, W, F, Sat
Easter Season 5
Proper 4, 7, 16, 26
All Saints' Day

Trumpets, etc.
Christmas, Proper III
After Epiphany 5
Proper 27

Trust(ing), Trustworthy
Advent 4
Christmas, Proper II
After Christmas 1

January 1—Holy Name, New
Year
After Epiphany 2, 7, 8, 9, Last
Lent 2, 5, 6
Holy Week—Tu, W, Th, F, Sat
Easter Day 1, Alt., Evening
Easter Season 3, 4, 5, 7
Pentecost 1, Alt.
Proper 4, 5, 8, 10, 12, 13, 14, 16,
18, 20, 21, 23, 27, 28

Truth(fulness)
Advent 3
Christmas, Proper I
January 1—Holy Name
After Christmas 2
After Epiphany 1, 2, 4, 7, 8, 9,
Last
Ash Wednesday
Lent 3, 4
Holy Week—Th
Easter Evening
Easter Season 2, 3, 6
Pentecost Alt.
Proper 4, 5, 12, 16, 21, 22, 23, 24,
25, 26
All Saints' Day

Turned Away
Christmas, Proper II

Uncertainty
Holy Week—Tu

Understanding
After Epiphany 5, 9
Holy Week—Sat
Easter Season 2, 6
Pentecost Alt.
Proper 8, 9, 10, 15, 18

Unexpected
Advent 1

Easter Evening
Pentecost 1

Unfaithfulness
Advent 3
Lent 1, 2
Thanksgiving Day

Unity
After Epiphany 3
Easter Season 3, 7
Trinity Sunday
Proper 4, 9, 15, 18

Universe
Lent 3
Proper 4, 14, 19

Valleys
After Epiphany Last
Lent 3, 5
Holy Week—Sat
Proper 23

Value(s)
January 1—New Year
After Epiphany Last
Holy Week—M
Proper 5, 8, 18, 21, 23, 24

Victim
Lent 6
Proper 21

Vineyard
Proper 20

Violence
After Christmas 1
Epiphany
Holy Week—F, Sat

Vision(s)
Advent 4

After Epiphany 1, 5, 8, Last
Lent 2
Easter Evening
Pentecost 1, Alt.
Proper 6, 11, 14, 25

Voice(s)
Christmas, Proper III
Epiphany
After Epiphany 1, 4, 5
Lent 1, 5, 6
Holy Week—Tu
Easter Season 3, 4
Proper 5, 13

Vows
After Epiphany 6
Easter Season 3
Proper 6
Thanksgiving Day

Wait(ing)
After Epiphany Last
Lent 6
Holy Week—Sat
Pentecost 1, Alt.
Proper 11

Walk
Advent 3
After Christmas 2
Ash Wednesday
Lent 1, 4, 5
Holy Week—Tu
Proper 4, 14

Wandering
After Epiphany 9
Holy Week—M
Proper 29

Waste(land)
Proper 13
Thanksgiving Day

Watch(ful)
After Epiphany Last
Lent 6
Ascension Day
Trinity Sunday

Water(s)
Advent 2, 3
After Epiphany 8
Lent 3
Easter Season 3
Proper 5, 6, 9, 14, 19, 20, 21, 26
Thanksgiving Day

Way of Life
After Epiphany 1, 6, 7
Ash Wednesday
Lent 4, 5, 6
Holy Week—Tu
Easter Evening
Easter Season 5, 6, 7
Proper 8, 9, 11, 18, 22, 26

Weak(ness)
Advent 3
After Epiphany 4
Proper 6, 12, 19, 29

Wealth (see also Riches)
After Epiphany 9
Proper 9, 14, 20, 22, 28

Weariness
Advent 4
Holy Week—W, Th
Proper 7, 9

Welcome
After Christmas 1
January 1—New Year
Lent 6
Holy Week—Th
Easter Day 1, Evening
Easter Season 3

Proper 8, 13, 16, 22, 23, 24, 26, 29
All Saints' Day

Wholeness
Advent 3
Christmas, Proper II
After Christmas 1
After Epiphany 3
Ash Wednesday
Lent 2, 5
Holy Week—F, Sat
Easter Day Alt., Evening
Easter Season 3
Proper 4, 11, 18, 23
All Saints' Day
Thanksgiving Day

Wickedness
Advent 2
Holy Week—Tu
Easter Evening
Proper 11, 13, 25

Wilderness (see also Desert)
Lent 1
Easter Season 7
Proper 20, 21
Thanksgiving Day

Wind(s)
After Christmas 2
Lent 2
Easter Season 2
Ascension Day
Pentecost 1, Alt.
Proper 14

Wings
Holy Week—M
Proper 6

Wisdom
After Christmas 2
After Epiphany 4, 5, 7
Ash Wednesday

Holy Week—Tu
Ascension Day
Proper 9, 22, 25, 29

Witness
Christmas, Proper III
After Christmas 1
January 1—Holy Name, New
    Year
After Epiphany 7
Lent 2, 4
Holy Week—M, Tu, F
Easter Day Alt., Evening
Easter Season 6, 7
Ascension Day
Pentecost
Trinity Sunday
Proper 5, 6, 7, 8, 9, 10, 11, 27
All Saints' Day
Thanksgiving Day

Wonder(s)
Christmas, Proper I
After Epiphany 5, Last
Lent 3
Easter Evening
Trinity Sunday
Proper 7, 24

Word(s)
Advent 4
Christmas, Proper III
Epiphany
Lent 5
Holy Week—W
Proper 4, 5, 9, 10, 11, 12, 22

Word and Deed
After Epiphany 4, 5
Holy Week—W, Sat
Ascension Day
Proper 12, 13, 15, 20, 24
All Saints' Day
Thanksgiving Day

Work(s)
  After Epiphany 5, 6, 9
  Lent 4
  Holy Week—M
  Easter Season 5, 6, 7
  Ascension Day
  Pentecost 1
  Proper 4, 20, 24, 29
  Thanksgiving Day

World
  Advent 3
  Christmas, Proper III
  January 1—Holy Name
  After Epiphany 1, 4, 5, 7, 8, 9,
    Last
  Lent 2, 3, 5, 6
  Holy Week—Tu, Sat
  Easter Day Alt.
  Easter Season 3, 5
  Pentecost Alt.
  Trinity Sunday
  Proper 6, 11, 12, 13, 14, 17, 24,
    25, 27

Worries
  After Epiphany 8
  Easter Day 1

Worship
  Christmas, Proper III
  After Christmas 1
  January 1—Holy Name
  Epiphany
  After Epiphany 1, 5, 7

Ash Wednesday
Lent 1, 3, 4
Holy Week—M, W, F
Easter Season 6, 7
Ascension Day
Trinity Sunday
Proper 4, 5, 6, 8, 9, 11, 12, 13, 16,
  17, 19, 21, 22, 24, 25, 26, 27,
  28, 29
All Saints' Day

Worth(iness)
  After Epiphany 7, 8
  Holy Week—M, Th
  Easter Season 7
  Proper 7, 9, 20, 23, 26, 28

Wounded
  Holy Week—F
  Proper 15

Wrong(s)
  January 1—New Year
  After Epiphany 6
  Holy Week—F
  Proper 19, 24

Yearning
  After Epiphany 5
  Ash Wednesday
  Proper 12

Yoke
  After Epiphany 5
  Proper 9

About the Author

The church's worship has fascinated Lavon (Burrichter) Bayler since she was old enough to stand on an Ohio pew, holding a hymnal upside down, singing words she did not understand. Her father was the pastor, and even before she was ten, he gave her an opportunity to read the Christmas scriptures in worship. As an Iowa teenager, she filled the pulpit on Youth Sundays and became a national leader in the Youth Fellowship of the Evangelical and Reformed Church.

Ordained ministry did not seem an option for a young woman in the 1950s as Lavon prepared to teach. Midway through college, missionary service became an option, but the call took on local church possibilities during a year as her denomination's Youth Associate. Her parents were supportive of her desire to preach, as she tried out Lancaster Seminary. There she met her husband, Bob Bayler, and the two continued their academic preparation at Eden Seminary, St. Louis.

The Baylers' first call was as co-pastors of four small congregations in central Ohio, halfway between their Iowa and Pennsylvania parental homes. There they became parents to David and Jonathan, who some years later welcomed brother Timothy to the family circle. Since 1964, they have lived and served in Illinois. Most of Bob's ministry has focused on health care. Lavon eventually moved from local congregations to the staff of the Illinois Conference, United Church of Christ, where she serves as minister of the Fox Valley Association.

Writing worship resources and hymns has been a fairly late addition to Lavon's interests, which have included music, photography, environmental, peace and justice concerns, sports, Indian finger weaving, and swimming. The last pursuit, begun in 1978, has her reaching for five thousand miles before the new millennium begins. Among the Baylers' delights in recent years is the addition of daughters by marriage and grandchildren with whom they keep regular "appointments."

This is Lavon's tenth book, three of which were coauthored with husband Bob.